Going Local

your guide to Swiss schooling

by Margaret Oertig

Bergli
books

Going Local
your guide to Swiss schooling

by Margaret Oertig

© 2012 Bergli Books, Basel
© cover and illustrations 2012 Marc Locatelli, Zurich

Bergli Books   Tel.: +41 61 373 27 77
CH-4001 Basel   e-mail: info@bergli.ch
Switzerland   www.bergli.ch

Disclaimer: Please note that much of this publication is based on information provided by websites (for which accuracy cannot be guaranteed) and the perceptions of many people (which are their subjective opinions). Although the author and publisher have made every reasonable attempt to achieve complete accuracy of the factual aspects at the time of going to press, they assume no responsibility for errors or omissions. The information is subject to change and should be verified with an appropriate source, for example, the school authorities concerned.

ISBN 978-3-905252-46-0 digital edition

ISBN 978-3-905252-25-5 print edition

Table of Contents

Introduction

If you have moved to Switzerland from abroad and are considering sending your child to a local Swiss public school,[1] this book is for you. It aims both to inform and to reassure. It will provide you with detailed factual information regarding the Swiss school system in its amazing diversity around the country. I provide input from teachers and school management and present the views of incomers and locals who have gone before you. I spoke to (or corresponded with) well over 120 parents around Switzerland who have children in local schools, and asked them to share their concerns, experience and wisdom. Each of their stories could have made a book in itself. The final content is driven by the issues that incomers have found most challenging and would have liked to have known more about when they were starting out. The aim is to help you feel better prepared for the move you are making and increase the likelihood of your child making a smooth and successful transition to a local school.

Going Local contains basic information about how the school system works in each of the 26 cantons of Switzerland. It provides the correct terminology in the local language(s) for each stage of school, and tells you at what age your child will pass through these stages. It is not an in-depth guide to any particular aspect of Swiss schooling, but rather, aims to provide an introduction for people who are not familiar with the system.

You may already have your child in local school but would like to be better informed regarding the challenges and opportunities ahead. This book will also help you think ahead about your child's education path and prepare for particular milestones before they are upon you. An example of this is the streaming of your child into one path or another around the age of 11 (in most cantons). Teachers will start observing his or her academic potential well in advance of this and it is important to know what they are looking for. I discuss what these key streaming decisions may be based on, apart from marks or external exams, and how you can support your child in this process.

The book also explains the alternative routes that young people can take in order to reach tertiary education at a later stage, if they are not ready for it earlier on. It is a very porous system and there will be a pathway that suits every level of motivation, interests and abilities at any given time. There are many routes that will get your child to his or her destination.

In addition to factual information, the book aims to inform you as to how local parents have handled the 'softer' school issues (which sometimes end up being the hardest ones). It refers to advice they receive from parents' organisations, books, magazines and the media as well as pedagogical and psychological experts. The concerns, experiences, opinions and reflections of parents from different countries are also presented, explaining how their children learned the local language, how they communicate with teachers and how they deal with particular challenges, such as bullying. Some of their children make a contribution to the discussion too.

Lastly, for anyone who has a more academic interest in the Swiss school system, this book also provides a sketch of the system as a whole, showing how it is slowly growing together. It outlines major themes common to all the cantons, summarizing the stages of schooling and how they are referred to in English and the local languages at national level.

Margaret Oertig
May 2012

Section one

Getting started

Chapter 1   Crash course in the Swiss school system

This chapter gives a brief overview of the stages of the Swiss education system, covering the ages of four to around 18 to 20, that is, from kindergarten until upper-secondary school. The terminology for all school stages in four languages can be found in Appendix 2.

In Switzerland, 95% of pupils attend public schools as the education is considered to be of a high standard. Pre-kindergarten, day care and playgroups for children under four are available, but are not part of the public school system. They all have to be paid for by the parents. It is unfortunately not possible to go into these in this book.

I recommend the English Forum (www.englishforum.ch), a community website with 60,000 members, as a starting point to ask for information and recommendations regarding day care, playgroups and private schools in general where you live.

The political background

There is no national Ministry of Education in Switzerland. Responsibility for compulsory education lies mainly with the 26 cantons, in four linguistic regions. 63.7% of the population speak German, 20.4% speak French, 6.5% speak Italian and 0.5% speak Rhaeto-Romansch.[2] The cantons may make school laws, but they delegate the main responsibility for funding and running the schools to the municipalities (*Gemeinde (D), commune (F), comune (I)[3]*) that is, the town and village governments.

In 2012 Switzerland had over 2500 municipalities. Many small municipalities are merging and it is expected that there will be fewer than 2300 by 2020. They vary in size from 20 inhabitants to 370,000 inhabitants. No matter their size, the municipalities have a lot of political power. They use their populations' tax money to fund schools and employ teachers. They also take responsibility for quality assurance in accordance with cantonal regulations. In some municipalities schools are governed directly by an elected board of lay persons, others have professional school offices with the post of a head teacher. Citizens can vote on all municipal government decisions related to schooling, including how their money is spent on schools. Some municipalities have a more limited school budget than others.

How names are used in this book

With regard to people's names, parents are referred to by their first names and in some cases a pseudonym is used. Their children are referred to by their first initial to protect their privacy. Older children I interviewed may be referred to by their first name. I refer to teachers by their first name and the first initial of their family name. Experts and people in official roles are referred to by their first names and family names.

Harmonisation of school systems

Alignment of cantonal systems is currently moving at a fast pace, at least by Swiss standards. In the old system, compulsory schooling covers at least nine years, from primary school around the age of six to lower-secondary school, which finishes around the age of 15. In the new HarmoS system (see box on pages 14 – 15) compulsory schooling lasts 11 years for the cantons that are implementing it, as it includes two years of kindergarten. Upper-secondary school after the age of 15 or 16 is not compulsory, and lasts a further three to four years, giving a total of 12 or 13 years in the old system and 14 or 15 years in the new system.

> **Numbering the years of school**
>
> Some cantons are already using the numbering of school years in accordance with the new HarmoS system. It is the aim of HarmoS to refer to the two years of kindergarten as 1st and 2nd class, rather than calling them the first two years of pre-school. This means that, in the HarmoS frame, the first year of primary school is known as the 3rd class. In this book I use the traditional term for the school year, and I add the HarmoS year in brackets, e.g. *3rd (H5)* class. The cantons counting in 'HarmoS years' are shown on page 253.

The school year

The school year may start any time from early August to early September, depending on the canton. It lasts around 37 to 40 weeks. Holidays vary from canton to canton, but there tends to be a short holiday period at Christmas, of around 10 days to two weeks, and the longest holidays are in July and August, lasting five to eight weeks. There may be an autumn and a winter week (or two) as well as ten days to two weeks at Easter. There are also a few days a year where there is no school, due to teachers' conferences, etc.

Travelling to school

Kindergarten and primary school are usually nearby and children are encouraged to walk there on their own, especially in German-speaking Switzerland. In rural areas, they may need to take a bus or boat, or even a cable car from a young age. Chantal (*see box on page 8*) told me that in her village in canton Valais, the children take the cable car down the mountain to kindergarten and school every day. One of the mothers accompanies the children for the first two weeks of kindergarten and, after that, they are on their own. Older pupils may either walk or cycle to school or use public transport, travelling longer distances than before by bus or train.

Kindergarten *(Kindergarten, école enfantine, scuola dell'infanzia)*

Kindergarten is the first stage of schooling. It is funded and governed by the municipality. It lasts for two years in most cantons and three years in canton Ticino. Children usually start attending some time before or after their fourth birthday, as stipulated by the cantonal authorities (see Chapter 27 for details regarding your canton). Some municipalities offer only one year of kindergarten, and others offer kindergarten for two years but only make it compulsory for one year, or not at all. In accordance with the goals of HarmoS (see 'HarmoS' on pages 14 – 15), cantons are encouraged to have two years of compulsory kindergarten by 2015.

Children have around 21 - 25 lessons (of 45 minutes each) per week. Please check with your municipality regarding the local distribution of hours. These can range from four to five mornings per week and from no afternoons at all to five afternoons. If both parents are working, you may need to organise day care yourself. School day care tends to be more readily available in larger towns.

The maximum number of children in a class varies from 20 to 26, according to the canton, but numbers are often lower. Each class covers two year groups, or cohorts, so that every year, the older cohort leaves and a new, younger cohort takes their place. (They are often referred to as the 'big ones' and the 'little ones'.) In the traditional system, the children will have the same one or two kindergarten teachers for two years.

Primary school *(Primarschule, école primaire, scuola elementare)*

Primary school is also funded and governed by the municipality. It lasts for six years, from 1st (H3) to 6th (H8) class in most cantons. Some cantons are phasing out five years of primary school (AG, BL, NE),[4] or even four (BS), and all cantons except Ticino will have six years of primary school by 2015, in accordance with the goals of HarmoS. I refer to cantons by the official abbreviations used for them. Please see pages 258 – 259 for a full list of the abbreviations and the cantons to which they refer.

Children usually start attending school some time after their sixth birthday. (See Chapter 27 for details regarding your canton). If they are very advanced both intellectually and socially, they can be tested by the school psychological services and start school a year early.

Pupils have around 21 – 25 lessons per week in the first two years and around 25 – 30 in the following four years. Please check with your municipality regarding the distribution of hours. This can range from four to five mornings per week and one to four afternoons. The maximum number of pupils in a class ranges from 22 – 28, depending on the canton, but numbers are often lower, in particular in rural areas.

There is usually a change of class teacher after two, three or four years, although this may vary. There may be additional teachers for specific subjects such as handicrafts, music, or languages. There may also be an additional special needs teacher, language teacher and speech therapist working with the class as needed. (Please see also Chapter 24 on special needs).

Lower-secondary school

The different names for this school level can be found in Chapter 27, pages 246 – 248. Lower-secondary school may be funded by the canton, the municipality, or both, at the canton's discretion. It starts in the 7th (H9) class in most cantons (with other models being phased out as mentioned above) and lasts until the 9th (H11) class in *all* cantons. Pupils tend to be around 12 years old when they start, and around 15 or 16 when they finish. They have around 31 – 35 lessons per week.

Pupils are selected for different lower-secondary school levels based on their marks and other criteria. In some cantons they go to different types of schools, in others there are different ability classes within the same school, and in a third model there are mixed ability classes.

The maximum number of pupils in a class varies according to the canton from 16 to 27, with the most basic ability levels having the smallest classes (e.g. a maximum of 16 pupils).

Upper-secondary school

This level is not compulsory, but is attended by around 90% of the population. It lasts from the 10th (H12) to 12th (H14) or 13th (H15) class. Pupils start attending around the age of 15 or 16. They may be finished by the age of 18 or 19, but could be a bit older, as it is very common to repeat years along the way.

Pupils are selected for different types of upper-secondary school based on their class marks, entrance exam marks and other criteria. The main types of upper-secondary school are gymnasium; vocational education and training (VET), involving an apprenticeship; IT or commercial school; and specialised upper-secondary school. School-based education is funded by the canton while the cost of apprenticeships is borne by the federal government, the cantons and the companies. School-based programmes tend to have a maximum of 22 – 26 pupils in a class and take place for around 33 – 36 hours per week.

In some German-speaking cantons, very mature, bright pupils may enter gymnasium immediately after primary school. The six-year-long gymnasium (*Langzeitgymnasium*) spans the lower and upper-secondary levels in one institution.

Different paths

This book will explain in some detail that the academic path through lower-secondary school is the most typical route to gymnasium and a traditional university, for which the entry requirement is a Gymnasial Maturity qualification. The middle path is the main route to a specialised upper-secondary school, commercial school or to the most challenging apprenticeships. Bright pupils may then go on to study at a University of Applied Sciences and Arts or do Professional Education and Training (PET) at tertiary level. The basic path prepares pupils for practically-based apprenticeships. There may be further variations in some cantons. In all cantons it is possible for pupils to change their path at various stages along the route if they have good enough marks, are motivated to do so, and are willing to put in the additional time and work that may be involved.

Cantonal diversity

This 'crash course' makes the stages of school sound fairly straightforward. You may be wondering why people say there is no such thing as 'the' Swiss school system. The reason is that when you look more closely at the stages of school outlined above, you will find that many aspects vary in one detail or another from one canton to another. As an example, different combinations of letters are used to name the classes or levels of lower-secondary school, such as R1, R2 and R3; P, E and A; VSB, VSG and VSO; A, B and C; E and G; or p, m and g. Neighbouring cantons may use different terms. The criteria for entrance to the different levels may also vary. It is difficult for parents to communicate across the cantonal divide at this stage. I therefore list the names of the lower-secondary school types and levels and their entry criteria in all the cantons in the cantonal tables in Chapter 27. The chapter covers a range of other practical matters too, such as the different cut-off birth dates for children to start kindergarten or school, and the year(s) in which pupils can start gymnasium in each canton. The broad overview of the school system for your canton will not be complete without referring to these tables.

A partial explanation for so much diversity with regard to the details may lie in the limits Swiss people set themselves in expressing their individualism. I spoke to someone at a Department of Education who explained the system in his small canton to me and commented, "We're a bit exotic." I came to the conclusion that all the cantons are exotic in some way or other. It has been my observation that individuals tend to prefer not to stand out too much in Switzerland, and that fitting in with the group is emphasised. It would appear that being special, different or exotic is transferred from the individual to the collective, and can be expressed to some extent at municipal or cantonal level.

HarmoS: harmonisation of compulsory education

This is a brief introduction to a fairly complex topic. This information given here should be read in conjunction with specific information on your canton (see Chapters 27 and 28). It is taken from the www.educa.ch and the www.edk.ch websites.

In Switzerland, the main responsibility for education and culture lies with the cantons. They coordinate their work at the national level via the EDK, the Conference of Cantonal Ministers of Education (*EDK, CDIP, CDPE*). It is referred to as the EDK in English on the official website. Legally binding, intercantonal agreements (known as concordats) form the foundation for the work of the EDK.

On the 21st of May 2006, the Swiss electorate and all the cantons voted by a majority of 86% to accept the revised constitutional provision of education. According to article 62 of the constitution, the federal government and cantons are required to work together and define key nationwide parameters. These include school entry, the goals of the educational levels, their duration and structure, the transitions in the education system and the degrees awarded. The Intercantonal Agreement on Harmonisation of Compulsory Education (HarmoS Concordat) is the instrument to fulfil these goals of the Swiss Constitution.

The individual cantons decide whether to join a concordat. A concordat is legally binding for the signatory cantons. HarmoS was adopted by the 26 members of the Swiss Conference of Cantonal Ministers of Education to be ratified by the cantons, in accordance with their own political procedures. As a consequence of several initiated referenda on a cantonal level, citizens of several cantons voted on whether their canton should join the HarmoS Agreement or not.

Once ten cantons had joined HarmoS, the concordance came into effect for all cantons. By 2010 15 cantons had joined, representing 76.3% of the population. Seven cantons voted not to join (AR, GR, LU, NW, TG, UR, ZG). Four cantons had by then not yet decided (AG, AI, OW, SZ).

A transition period is now in place until 2015. In 2015 the EDK will assess the extent to which the goals of Article 62 of the constitution have been realised.

HarmoS measures

Under HarmoS, there are 11 years of compulsory schooling: two years of kindergarten, or pre-school, 6 years of primary school and three years of lower-secondary school. Children who are four years old by 31st July will start kindergarten the same year. In many cantons the cut-off date is earlier, and is being postponed by two weeks to a month every year until 31st July is reached. In other cantons (GE, NE, TI, VS), the cut-off date is later than 31st July.

While most cantons already have six years of primary school (whether or not they agreed to HarmoS), the cantons of Aargau, Baselland and Neuchâtel are changing from five to six years, and Basel-Stadt from four to six years. Only Ticino will continue to have five years of primary school. The EDK website provides an interactive map of Switzerland with diagrams of the school system in each canton for the current year.[5]

HarmoS also aims to set national educational standards to be reached in the areas of the school language, foreign languages, maths and natural sciences by the end of the 2nd (H4), 6th (H8) and 9th (H11) years. The aim is that the majority of pupils will exceed the basic competences defined. A first foreign language will be taught from the 3rd (H5) class and a second one from the 5th (H7) class. These are a second national language and English. In Ticino and Graubünden there may be a third national language.

A further aim of HarmoS at kindergarten and primary school level is to promote teaching blocks of full mornings, lunch and school-based day-care facilities, in accordance with observed local needs. This is an ongoing process, and the use of services generally incurs a fee. Cities tend to offer more supervision, but there may be waiting lists. Working mothers have a stronger argument for being given a place. It can be worth checking up on what is on offer before you move into an area. In some municipalities, extra care will be offered as a range of modules to choose from. For example, if your child is in kindergarten from 8 till 12, the modules could run from 7 till 8 am, then lunch from 12 till 2 pm, then afternoon modules, from 2 till 4 and 4 till 6pm. In other cantons, or municipalities, there may just be lunch on offer, or nothing at all. The school will close and your child will have to come home for lunch and stay at home some afternoons too.

Chapter 2   Making the move to a local school

What does transition involve?

People who come to Switzerland with small children tend to have the easiest time with the local system. Their children may lead a 'double life', experiencing different ways of doing things at home and outside the home. They first go to local day care or playgroup with children from the neighbourhood and soak up the local language and culture almost by osmosis. As an example, Helen is from England and lives and works in Zurich. She and her husband speak English at home to B, their two-year-old son. He goes to local Swiss day care and his first words were Swiss-German ones. He is hearing stories in Swiss German and learning local nursery rhymes. B will already be both bilingual and bicultural when he starts local kindergarten.

The situation is different for parents and children when the child moves from a local school in their home country to a local school in Switzerland, or from an international school in Switzerland to a local public school. Both the parents and their child go through an adjustment process. The child will be learning a new language and will get to know the teacher and other children using this new language. Communication styles will be different. Language is the aspect of adjustment that we can see and can most easily judge progress on. There are cultural aspects going on beneath the surface too. Some children will need time, patience and plenty of support and encouragement as they get used to a culturally different school environment.

As an example of a different environment, a key aspect of Swiss education is the emphasis on children learning to be self-reliant. This can be seen in the custom of encouraging them to walk to kindergarten or school without parental supervision in some parts of the country. There is also the expectation that a kindergarten child will learn to zip up her own jacket and tie her own shoes without help at the end of the morning. (Shoes and jackets with Velcro fastenings can come in handy at this stage).

Cultural differences

Example 1 - Giving comfort

My daughter tells the story of how, when she was three years old, she banged her knee on a chair while she was playing with L, a neighbour's child, who was also three. To her surprise, L offered her four options to 'make it better'. "I can blow on it, kiss it, stroke it, or sing *Heile, heile Segen*."[6] My daughter found the offer a bit strange but opted for all four anyway. L was Austrian, and had lived in the USA till she was two. Then she moved to Switzerland. She had already worked out that adults had different ways of comforting children, and that children had different preferences when being comforted.

Example 2 - Communication styles

Lorna taught English from home to five to eight-year-olds from her daughter's classes. She found it difficult to get them to behave and do what she wanted. When she watched her daughter's teachers work with the children, she realised they were being much more direct, using commands, rather than polite requests. "Sit down, Sara." or "Luca, put that down." She had been giving instructions that began with expressions like "Could you please…"

Resocialisation of parents

The process of cultural adaptation can be referred to as acculturation or even *re*-socialization for the whole family, as there may also be an adjustment for parents regarding what the school expects of them. They may be socialized in one country to get involved in the work of their child's school, taking part in classroom activities, even helping groups of children with reading aloud. Then, in another setting, they are resocialized not to get involved in the work of the school, but to leave it to the professionals. (Please see also sections three and five of my first book *Beyond Chocolate – understanding Swiss culture*[7] for further information on cultural differences that may be relevant). Until they get used to it, parents can experience their new hands-off role as disempowerment.

As well as the expectations of the school, the attitudes of other parents contribute to the resocialisation of parents. Alexandra Muz is a Swiss journalist who lives in Mexico City. She describes in an article how she became a 'tiger mum lite', a mild version of a 'tiger mum', as a result of sending her seven-year-old daughter to a prestigious private school there.[8] She ended up enrolling her daughter on a maths tutoring programme, like the other mothers around her. The children practised maths for 15 minutes every day all year, usually only with a lot of pressure from their mothers. Alexandra Muz comments that by the summer holidays her daughter could do as much maths as her cousin in Switzerland who was a class higher than she was. In Switzerland, if there is any pressure, it comes later, and it is mainly driven by the teacher. In this book you will read about children doing 15-minutes-a-day speed maths calculation homework under time pressure around the age of nine.

When should you make the move?

Given that the transition to a local Swiss school may involve both learning a new language and adapting to a new culture, whether and when to move should be considered carefully. It may be that you are on an expatriate contract and are not yet sure whether you will be staying in Switzerland. Some parents find sending their child to an international school makes it easier when they transfer their child to another international school in the next country. It is also easier for the children of native English speakers who will be returning home and going to school in their local system in the same language.

There may also be curriculum issues to consider. Some parents prefer to keep their children in an international school if they know they are going to be going back to a country where academic learning starts around the age of four or five. Children educated in the Swiss system may have some catching up to do if they go back around the age of six or seven. Many parents with older children say that, somewhere between the ages of eight and ten, the gap closes and children educated in Switzerland are doing as much or more than their peers in countries with early academic learning.

The view that the gap closes can be reassuring to parents who are concerned about the quality of the Swiss public school system. Kaya Usher-Samayoa is a senior consultant for the relocation company Ready Steady Relocate.[9] She explains that public schools do not have the best reputation in some countries and expatriates therefore do not expect them to be good in Switzerland. They think, 'It is bad there, so it must be bad here.' They are then pleasantly surprised to discover that their assumptions about Swiss public schools are wrong.

Another issue to be considered if you will be in Switzerland short term is whether your child will be learning only one language or a language and a dialect too. I found that parents in the French and Italian-speaking parts of Switzerland are happier to expose their children to a new language, even if it is possibly only for one or two years.

In the German-speaking part, people are more hesitant to do this as, especially at kindergarten, children will be exposed to both High-German and Swiss-German and it can take a bit longer to sort the languages out.

All over the country, once people know they are staying permanently, they often decide to 'go local' and transfer their children to a local school. One reason may be that they would like them to feel at home in the local culture. In many cases, the company is not willing to continue paying the fees for private school long-term. Some try to do this as soon as they know they are staying, to help their child start to learn the local language and get used to local ways.

A first key milestone is around the age of four when the child starts kindergarten and another at the age of six, when children tend to start Swiss school. In school, a group is formed and children get to know the classmates with whom they will be spending around six years in a fairly close-knit group. A third important milestone is when the assessment process begins, around the age of 10 or 11 in many cantons, to stream the children into different schools, classes or achievement levels. If you have the chance, it can be helpful to have your child already settled in a local school with a good grasp of the language, when the assessment process begins.

Juggling your lives

Sanjay and his wife are Indian and were both relocated by their company in India to Switzerland. He points out that, if both parents are working, this could influence the decision to go local as the issue of childcare arises. In the cases I came across where both parents worked full-time, they either had childminders or live-in nannies for their primary school children, or else they made sure that they lived somewhere that offered lunch at or near the school, as well as childcare before and after school.

The best of both worlds

Some expatriate parents send their children to international schools and later transfer them to local schools. Barbara is German and she and her Hungarian husband and their daughter all speak German at home. Their daughter spoke English at the international school she attended until she was ten. Barbara describes what she appreciated about the international school:

> They motivate the kids, focus on their strengths, and have the vision to educate them to be explorative, challenging children. It is brilliant how they inject into kids a fascination for reading and writing, learning it early. An example of this is already in kindergarten where they read books with five to ten words per page and feel successful because they have read a whole book. They make learning fun for the children. They integrate the use of computers in the different subjects. There was a Science Day in 1st grade which provoked a lot of independent thinking and exploring. Our daughter gave her first PowerPoint presentation in 2nd grade.

Barbara and her husband were aware that they would need to change to the Swiss system at some point. A basic driver was that the company was going to stop paying for their daughter's private education. The question was finding the right time to move:

> We found out that in canton Schwyz, the key age is twelve, or the 6th class, when they change to a different school type. So we

worked backwards from there. The decision whether to take the exam to get into *Gymnasium* is based on marks at the end of 5th class and after the first half of the 6th class. So we changed her in time to enter the 4th class, to give her time to fill any gaps, then the 5th class would count and the 6th class was the decision year.

When they changed to the Swiss system, Barbara got extra maths lessons for her daughter from a local teacher who knew how maths was taught at the local school. She had heard from many people locally that kids were a lot further on in maths in the local Swiss system by the 4th (H6) class. She did not worry initially about her daughter's language, as they spoke High German at home, but realised later that there were gaps in her German grammar. All in all, they appreciated the international school but were also happy with the move, and the solid foundation provided by the Swiss system:

> My husband and I have discussed this. We think the Swiss school system is like going on a hike. You prepare well before you get moving. The children have their 'education backpack' packed properly. They put on the right shoes, and then they walk. They don't try to impress people by walking too fast at the beginning.

Barbara's daughter was a native speaker of German and there was no issue regarding having to learn the language of the new school.

It was the language issue that Kate kept in mind when she and her husband moved from the UK to canton Zurich with their two sons, J who was eight, and C who was six-years-old. They started them at the international school. The company was paying for their schooling and neither Kate nor her husband spoke any German, so Swiss school did not seem like an option. Kate appreciated her children's creative and imaginative teachers at the international school and the standard of English and maths was good. She also benefited from the very friendly support network of parents there, as there was no language barrier.

At the same time, their neighbours in the village were friendly from the start and Kate and her husband soon started to feel at home there. When J was nine, they started thinking about changing the boys to local school in the village. Kate had read somewhere that if it was left beyond the age of ten, language integration was much harder, so she was aware of the clock ticking for J. She describes the main reasons for moving them:

It was meeting Swiss people who had such command of so many languages that was the deciding factor. I wanted the boys to grow up understanding cultural differences, and different languages, and I realised that being able to speak them is a huge advantage when it comes to employment. Also I was fed up with driving everywhere for play dates. In my mind, I wanted them to have friends round the corner, particularly now we were living in a country where playing outside is still considered the safe and normal thing to do.

They then moved their sons to the local village school, where they joined the 4th (H6) and 2nd (H4) class respectively. At the same time, Kate and her husband remain good friends with at least three families they got to know through the international school, as well as two of the teachers. As she puts it, "I now feel we have the best of both worlds."

Kate gives a highly entertaining as well as extremely informative account of her own and her sons' transition process and experience of Swiss school in her blog, *Swiss Family Taylor*.[10]

A gradual transition

International and bilingual school websites are in English and it is relatively easy to find out about these schools' profiles and what they are offering. It is more difficult to find out about the local Swiss schools if you do not speak the language. Stephen is Australian and his wife Renate, is Dutch. They moved from the Netherlands to canton Basel-Stadt with their four-year-old son, J. Even after over a year in Switzerland, Stephen still describes the transition process they face as a challenge: "Before we came to Switzerland we had a bit of an idea what the international schools entailed. But now, with the transition to the Swiss system, it's just the unknown."

J spoke both Dutch and a little English when they arrived, but no German. Renate told me that they sent him to a bilingual school first to make the transition smoother: "For us, the bilingual aspect was attractive, because at this age you can pick up the languages a lot quicker, and it is done very playfully. Once he has a proper basis of German, it is easier to go to the Swiss school."

After one year of bilingual school, J speaks reasonable High German for his age. After another year they hope to move him to the

Swiss school in time to start the first class of primary school. At a bilingual school, children get a head start in both the local language and the culture. Some of the teachers are Swiss and the children will get used to their approach to teaching as well as local customs – for example, having to shake hands with the teacher when they arrive and leave.

Tünde is Hungarian and she and her Austrian husband lived in the USA until their daughter S was two-and-a-half. She had been diagnosed as speech-delayed in the USA, and they were advised to speak only English to her. Therefore she had no German at all. When they arrived in Switzerland she started attending a German-English bilingual day care centre. They wanted her to be in an environment where English was also spoken so that she would feel comfortable and have a smooth introduction to German as the new language. She was happy there, but was not picking up any words in German. After six months she started attending a German language Swiss day care centre for part of the day. She enjoyed it as much as the other one although she was still not speaking German. After ten months she started local kindergarten, which she enjoyed very much, and things took off. Within weeks she was telling her parents things in German. Parallel to this, her English kept improving. She speaks it a lot at home and is developing both at the same time.

Children can also learn the local language at an English-speaking international school. Kimberly is from the USA and originally moved to Zurich with her husband for a three year assignment. Their daughters, then eight and six years old, attended an international school, where German was one of their subjects. Once her husband's contract switched to local, it was decision time. Kimberly reports:

> We went through the agonizing choice of switching them to local school. We made the right decision, and moved them. B had just finished third grade and M fifth grade. They first went to the transition class with intensive German. They were only there until the Christmas break then moved to the 'regular' classroom. The German they had at the international school allowed for them to have a very short transition time.

Some parents with children of different ages try a combination of approaches. Karen and her husband moved from England and settled in canton Basel-Stadt six years ago with their six children, then aged eleven, ten, seven, five, three and one. As a teacher herself, Karen found the idea of a completely different school system quite intimidating. "You're scared. You've taught in your own school system. You believe in it, you know how it works. We were told by others that we didn't need to know about the Swiss school system."

Their eleven-year-old started at the international school and stayed there until he had taken the International Baccalaureate six years later. He was already performing at a high level in English and they did not want to risk changing him to the local system. Their ten-year-old son and seven-year-old daughter went to bilingual private schools in preparation for changing over to the Swiss system. After three years, when their daughter was nine, Karen wished to transfer her to the 3rd (H5) class of Swiss school. She contacted the local school authorities.

> I asked their advice and they said that she might have to go down a year. I suggested getting her German teacher to write a report with examples of her work and they agreed to this. "Send it to us and we'll consider it." When they saw her work they said, "Fine, she can go into the 3rd class."

Although they were not encouraged to do so by others, Karen and her husband sent their fourth child to local kindergarten. There she was given extra German lessons. The two youngest children also went straight into the local Swiss system when their turn came and were given extra German too. Looking back, Karen says she would have gone local immediately with all six children if she had known more about the system.

In at the deep end

In some cases, expatriate parents do not know whether they are staying in Switzerland long-term but are still willing to give the local system a try. Especially in the French and Italian-speaking parts of the country, where there is little or no dialect, it can be fairly easy for children to go back home with a new language under their belt. Angela and her husband moved from England to French-speaking canton of Vaud when their son was eight and their daughter was seven. They moved to a very multicultural area by the lake, with many expatriates, where around 80% of the children do not speak French at home.

> We were relocated by my husband's company and were expected to use the international school. However, it had no places and we were not happy about the education on offer elsewhere. At the international school, the fees would be paid on a sliding scale with the company's contribution decreasing every year, so we would have had to move them later to the local school. So we thought we would try the local school right away, for a year. It was good immersion for the language. They had done well at their level in the UK, so wouldn't be behind. They were to be given three hours of extra French lessons every week.

> I was terrified. It was a huge leap of faith and the children were the ones making the leaps. I had a sick feeling in the pit of my stomach every day when they came home for lunch in case it hadn't gone well. But it did. Now the international school has offered us places for them if we want it. We asked the children, and both were adamant that they wanted to stay in the local school. They like coming home for lunch every day for two hours and they like having Wednesday afternoons off.

Hannah was 10 years old, and in the last year of primary school in England when she arrived in Switzerland one Easter. She was very bright for her age and was put in the 5th (H7) class in Basel-Stadt. "In the beginning teachers came over to explain work in English," she told me. "Later they said it in simple High German. If I didn't understand anything, I just went to the teachers, they were all really helpful."

Many of the people I interviewed who now have older children are proponents of the 'deep end' approach. Looking back, they say things like,"If you are planning to stay, it is worth going local as soon as possible" and "Jump in while your children are small, before they get used to another way of doing things." The fact that there is now much more support in learning the language makes taking the plunge a lot easier than it used to be. More is said about this in Chapter 4.

Views of children who make the move

I conducted an interview in English with a group of eight 10- and 11-year-old girls who are now in local schools. They came to Switzerland from different countries and some have been in international schools too. Below, I provide a selection of their comments and their advice to any children who are going to start Swiss school. R (11) is British and started Swiss school at the age of nine:

> If you move to a new school you're obviously going to be upset that you're moving away from your friends. And the first time you go into a new class, everyone looks at you and you don't know what to say. You want to be nice and fit in but you can't. (I just wanted to go back out, and go home). But then after two weeks you're not scared any more. You're just a normal child, you're like them and it just takes some time to learn the language. But you'll learn it some time. Because they speak to you and you just pick it up from the other children. I think you shouldn't be scared because everybody's basically nice over here.

J (10) is English and started French school at the age of four:

> At first it's scary but you should be confident because you'll soon learn the language. They explain it to you. I learned the language really quickly, so when I was six I could speak it fluently. And if I don't understand I can just ask.

M (11) is Hungarian and started Swiss kindergarten at the age of five:

> When I first came here there was a girl in my class who also spoke English so I was happy there. And every day I had German with the teacher and it really helped me. And in school every time a new kid comes, they can learn German really fast because they are surrounded by lots of German-speaking people. I really like it that you stay a long time with the same kids and the same teacher. Because you get used to them. For me, my class is like a family because I have been so long with them and I enjoy every bit of being with them.

E (11) is Brazilian and started Swiss school at the age of ten:

> When I first went to the Swiss school I learned German better when I just started talking more and reading books. I got some books from the bookstores and the library. At home I wrote down every new word to memorise it better.

D (11) is Columbian and started Swiss school at the age of seven:

> When my parents told me we were moving to Switzerland, I got very sad because I couldn't be with my best friend any more. I thought in the new school I would just sit around and look at the other children playing together and I wouldn't have friends. But it was completely different. On the first day I got really nice friends. Every girl who comes here thinks too she won't have friends, but she shouldn't think that because you will get friends.

These girls had mainly positive experiences. Most of them joined classes where there were other foreigners, many the children of other expatriates. Other young people report that making friends will not happen so quickly. It may be partly a matter of age if children are less open to newcomers as they near puberty. It could also be partly due to the peach and coconut phenomenon I describe in my first book, *Beyond Chocolate*.[11] In a 'peachy' environment it is easy to start getting to know people, but relationships may not be long-term. In a 'coconut' environment, people may be more cautious and possibly distant at first. It takes time to build relationships, but once they are established, they are enduring.

A is an 11-year-old English girl who started Swiss school at the age of 10. Her account shows how this may work in practice:

> When I first came here I was really lonely. I tried making some new friends at Swiss school, but they mostly laughed at me, probably because I said something that was funny in German without meaning to. As time went on and I learnt more German, I could speak more to everybody. It helped when I kept changing seats in the classroom every two months because then when I needed somebody to help me with things I didn't understand, I had different people to ask.

I soon made some new friends and I now have two good friends at school. I sit next to one of them at the moment and when we next all change places I will sit next to the other one. Though I now have friends, I will never forget how it felt when I was so alone. So now, when some of the girls in my class fall out for a while, I sit with the girl who's alone as the other one will have lots of people on her side – I won't let anybody else be alone like I was.

A's mother Claire commented on the turning point, from her perspective as a parent:

I think the big change happened for A when the class went away for a week to a cabin up in the mountains – she was forced into a situation where she was surrounded by her class-mates for a week, had to speak German (and some Swiss German) and had to socialise with the other children. Before she went she was very hesitant about going and was very unsure of herself and how she would feel being in that situation – however, the change in her when she returned was incredible.

All of a sudden there was a lot of, 'B did this' and 'C did that' and since then A has felt more part of the class and settled into school life more. I think a large part of the problem with foreign children being integrated into Swiss school life has to do with the fact that all the children in the class will have been schooled together since kindergarten and therefore have formed very close friendship groups. It is natural that is difficult for 'outside' children to find their feet in those groups, but once they are accepted they seem to be totally accepted.

Kevin is Irish and goes to local school in Basel-Stadt, where he was born. When he was 13 he spent two weeks at a local school just across the border in France. It was part of an immersion pro-gramme called *Sprachbad*. He commented on how the children in France were a lot friendlier to him as a newcomer than he would expect his peers back in Basel to be:

In breaks they crowded around me. They tried to speak German to me and asked me loads of questions. They also will-ingly gave me information about themselves. Swiss kids wouldn't do this. They like to stay together. Once they have their own friends, they don't need anyone else and don't reach out to others.

Hannah experienced the approach to newcomers as quite different in Switzerland than in her school in England, and gives the following advice:

> Unless the teacher tells the other children to show you round, they stick to their groups. These are strong and hard to break into. Don't wait till they approach you, it's not going to happen. Go up to someone, try and talk to them, go around with them if they will let you, go with them if they ask you and laugh with them, try and be part of the group. In England in my school, if you had a new girl, everyone would follow her around. It was exciting, the new girl was fussed over and people fought to be her best friend. After the excitement wore off, they decided if they really liked them or not. In Switzerland you have to fend for yourself, and make the first move. There are no ready-made friends.

As Claire mentioned, it seems to be easiest for children to integrate if they join a class as it is forming – for example in the first year of kindergarten or the first year of primary school. After that, it is still easy to integrate if new children are regularly joining the class. The other, newer children are likely to be the most open. Joining a class where everyone else has been together for years involves being proactive, as Hannah describes. It can be an advantage to go to a school where there are regularly new children shaking up the class dynamics.

Chapter 3   Which school will your child go to?

No shopping for schools

When parents hear that they will be moving to Switzerland, they may join an online group for expatriates such as the *English Forum*,[12] *Expat-Moms-in-Switzerland*[13] or the *Yahoo Swiss schooling group*.[14] Very often, the first question they ask is: "We are moving to such-and-such a town and will be sending our child to the local school. Can anyone recommend a good school?" They inevitably get the reply: "You can't choose your school in Switzerland. You can only choose where to live and are then allocated a school." This is the case during the nine years of compulsory education. Allowing parents to choose the school they want their child to go to was the subject of an 'initiative' the Swiss people voted on in September 2008. They voted against it. Another initiative about this is under-way as we go to press.[15]

The fact that there is no 'shopping for schools' makes Switzerland quite different from countries where parents have become used to having a greater degree of influence in the sphere of education. As an example, in England and Wales, the Department of Education and Science introduced the *Education Reform Act of 1988*, "to reduce the dominant role of local authorities in education and increase the influence of the consumers – the parents and children – by intro-ducing market principles into the schools system."[16] As a result, parents, industry and commerce all have more say as consumers in the policy and practice of schools there. The emphasis is on pro-ducer accountability to consumers, value for money, effectiveness, efficiency and market forces. Similarly, in the Netherlands, parents are clients and can actively participate in developing the school, as reported by Micheline Ruggle, a Swiss teacher there.[17]

The fact that you are just allocated a school in Switzerland is probably the biggest adjustment for expatriate parents who decide to 'go local'. Some have previously had to choose between private schools and want value for money. Others come from countries where public schooling is not assumed to be of an equally high standard across the board, as was mentioned earlier. It is the parents' job to exercise their consumer rights responsibly and do research on the quality of the schools to try to choose the best school for their child.

School across the border

German, French and Italian incomers may have more choice regarding school if they live at the border near their country of origin. Anja is German and lives in canton Thurgau. She told me that she considered sending her children to school in Germany, partly because more children can go to gymnasium there. In the end she decided to send her children to the Swiss school so that they would learn Swiss-German, get to know children in the neighbourhood, and be integrated in the local community. However, she stresses that you have to decide for yourself. There is no right way to do it.

No league tables

In Switzerland there are no league tables available to parents regarding which schools are the best. The profession is protected to a greater extent from the opinions of the public and is less accountable to them. There are, however, studies done and data generated by education research institutes for quality improvement. This is an internal matter for the professionals; the teaching staff, schools of education and the education authorities. Parents and pupils often report that the differences are between individual teachers rather than between schools.

In the Romandie, or French-speaking Switzerland, there are canton-wide exams (*épreuves cantonales de références*) that provide schools and teachers with internal comparative data about the performance of municipalities, schools and classes. These are also being introduced in German-speaking cantons and may be referred to as *Vergleichstests*). However, the data is not released to the public.

Angela comments that she was only informed about her own child's performance:

> I was obsessed with comparisons, SAT results and league tables. People said they don't exist here, but in Vaud like the rest of Romandie they actually have canton-wide exams at the end of two years and also six years. I would like to have picked the school that was above the cantonal average. My daughter took the exam in Maths and French, we got the results back, and they said how she did compared with the cantonal averages. The teacher wrote me a note. My daughter was slightly below the cantonal average, but passed everything.

Making contact with a school

All around the country, children are allocated a nearby kindergarten or primary school by the school authorities where they live. When you move to Switzerland and choose somewhere to live, you have to register with the local city or municipal authorities (*Gemeinde, commune, comune*). They will then allocate you a school, or give you a contact person if your child has to attend a special foreign language class (also sometimes known as integration or transition class), to learn the school language first. In smaller municipalities, there may be no choice as there is only one local school for your child's age group. In bilingual cantons (Bern, Fribourg, Valais) and Graubünden, which is even trilingual, it may be possible to choose a school where teaching is conducted in a particular language.

Officials are down to earth and close to the people in Swiss communities and expect to be approached by them. Ursula L. is in charge of intercultural education in the Education Department of canton Baselland. She emphasises that *talking* to the school is really important when you arrive. She recommends that parents go and see the director of the school in the municipality they are moving to, to discuss their child's educational ability and the options available. A government official in canton Vaud commented to a colleague of mine in an e-mail: "These are public schools, dedicated to the public: if parents want to know anything, they can ask their kid's specific school: the secretaries, or teachers, or deans or director – all these people will be delighted to help."

If you are moving to Switzerland just before school starts, some municipalities would be willing to send you the forms you need to fill in by email, while others will want you to actually move in before they get down to business with you. Sarah explains the tight timeline for her and her family. Her daughter H finished school in England at the end of July and they moved immediately after that. She could not find a website for the school but found the email address of the school administration on the web site of the Baselland municipality they were moving to:

> I emailed the principal of schools two weeks prior to us moving and I said, "Help, what do we do, how do we find a school?" I was told that I would need to email and get in touch with him once we had moved. So, on the 11th of August, we met him and discussed our reasons for wanting H to attend a local Swiss school. He explained the hours of school and rules, and then we filled out a form and that was it! H was enrolled and started four days later. We received all the paperwork and information about the school a week after she started.
>
> School started at 8am on her first day and I took her along to make sure all was well. At 10am that morning I was invited back by the principal to see H welcomed into the school along with other new students. All new students got a flower windmill to put in their garden. It was really lovely and I have never experienced anything like it before. Even though we couldn't understand the songs or the ceremony, we still really enjoyed it and all the children seemed to too. It was also a great way to meet all the teachers in the school.

Claire moved from England with her children to Baselland.

> I didn't speak to the authorities, I contacted the school direct during a visit to Switzerland. In the UK, you phone up the school you want your child to go to. My husband was already here. He moved out here a year before we did. So I spoke to the school in advance, and said, "We're moving to Switzerland, can we come and speak to you?" So we went in to the school office and filled in the forms there and then before we moved over.

It is difficult to navigate your way round school authorities' websites if you don't speak the local language. If you cannot find the municipality website, or a school's website, I recommend that you start at the top and phone the cantonal Department of

Education for your canton to ask your first questions. They will give you the telephone number of the school administration in the municipality you are considering living in. A list of telephone numbers is provided in Appendix 1. As you will see, the Departments of Education have many different names. Sharon explains how she phoned this number for the canton of Zurich, and was put through to the school administration, who asked her a few questions. They then put her through to the integration department to discuss her children's language learning needs. They wanted to know which *Gemeinde* (municipality) she was thinking of living in so that they could put her through to the school itself.

Influencing the allocation of a school or class

Swiss parents tend to assume their child will be going to a good school to be taught by a good teacher and they accept the luck of the draw. Some will try to influence the class their child will be sent to by choosing to live in a middle-class catchment area in the suburbs rather than in the city. Others choose to live in the city where there is more diversity and where there is lunch on offer near the school as well as more after-school care.

In some towns, it will end up that all the children living in 'the detached houses at the edge of the forest' will go to the same little kindergarten and school, while those living on the busy main street will go to a different one. However, even this is not certain. Some municipalities will divide the town in such a way as to get a mix of children from both areas in each school.

In addition, logistics play a role. Many local authorities aim to give all children a place at a school within walking distance of their house. This could mean that the places at the little school just a one minute walk from family A's house may be needed for the children of families B to F, who live in the north of the town, where there is no school nearby. The children in family A may then be allocated another school further south that is a 15-minute walk away. Everyone then has to walk a bit.

It may be that you are signing up your child for day care offered by one of the schools. In this case, your child will be allocated to that school. (Day care can be in great demand, and you may only be given a place if both parents have a job.) Another factor that may influence the allocation process is that some school administrations allow children to choose one or two friends they would like to be with when they change from kindergarten to primary school. They will then try to make sure the child is together with at least one of those children. (If three children all name each other, they may all stay together.)

Requesting a school

Swiss parents may write to the authorities to request a particular school or teacher/class, giving a reason for their preference. Requesting a particular school or teacher will only make sense for you if you are already living in a particular neighbourhood and know something about the schools or the teachers. Then you may have a reason for a request. It is important that you do not suggest to the school authorities that you think you have a **right** to choose your school or class. This does not go down well. It also varies from one place to another as to whether you are allowed to visit the kindergarten or school with your child before the summer holidays. There may be an open-door day for visitors. You can ask about this.

Reasons parents may give for their request for a particular school include the following:

- Our child's older sibling is attending this school.
- My son has made friends with a neighbouring boy who is attending this school. It would be nice for him to go to a school where he knows someone.
- I am a working mother and wish my child to be able to go to the organised lunch offered near this particular school.
- I am a working mother and my childminder lives near this school.
- I am concerned about my child managing the local language and I have been told that teacher XYZ in school ABC is very good at helping English-speaking children to settle in.

Finding a neighbourhood that suits you

Parents who start with temporary accommodation have a good opportunity to first sort out the educational issues and then find somewhere to live. An example of this approach is when Dana arrived with her family from the USA in the month of May. Her husband's company gave them temporary accommodation, which gave her time to research where it would be best to live. She describes how she made contact with other expatriates who had their children in local schools to find out which areas they recommended:

> In the States, the quality of schools can be dramatically impacted by the neighborhood, so I had some biases. Once we had decided on local schools, I attended expat events and joined groups (on-line and play groups) and talked to as many people as I could to find out about their local area schools. I also took the children to play at local parks in the areas I was considering. I found parents with older children didn't necessarily know current information and based their opinions on outdated experiences. I also contacted and visited Swiss playgroups and Swiss school offices. I asked teachers where they send their kids to school. We then moved to what people had told us was a 'good' neighbourhood.

The neighbourhood to which Sara moved has a high percentage of pupils going to gymnasium (the academic path). This varies from one municipality to another in many cantons. The canton of Zurich publishes statistics on how many pupils in different municipalities go to gymnasium.[18] For example, in Zürichberg 57.8% of pupils went on to gymnasium in 2008, compared with 22.9% in the whole canton that year. In Kilchberg it was 50.4% and in Küsnacht 48.6%, while in Letzi it was 22.5%, around the cantonal average. In Limmattal it was 19.6% and in Affoltern it was 18.7%, both a bit below the average. In Schlieren it was only 12.8% and in Volketswil it was 11.2%. Most cantons do not publish data like this.

Other parents appreciate the childcare on offer in cities, as well as the diversity and intercultural skills resulting from living in a multicultural city neighbourhood. Andrea is Swiss and settled with her Ghanaian husband and three children in the city of Basel, in St Johann, a very diverse neighbourhood with different religions and cultures. Her children spoke Swiss-German to her at home. Andrea explains her perspective:

> I am a fan of the city. Everything is nearby, shops, cinemas, theatres and so on. There are plenty of parks and playgrounds, and children play outside together. School will always be nearby, even upper-secondary. You never have to travel far to get to it. Our three children took part in an integration project at primary school in the St Johann neighbourhood that fostered the development of their social and intercultural competence. They have a wide circle of friends from many cultures, with a mix of backgrounds and living standards. I think it is good to have this mix.

Andrea appreciated the very committed teachers at her children's school. She sees the attitude of the class as influential too. If a child has classmates who are ambitious, the child is more likely to be ambitious too. She found ambition levels varied in her children's classes, and that they were influenced by the attitudes of their peers. Her sons were tired of school after nine years and wanted to do apprenticeships, while her daughter went on to an upper-secondary specialised school.

Alfredo is from Brazil and lives in Geneva. He expressed appreciation that his children meet others from many countries and cultures at their school. "They have good Muslim friends and were surprised to learn about Ramadan fasting," he explained. "There is an emphasis on respect and early training on democracy through class and school assemblies." Martin is from Germany and has two children in local school, also in canton Geneva. He also comments on the emphasis on social cohesion in their multicultural community:

> The schools belong to the community in which we live and contribute meaningfully to greater social cohesion in the neighbourhood. The efforts for social integration of people from abroad have been excellent in the Geneva canton. The quality of the education has been – it seems to me – better than in Germany with a stronger emphasis on social relationships. Parents coming from abroad may need to know that there is a certain Swiss understanding of discipline and behaviour – not so much in Geneva with the strong presence/influence of people from abroad (in a class of 20, there were at times only five Swiss children, all others had parents coming from abroad).

Moving to the country

My family and I sometimes watch British TV programmes showing a couple planning to retire to the country, or somewhere abroad, and being shown properties to choose from. We are always surprised by the way the focus is only on the property itself. No reference is made to the community the couple will be living in, or the neighbours they will have. In Switzerland it is really important to investigate this.

If you are considering moving to the countryside, you may be delighted to discover idyllic little Swiss villages with views to die for and reasonably priced houses and low cantonal and municipal taxes. However, the fact that the reasonably priced houses are not being snapped up by financially astute Swiss city dwellers might suggest that they are not always the easiest places for 'outsiders', Swiss or foreign, to settle in. It can be challenging for city dwellers to live in a community with traditional values that is not used to receiving incomers. Small close-knit communities may have generations of several families or clans in the same village. Everyone will seem to be related to everyone else, including the school teacher and the village council who make both administrative and political decisions related to running the local school.

With regard to explaining how things work, local people may consider many things to be self-evident that are a complete mystery to you. This was experienced as a challenge by Jennifer and her family, who are bilingual in French and English. They spoke no German when they arrived in their small German-Swiss village, although Jennifer learned it quickly. She found it hard to find the information she needed:

> The school system itself is good, once you get to know it and see what they're doing. I think the curriculum is good and my son is enjoying it and doing well. I just wish the school system had not been so hard to get acquainted with. The village was not used to having non-German speakers and there was no real school head and no one used to explaining how the system works, provision of language classes, choices after primary school, or telling you more basic things like the plimsolls needed for gym classes, or even that the gym classes were held in a building 200 metres away from the school.

My overall feeling is that you should be aware of the challenges and know you are the sort of person who wants the end result of thorough integration. Going it alone as non-German-speaking (and not married to a Swiss) in a small village is very, very hard work and you have to have balls and confidence. I am not good at sticking my neck out and found this very hard in the beginning. The rewards are huge and our integration, after five years, is very much better than the few other expats I have got to know, but it came at a price emotionally. You have to be gutsy to ride that out long term, and I do not think I am. We are moving now to a French-speaking Swiss town. Our younger son is going to attend a special school for children with developmental delay. I could not face navigating the special school options in this village in German! I know when I am beat.

I interviewed Stephan, a Swiss father of young children whose job involves working with small villages. Generally speaking, he finds it much better to live in a village than in the city because of the beautiful countryside and the high quality of life. It can also be an advantage that you will get to know the neighbours fairly quickly. However, for foreigners, he would only recommend villages that are open to change:

In some villages in Switzerland a hundred new houses are built every year, and well-heeled, highly-qualified people move in who work in the city. The inhabitants are more open towards another culture. A way to know if a village is like this is to see how many new houses have been built recently and how many newcomers have been settling in the village over the last few years. It is a very positive indicator if a village organises a *Mittagstisch* (organised lunch for school children). This shows openness to the idea that both parents can work outside the home. In a village I know, the men will say, "We don't want a *Mittagstisch*. I want my son to be able to come home for lunch."

It is Stephan's opinion that in small villages with up to 2000 inhabitants it is a tradition that everyone knows exactly where everyone else is at any given time. (You could consider whether you would like to be the village's main source of entertainment.) In villages of 2000 to 6000 inhabitants, people all know each other but don't check up on each other so much.

Stephan recommends that incomers to a village enrol their children in sports activities such as the local football club, or a music class. That way they will be known more quickly and accepted by the local people. It is ideal if parents can take part in local activities too (see also Chapter 5 on learning the language). Stephan also suggested checking for language classes organised by the village municipality, or another village nearby, for mothers and their small children. This means the mothers do not have to find a babysitter if they want to learn the language. This can be helpful for the family to start getting to know other foreign families who have recently moved in.

One last piece of advice that may be useful to incomers settling in a village comes from Jonathan, who is English and lives in a small village. He emphasises the importance of supporting local business, and not 'going to strangers' for your shopping. (He jokingly calls this *fremdgehen* in German, which actually means 'having an affair'.) He and his wife often do their grocery shopping in the village shop and buy wine from the local wine dealer.

Fitting in time to work

As well as the symbolic value of having lunch provided near the school, it is worth considering whether you need to have child care out of school hours. Does the canton or municipality you would like to live in have child care on offer and will there be places available? "The school days are really short here," one mother commented. "I fitted in a part-time job in the UK. I can't do that here." Her ten-year-old daughter comes home for lunch and often does not have school in the afternoon.

High hopes

Although they may choose where to live, and occasionally request a particular school, Swiss parents otherwise accept that their children will go to the nearest local school. They will focus their energies on helping their children to do their best in the school they happen to be in. They may hope, but not assume that their child will be one of the 20% of pupils nationwide who end up on an academic pathway to gymnasium and then university. They are aware that young people who do an apprenticeship can have excellent career prospects too, as will be discussed in later chapters. This book will tell you a lot more about the different pathways and will also show how other parents have supported their children along the way.

Chapter 4   Learning the school language

This chapter is named 'Learning the school language', rather than the local language. Some cantons (Bern, Valais and Fribourg) are bilingual, and others (Ticino and Graubünden) are trilingual. It is likely, but cannot be assumed, that the language of the school is also the language of the local neighbourhood. Wherever you are, provision will be made for incoming children to learn the school language. In this chapter, I first outline different types of provision offered and then go on to provide specific examples in different cantons or municipalities based on interviews with teachers and parents. There may also be other approaches to provision that I have not heard of.

> **Graubünden: a special case**
>
> At Romansh and Italian-speaking schools in canton Graubünden, children generally start learning German as a foreign language in the third class. Language lessons for incomers may therefore be Romansh, Italian or German, depending on where the school is. For this reason they are referred to as *FfF*, or *Förderung für Fremdsprachige* (support for speakers of foreign languages) rather than *DaZ* or *Deutsch als Zweitsprache* (German as a second language).

At kindergarten level, children usually join a regular class and have extra one-to-one or small-group support from a language teacher in the classroom during class time, for example, during free play. Some incoming children are completely fluent in the school language by the time they start school, and can then learn to read and write it as native speakers. At primary school level there are two main approaches. The first is to place the children in a regular class immediately and take them out of class for extra lessons in the local language. It is important to find out how many hours of extra lessons your child is entitled to in your canton. The municipality usually covers the extra cost (via the taxes of residents).

The other main approach is to allocate children to two classes: a special mixed-age class to learn the language as well as a regular class. The special classes are known as foreign language classes (*Fremdsprachenklassen*) or integration classes (*Integrationsklassen*) in High German, and reception classes (*classes d'accueil*) in French. This approach is used where there are a lot of incoming children. It is standard practice in Geneva and some other parts of French-speaking Switzerland, and is also found in German-speaking Switzerland. The teachers can teach all subjects, but are specialised in teaching German or French as a foreign language. They simplify their language in order to be understood by the children. Initially the children spend more time in their integration class, learning the language. At the same time, they start attending lessons in their regular class – for example, sports and art classes, which are less language-based. They usually stay in the special class for six months to two years.

A third approach, which is becoming less common, is to keep children completely separate from their future class in an integration class where they have no contact with a regular class. In this case too, transfer to regular classes may take place after six months to two years.

Throughout the country at lower-secondary school level, it is most common to allocate children to a special integration class, where they first learn the language. It is thought that the subject matter is too complex to pick up without first obtaining a solid language foundation. In Ticino, however, children may be allocated to a regular class and be given extra language lessons. Please see chapter 15 for an example of this approach at the gymnasium level in canton Basel-Stadt.

At primary and secondary levels, it is sometimes recommended that the child go back a year, joining a lower level class where the school work is easier. Then they can concentrate more on learning the language. Incoming parents may be alarmed by 'losing' a year, but there is no 'age race' or stigma attached to repeating a year in Switzerland. Many children do this at some time, either to make sure they have a solid educational foundation to build on, or to give them time to become more mature. Teachers want them to have a sense of self-mastery, feeling self-confident at each level, rather than overwhelmed. Young adults finishing upper-secondary education may therefore range in age from 18 to 20, or, a bit more rarely, 21.

No matter which type of provision your child experiences, learning the language is a very individual matter for both adults and children. Some children will start to speak almost immediately, while others will say nothing for a very long time. Kirstin comments that her children were in local school for nine months before she heard them speaking understandable phrases in French, although it was clear they understood much more earlier on. Some children want to be able to say a proper sentence, she comments. You have to give it a certain amount of time before you can decide whether it is working. For one child it may be three months before they feel comfortable speaking, while for another it may be two years.

Learning the language at kindergarten

Learning the language may be easiest at kindergarten. Caz describes how her older daughter started kindergarten at the age of four, with very limited Swiss German. Although she had gone to Swiss day care for a few hours a week, many of the staff had spoken English to her. In spite of this, she learned German easily, as Caz explains: "By attending Swiss kindergarten, she sorted the language out fairly quickly and through the themes that the teacher used was able to learn a great deal." Caz describes how all the children extended their vocabulary, for example, by learning about caring for their pet mouse, or a jungle theme.

Corinne H supports class teachers by teaching High German as a foreign language at kindergarten level in canton Aargau. There is a budget of one hour per week per incoming child who needs to learn German. She works six hours a week with the incoming children from two different classes, during time scheduled for free play. Although she focuses on the foreign children who speak little German, she uses a language programme that promotes phonological awareness in High German that

Swiss-German speakers can benefit from too. They start with rhyming sounds. Corinne H. shows a doll (*eine Puppe*) and asks in High German, "*Ist es eine Suppe? Ist es ein Pullover?*" (Is it soup, is it a pullover?) Children then shout "*Nein!*" to correct her, even the children who are still very shy.

At other times, if Corinne H sees that one of 'her' children has nothing to do, she takes him aside and does some language work with him in a fun way. They talk about what is going on around them. She does an analysis of the particular child's language level and needs. For example, if a child can make herself understood, but makes mistakes with prepositions, she focuses on that. If they do not understand the prepositions or conjunctions, they may misunderstand important points. Sometimes someone brings a book to her and she reads it with them.

In some German-speaking cantons, only High German is spoken at kindergarten level, while in others, both High German and Swiss German are used. Corinne H comments that children may mix up the two variants for a while, but will have usually separated them by the time they finish the first class at school. At school they have their classes in High German and also learn to read and write in High German, but will probably speak Swiss German in the breaks.

Incoming children who have attended kindergarten tend to speak both variants, while those who start learning the language in primary school may not speak dialect, even though they understand it perfectly. They often show increased interest in speaking dialect as they reach puberty to show they belong to their peer group.

Below, I provide examples of how learning the language has worked in practice for some children around the country. Both parents and children react differently to the types of support that are offered, and my aim is to help prepare you for different possibilities. It may be handled differently again in your canton, in your municipality or at your school.

It is worth making an appointment to discuss the language learning options with your school authorities. If your children already have the basics of the local language, they may be placed straight into a regular class.

Joining a regular class

Kate's two sons started attending local school in Canton Zurich when J was nine and C was seven years old. Kate and her husband had a meeting with the *Schulpflege*, the school authorities, to assess their children's language needs. At the international school, both boys had lessons in High German four times a week, so they entered Swiss school with a smattering of it. The school authorities said they would provide J with three lessons of German (*DaZ*) per week and C with about five to six lessons. I asked Kate about their progress three years later, when J was 12 years old, in the 6th (H8) class and C was 10 years old, in the 4th (H6) class.

> Looking back, I reckon it took six months for J to get to reasonable grips with the language, and a full year before he was confident, but then it was in both High German and dialect. J is now officially no longer in need of German lessons – but he is gifted with very strong language skills, and finds life impossible if he can't communicate, so he is very motivated to learn the language. C will have only two hours a week this coming term. He was still unsure after two years but has made huge progress in the last year. He understands, but is much more reluctant to speak – partly it's due to his personality. C's Swiss German is still weaker than his High German, partly because he reads a lot, which is always in High German. He's getting there, but it's slower. Every time there is a school holiday and he spends the time communicating in English, the first week back is a killer. That said, he is now being given a mark for German, and his marks are as good as I could hope for him. He is much more confident about his own ability to improve in the future.

C was 'signed off' his *DaZ* course after three and a half years. Kate is not sure whether this is because he had his maximum allocation of *DaZ* funding, or if it is because he was deemed proficient in German. But since he achieved a very high mark in a standard German class test, she assumed the latter.

Angela in canton Vaud described how her seven and eight-year-old children went to special French classes one morning a week, for three hours, at a different school in the small town they live in.

They are taught in age groups, and concentrate on pronunciation and the nitty-gritty of the language. In addition they are taken out of their regular class for half an hour once a week to have one-to-one teaching, playing games in French. After nearly a year, my daughter matched the native speakers and didn't need the class any more. The teachers are really happy with her progress. My son continued a bit longer. Now they both have only 30 minutes of one-to-one tuition per week.

It may be that there are cantonal regulations regarding provision of language classes, but that the municipal authorities are unaware of them. Jennifer describes how, in her small village, the language support teacher kept saying her son didn't really need any language help as his language was better than most of the rest of his primary school class:

> That really irritated me. I do not compare him with other children, I compare him with himself and the best that he can be. So at that point, I armed myself with the cantonal regulations and sallied forth! I got him one hour a week. After three-and-a-half years in primary school, they told us the classes were at an end. So again I popped out the regulations, and now he is continuing with the classes.

Lise is Danish and lives in a village near Lugano in canton Ticino. She explains how her older son got extra Italian lessons in primary school, although he was not entitled to them any more:

> He should have had two years of extra Italian at *asilo* (kindergarten), although I did not know this and he didn't get it. He wasn't entitled to any more in school. However the teacher thought he would benefit from more and wanted me to send him to Italian classes after school, and pay for them. I thought this would be too much for him in addition to school. It was not fair to add more hours to his day. Then a new boy arrived from German-speaking Switzerland and my son joined him for his extra lessons during school hours. He ended up getting top grades in Italian from the 2nd class. My second son took longer to learn Italian, although he did three years of *asilo*. He did not have extra classes at all and was still struggling in his first year of school.

Enrolment in two classes

Sarah M is in charge of the BAEP (*bureau d'accueil pour l'école primaire*), an office responsible for informing incoming parents in Geneva about primary school. She explains that in Geneva, from class 3P (known elsewhere as 1st class, or H3) children who cannot speak French (known as *allophones*) may be enrolled in two classes at the same time (*double scolarité*). From class 4P (H4), they are systematically enrolled in two classes:

> Firstly, they attend the *classe d'accueil* (welcome class) for half a day every day, two mornings or afternoons per week, to learn French. This is a mixed-age class for primary school pupils aged six to twelve, with maximum 12 pupils in a class. Depending on their age, they might learn to read and write, or do geography, using French. At the same time they are allocated to the *classe ordinaire* (regular class) according to their age. They will, for example, do maths in this class.

Integration classes

In 'integration classes' or 'foreign language classes', children are kept relatively separate from their regular class until they are fluent in the language. Jo is from Australia and told me that her seven-year-old daughter only had seven months in such a class in Basel-Stadt before being transferred to the 2nd (H4) class of primary school. Some of the other children stayed in the integration class for two years.

One of the reasons Jo's daughter learned German so fast was that Jo had hired a German-speaking nanny from Basel to look after her children. She helped the girls to integrate by explaining some local customs. Jo and her husband both worked full-time so the children had ten hours a day speaking German – four at school and six at home. The nanny helped them with their reading and other homework.

Kimberly describes how her daughters, M and B, were the only English-speaking children in their group in their transition class in canton Zurich. German was the only common language the class spoke. It did not deter them from finding ways to play together, however, and the girls bonded fairly quickly with the other children. Because the girls had a foundation of German from the international school they had previously attended, they were able to transfer to the regular school class after Christmas break. There, they both received two extra lessons of German a week – one during school and one after school.

In the end, it was maths rather than German that raised a question about the class B should attend afterwards. Kimberly communicated intensively with the teacher to persuade her that, at the age of ten, B was ready for the 4th (H6) class.

> The transition teacher was not initially supportive of B going to 4th grade because she had not completed the division portion of the initial math test given to her in August. I was able to change her mind and gain her support through showing that I had purchased the standard math books (*Schweizer Zahlenbuch*) and that the girls were doing a page of math at home per day so that they would not be behind when they joined the other class.

> I also explained that B had not completed the division portion of the initial math test because she was not familiar with how the problems were written. It was not that she didn't know division. Thirdly, she was going into a mixed-age class which combined 4th, 5th and 6th grade, so if she wasn't ready for 5th grade at the end of the year, she could easily remain in the 4th grade within the same class. Everything worked out very well. Both girls adjusted well to the new classrooms and ended up completing the school year with good grades.

The type of school that works best can vary from child to child and it cannot always be predicted in advance. Val and Ian are British. They were not comfortable with the concept of the integration class because it meant that their seven-year-old twins had no contact with local children.

> We moved to a *Gemeinde* (municipality) in Baselland in April because people said it was a nice area. Our twins were allocated to an integration class of 12 foreign children between six and thirteen years old. As soon as they were proficient in High German they would be transferred to a proper German-speaking class. After six weeks we realised that they were not integrating in the integration class. They weren't making any friends and they felt isolated. They were also not speaking High German. It felt like they were segregated.

Val and Ian then met with the teacher, who was also the programme coordinator, and spoke to him through an interpreter. He estimated that their children would need to stay in the class for another year after the summer, as they were not picking up German quickly. Val was not confident that they would pick up German at all this way. She then made enquiries and an English mother living in Riehen, in canton Basel-Stadt, told her that her children had gone straight into the local school as soon as they arrived there. They had been given free extra German classes by the school. Val then contacted the schools department in Riehen:

> They told us that if we moved there, the children would go into the second year rather than the third. They would also be given three hours of extra German every week, for a total of 40 hours in the first summer semester. If they needed more, they would be given more. So we moved to Riehen, and that is what happened. It lifted my spirits when our kids went straight into school. I felt we were part of the community, not on the periphery any more. As it turned out, they only needed the 40 hours. Their German was fine by Christmas.

Val and Ian started out in one of the few municipalities in canton Baselland that ran an integration class at that time. Ursula L. describes it as 'double integration work' for the child to adjust to both a new language and a mixed-age group. She reports that it has become the norm in Baselland to place children in regular classes, but that there are a few areas where there are so many foreign children that integration classes are needed to accommodate them all. However, an effort is now made to allocate all children to a regular class at the same time.

Children may respond differently to mixed-age teaching. H is from England and is ten years old. She had a very positive experience of her first three months of an integration class in Baselland. Speaking about the children in her class, she said, "Our oldest is fifteen, our youngest is six or seven. It's like a family with kids that are younger and older." H's mum also commented on how well it had worked:

> She's just grabbed hold of it. She's running with it. She loves the whole experience. And to her it's just like a massive adventure. There are children there from six-years-old to fifteen, she plays with

them all, she talks about them all. There are so many other nationalities in the class – Italian, Spanish, Turkish and so on. She is the only
English-speaking person in her whole class. The teaching assistant
can speak English. She's very good, but they speak German from
the minute they come in. They shake hands, they greet every child,
they sit down and they go through everything in German.

H also describes how the integration class can be fun as well as
hard work:

> Today we did maths. We have a worksheet. The younger ones
> have easier ones. They might be adding up a few things. But in
> the integration class it's quite different because in England you
> hardly ever went on trips, and here I've been to the town twice
> now. And we've bought bread and fruit and things, and worked
> out the change and how much it cost and everything. And we've
> taken what we bought back to class and eaten it.

H's mum, Sarah, appreciates the life skills H is learning, in order to
be able to get about in the local environment:

> The teachers give them ten Swiss francs and take them out. You
> don't know till they come home from school that they were on a
> trip. "We've been to town," she says. "We bought this and that
> in the supermarket and we made a fruit salad." They are literally
> teaching them how to do things in German, the way you would
> teach them in your own language, from shopping to going to
> the hairdressers. They do the whole thing across the board. And
> she's loving it.

In some cases, there is different provision for primary and
secondary level. Claire describes how her ten-year-old daughter
A was given the chance of ten weeks of German lessons, full-time,
one-on-one or a small group of three. She was lucky. After five and
a half weeks they said she understood enough to start attending the
regular primary school class. Her older sister, who is thirteen, has
to travel by bus to a different municipality to attend the specialist
integration class there for lower-secondary level.

Integration classes at lower-secondary level

Vicki's daughters were 11 and 14 when they joined a *classe
d'accueil* (welcome class) in canton Vaud. They were in a class of

mixed ages, ranging from 11 to 17, with between 8 and 12 pupils in the class. They were taught French, poetry, music, art and physical education. There was also a subject that covered history, geography and science. The main objective was to get their written French up to speed. Maths was also very important and Vicki's older daughter was put in a regular class for this. French and German were also tailored to their ability:

> Once they knew that my daughters were bright and hard working, they pushed them as fast as they could go in French. Each pupil worked at their own level and pace on the French, it was very worksheet-based but it was very effective. After meeting with their teacher in November, it quickly became apparent that they were headed for the academic stream of regular school. They started German too, at a different school (known as an *appui*, or support class) some months later. The German taught in the school they were in at first was for the other two streams.

> They both spent a year in the *classe d'accueil*. They both have a very good foundation in French. I would say they were probably slower on the spoken French than if they had gone straight into regular school (they were initially mixing with other non-French speakers in their class) but for me the fact that this integration class was offered was a deciding factor in bringing teenagers into a French-speaking school system.

The role of dialect in German-speaking schools

In the French and Italian-speaking parts of Switzerland, standard French and Italian are spoken at school. The situation is different in German-speaking Switzerland. Here there is a situation of diglossia, which means that two dialects or languages are used by a single language community. High German is used in formal situations, like making a speech, or reading the national news on TV or radio. The written standard is also High German. Swiss-German speakers use their local dialect everywhere they can: at home, at work, in meetings, on TV – in short, in all situations where they think it will be understood by their listeners. (Teachers sometimes automatically start speaking in Swiss-German at parents' information evenings. They should not be doing this, and you should put up your hand *immediately* and ask them to speak High German).

There are many regional dialects and no standard Swiss German language. In the following chapter on learning the language, you can read some examples of the differences between High German and the Swiss dialects.

Cantons usually define their policy about diglossia. At kindergarten, Swiss German is still spoken some of the time in class in some cantons. Children tend to speak Swiss German to each other at this stage. High German is spoken in the classroom from primary school onwards. If your child is having extra language classes, these will be in High German, and the teacher will speak High German to parents. There will however be a certain number of Swiss-German words used in relation to school, like 's'nüni' (snack) that you will not find in the dictionary. Examples of a few of these can be found in the list of Swiss-German words (see Appendix 3).

Swiss German and youth culture

While older people tend to write in High German, most young people use their local variant of Swiss German in all their written communication with each other, including their text messages and on Facebook. It provides a double sense of identity, first their identity as a young person, and second, showing where they belong geographically. There are many variations in Swiss-German spelling as there are few set rules about how to write it. My daughter explains how she sees it:

> Any communication with people around my age is in Swiss German. We only write High German to older people, for example, over 30, because that's what they do. Most people I know under 30 write Swiss German to each other. Even an invitation to a wedding might be in Swiss German. I tend to write notes in High German, for example, the minutes of a meeting or even a shopping list.

Children who go through local kindergarten usually end up speaking both Swiss German and High German, while those who enter the Swiss system later only learn High German. Swiss children will usually speak Swiss German to each other in the playground, and possibly in the classroom too if the teacher is not around. However, they switch readily to High German if other children cannot speak Swiss German.

The group of 10 and 11-year-old girls I interviewed mostly agreed that it is important to learn High German and not necessary to learn Swiss German too. You can be understood with High German everywhere. However, in practice, all of them understand Swiss German to some degree, and some of them use some Swiss German words. As M explained, "Most of the time kids speak to us in High German because they know we come from other countries. I think you anyway will learn Swiss German on the street." D had only learned High German at school, and told me that she was learning Swiss German from her little brother who went to kindergarten. She also commented, "I think there are different kinds of Swiss German, because there's one that I really don't understand." Someone in her class was probably speaking a different dialect than the local one she was becoming familiar with. A also commented, "It's better to learn High German first because Swiss German is different in Zurich and Basel. It is more a slang."

As they reach their teenage years, young people may want to be the same as their peers and may prefer to speak and write Swiss German. If their High German is good, this may be the right moment to encourage them to activate their knowledge of the dialect. It might be helpful to let them have the opportunity to practise with one person, someone who will be patient with their first attempts. My Swiss husband once spent an afternoon playing board games with a 13-year-old boy who spoke High German and wanted to try out speaking dialect to a sympathetic listener. The boy found out he could do it and then changed to dialect with his friends.

Chapter 5 Language learning for parents

If you do not think you will be staying long in Switzerland, learning the local language may not be at the top of your priority list. However, making a start on this early not only helps you feel at home, but also makes it easier to change over to the local school system if you do end up staying permanently. English is not a *lingua franca* in Swiss schools. The authorities and some teachers will speak to newcomers in English when they arrive, but will expect the incomers to start learning the local language. They often feel very strongly about this, even if they express it mildly. There may be interpreters available at parents' meetings and some teachers may be willing to conduct conversations in English, but they think that after a while communication on school territory should take place in the school language.

A dual approach

I am an advocate of learning the language, as you will see in this chapter. However, I think it is also important to have some people you can chat to in your mother tongue or another language you already speak fluently. This was confirmed by Valerie Alexander, a personal coach and counselling psychologist.[19] She comments that moving to a new country can give you a sense of discontinuity because life as you knew it has stopped. She recommends using networks or information centres to find people with similar interests who can speak your language. "If you seek out like-minded people, this will help you not to feel alienated in your new environment. Then you can feel comfortable as you venture out to get to know the local people."

Expatriates are usually offered a budget for language lessons by their company when they first arrive in Switzerland. However, if the working parent(s) have a long working day and also travel a lot, it can be difficult to find time to learn a language they do not need in order to be good at their job. It is often the home-based parent who starts learning the language first, as he or she (as is more often the case) is spending the most time interacting with the school and may also have more time to attend classes.

There are, however, many good reasons for both parents to sign up for classes. As Doreen, a British mother points out, her children are grappling with the challenge of learning a new language and using it to interact with others at school. They have no choice in the matter. It is an encouragement to them if their parents are setting an example by doing the same. There are very good reasons for both parents to learn the language, as I explain in more detail below.

It is good for family cohesion if the whole family is able to mix with the locals and speak their language. Dana is from Chicago in the USA and is sending her son to local Swiss kindergarten. She comments that, with regard to diversity and acculturation, Switzerland is like the United States. "You need to assimilate and learn the language to get by, but then you realize so many people are from all over the place and speaking something different at home."

Nicole von Jacobs is in charge of diversity and integration for the cantonal government of Basel-Stadt. "We appreciate the people who come to live in Basel with their different talents and experience and the enrichment this brings," she explains. "We want to get to know them and introduce them to the diversity that Basel offers." Nicole von Jacobs emphasises the importance of newcomers learning the local language. "It improves your quality of life," she tells new-comers to Basel. "If you can talk to the people around you in their language, you gain insight into how they think. There is also a wider range of people who can become your friends."

It can also be of great benefit to children if their parents can function as a team with complementary skills when liaising with the school. It is tough for the home-based parent to have to operate as a 'single parent' when it comes to school matters because their partner cannot participate at all in school life. This is particularly difficult when there are no supportive relatives nearby who understand the issues. If a couple can tackle the language challenge together, they can both obtain an inside view of the school system. They will understand how the school works, build a relationship with the teacher (and other parents), and be able to express their opinions regarding their child's needs. They will take in new information at parents' evenings and be able to read school brochures and research school pathways online.

Robert and Heather came from England to Switzerland with their three daughters. As parents they took one-to-one lessons alternately on a Saturday morning, taking turns to stay at home and look after the children. Robert had three years of school German and explained to me why it was important to him to build on this:

> We wanted the girls to integrate into the society around us. School is, of course, a great way to get to know other parents and I wanted to be able to follow the kindergarten playlets and so on which the children took part in. So it was a further motivation to keep going with the German, and in particular to pick up enough Swiss-German to be able to follow what's going on. You're right that it's normally the mothers who take on this kind of thing and Heather has certainly learnt much more German and Swiss-German than I have. She's also better than I am at languages. Nevertheless, I'm glad that I've learnt as much as I have.

Kirstin Barton is an expatriate coach in the Basel region.[20] She comments that it is helpful to have both parents engaged in learning the language and able to communicate with the school or help with homework. "One parent may be more bogged down in the nitty-gritty of daily school life and may get worn down by this. The other parent may have more distance and a different perspective. It can feel like a heavy responsibility to be the one doing all the communicating, especially if there are problems."

Why is it so difficult?

Native English speakers from western cultures are at a disadvantage in learning a foreign language if they never learned one properly before and have not been taught much grammar about their own language at school. They may know next to nothing about articles, tenses and cases. An additional psychological barrier for native English speakers is that speaking a foreign language is considered by many to be a specialist skill. It is for gifted people and on a par with being able to paint landscapes or play the violin.[21] The argument is that some people are born artists or musicians and others are born linguists. In Switzerland, learning a language is seen as a more basic skill that you learn, like being able to drive a car or use a computer. You are expected to invest time and effort in it (and possibly money too) whether you are particularly gifted or not.

Another factor in making language learning difficult is the high demands expatriates make on themselves. They can then easily get discouraged. Bob is Irish and has lived in Switzerland for 16 years. When he first arrived, he started German classes, paid for by the company. He was given a budget and had to find a teacher by himself. He was quickly discouraged by his lack of progress. "I wanted to learn it too quickly. When my teacher arrived, he would try to make conversation with me and it just didn't work." After six months, or 40 hours of German, Bob's ability did not stretch to this. Before he could chat about his weekend, he would have needed to learn the past tense. He still needed structured dialogues and was not ready for fluency practice.

Bob had the impression that he was not making progress quickly enough and gave up. His wife was learning the language successfully and was managing the school issues. Looking back, Bob thinks it would have helped him to have a coach to address the psychological aspects of language learning. Companies are otherwise very good at helping people to develop their potential. He describes himself and many of his colleagues in his company as high achievers, even perfectionists, who find it hard if they make mistakes or do not make progress quickly.

Being too busy is also an obstacle. Bob told me about a new British colleague who was working a 12-hour day and was also learning German. "He was running out of the office early once a week to go to his class," Bob observed. "He would be stressed if he hadn't done his homework. It would be even harder if he had children."

How do people manage it?

Kirstin Barton offers expatriate coaching on the topic of 'Getting to grips with the language.' She explains her approach:

> I encourage people to keep it simple in the early days and see language learning as a series of short-term projects relevant to their immediate needs. I invite them to set goals that they feel motivated to achieve. People tend to assume taking lessons is an isolated thing. It's not. The language is all around you. I suggest they can look for opportunities to learn and practise with people around them and do things they find interesting or fun. I also say, 'Be ready to stretch yourself out of your comfort zone. Just plan to take small steps, very often. It is important that you ask for the support you need, including from yourself. Don't be your own worst self-belief thief!'

Kirstin also emphasises that learners may need to insist that people speak the new language to them rather than English. The learner's need to learn the local language for the sake of their children should have priority over the local person's wish to practice their conversational English.

As Kirstin suggests, it is important to complement a language course with practice outside the classroom. Bob is now starting to speak German to a local farmer. He grew up on a farm himself, and he sometimes pops over to the farm and has a chat with the farmer about the cows, armed with two dictionaries: one to translate from English into German and a second one to translate the farmer's Swiss German into High German. He is very motivated. His family are amazed at his growing specialised farming vocabulary.

Brian is an American who lives in Neuchâtel. He speaks English everyday at work, so it was a real challenge for him to learn the language. He took a French course online, run by a native French-speaking couple who teach courses using Skype.[22] He took the course from his desk at work or from his home office. It worked very well with his busy work schedule. He also tried to speak with the parents of his children's friends in French, and chatted to the farmers and vendors at the outdoor market in town. He is passionate about music and joined a group of Swiss jazz musicians and played the saxophone at a weekly jam session.

Robert and Heather are churchgoers. Robert describes how joining a local evangelical church helped them learn German:

> We had decided at the outset when we moved here that we wanted to go to a German-speaking church. It didn't much appeal to us to base our lives around an expat community with all of the changes that implies; just as you get to know someone, they up and off to another country. We came with the intention of staying a minimum of 5 years and of getting to know local people. That became a second strand in learning, next to language classes, and probably the most important one. I used to go to church with an English Bible, a German Bible and an English/German dictionary and try to follow the sermon.

For those who are not into farming, jazz or churchgoing, there are other ways to get exposure to the language. Mike is Australian and has attended an intensive course in German. He is now picking up the language by reading his son's school books that he brings home when he has homework. He describes attending language classes as something that needs commitment, just like going to the gym. "It is doable if you are determined. You have to schedule the classes and then be firm about keeping the slot free, for example, refusing to schedule meetings then."

A reasonable time frame

It is easy for people to imagine it will not take long to learn the language when they read advertisements for language learning software promising to help clients 'learn a language in three months'. In fact, it is estimated that it will take an average learner at least 350 hours of guided language study to reach the Common European Framework of reference level B1 and become an independent user of a language, as can be seen in the table on the next page.[23] The number of hours needed for individual learners varies greatly in practice, depending on age, level of motivation and the extent of exposure the lerner has to the language outside the classroom.

Level[24]	Description	Hours of guided study
A1	Basic user	Approx. 90-100
A2		Approx. 180-200
B1	Independent user	Approx. 350-400
B2		Approx. 500-600
C1	Proficient user	Approx. 700-800
C2		Approx. 1,000-1,200

Table 1   Hours required to learn a language.

According to the Common European Framework of reference, a B1 *independent user* of a language can understand the main points of clear standard input on familiar matters regularly encountered in work, school, leisure, etc. They can also deal with most situations likely to arise while travelling in an area where the language is spoken and produce simple, connected texts on topics which are familiar or of personal interest. Lastly, they can describe experiences, events, dreams, hopes and ambitions, and briefly give reasons and explanations for opinions and plans. This could be a good mid to long-term goal for parents of young children who will later be attending local schools.

Swiss German grammar and vocabulary

In the last chapter I talked about the situation of diglossia, where both High German and Swiss German may be spoken by the local people. It is difficult for adults to learn High German in an environment where Swiss German is spoken a lot.

Swiss German speakers are often unaware of how big the jump is from High German to Swiss German and how much variation there is between the different dialects. Although many of them are skilled language learners, they forget that consistent input (repeatedly hearing exactly the same words and structures) is the key to mastering new vocabulary and grammar. This is exactly what you do not get if you listen to people with different dialects, as both the grammar and vocabulary may vary from the standard language.

I experienced the variations of vocabulary living in Basel with a husband who speaks a St Gallen dialect. Friends and neighbours spoke High German, a Bern dialect and a Zurich dialect. I can remember when I said *'füf'* in St Gallen dialect as part of my telephone number, Basel people repeated *'fünf'* back to me. I asked a Canadian friend whose husband was from Zurich what she said, and she replied, *'föif'*.

Grammatical constructions raised similar problems. When my husband saw our baby daughter trying to open the fridge, he asked, *"Wa wötsch?"* (What do you want?). My friend from Basel would say *"Was willsch?"* while my German neighbour would say, *"Was willst du?"* In each dialect the verb changes (besides *wötsch* and *willsch*, *wotsch* is another possibility) and, as a grammatical difference, the *du* (you) that is used in High German is missing in dialect for question forms. I imagine it would be a similar experience to learn English from Scottish dialect speakers in Scotland, who might refer to a bag as a *'poke'* or say *'Amn't I invited?'* instead of *'Aren't I invited?'*

This diglossia situation in German-speaking Switzerland is a problem for people from the French- and Italian-speaking Switzerland just as much as for people from other countries. I would like to suggest a way for language learners to deal with it.

- First of all, to encourage yourself, assume you will only ever have to speak High German and learn this. Many Germans only speak High German, even if they live here for 50 years.

- Secondly, ask people to speak High German to you as much as possible, to give you a chance to hear this all the time. It would also be ideal if they would speak it to each other in your presence, so that you can benefit from listening in. However, they may feel uncomfortable doing this.

- Thirdly, do not accept it when people refer to your learning 'the language'. Make it clear to them that you are actually receiving input in what are, for learners, two mutually incomprehensible languages. (I spoke High German when I came to Switzerland, but I only understood the occasional word when people spoke Swiss German). For this reason, your progress will be slower than if you were learning German in Germany, French in the French-speaking region of Switzerland or Italian in Ticino.

As shown in the previous chapter, schools are now providing a good example of how language learning can be done. Local children accept that they should speak only High German in the classroom and even make an effort to do so in the playground. This is a help to children who are learning the language. German-Swiss adults need a bit more persuasion. They may experience it as a threat to their linguistic identity if they have to start speaking High German to each other for the benefit of learners. If you find people who are happy to do so, it will help you learn faster.

Section two

Kindergarten and

primary school

Chapter 6   The kindergarten curriculum

Building the foundation

Many foreign parents comment that their children just play at kindergarten and do not learn much there. For some, this confirms their suspicion that public schools will be of poorer quality than private schools. A good metaphor for the first years of Swiss education is that it is like looking onto a Swiss building site where a house is being built. The excavation work has been carried out to build the garage and cellar floor below ground. There are workmen down there, and they seem to have been digging around in the hole for a year, but you can't yet imagine what the house is going to look like.

Kindergarten is a bit like this. You are looking at a hive of activity 'below ground' of a foundation being built. Children are working and playing together in pairs and groups, using paper and paint, scissors and glue, fretsaws and hammers, or playing 'let's pretend' games with the teacher guiding them. A lot of time and energy is being spent building a strong educational foundation, but not much is yet observable to parents on the surface level. The children are not bringing home academic products as proof of learning. However, just as with Swiss houses, once the foundation is there, the ground floor will duly be built and people will start to notice the house. Things will move faster after that as the various floors take shape, just as parents may be taken aback by the way school ramps up and greater academic demands are made on children a few years later.

Swiss kindergarten prepares children gently for school. A main goal is intellectual development rather than academic development. An example of academic goals would be doing worksheets to learn and practise the alphabet while, according to Louise Katz, an expert on early childhood education, "... intellectual goals address the disposition to make sense, analyse, synthesise, theorise, speculate about cause and effect relationships, ponder, conjecture."[25] Katz believes intellectual goals are more likely to be met in project work than in doing worksheets. This fits with the kindergarten approach.

Swiss kindergarten may be misunderstood by newcomers because its goals appear to be implicit. You might find information about the curriculum on your cantonal website, or order a brochure somewhere, but teachers are unlikely to spell out their educational goals. As the kinderten teacher Corinne H commented, at parents' evenings teachers are likely to tell parents what special events will be taking place, what kind of snacks their children should bring, or what clothes they should wear to play in the woods. They are less likely to give an overview of the subjects taught, or explain specifically how the children's linguistic and mathematical abilitiy, social skills, personal competence and knowledge are developed. The best way to understand what is going on is to visit and see a class in action. Karen Dyson is a senior consultant for Ready Steady Relocate, based in Basel. She used to be a primary school teacher in England. She expresses her observations of a kindergarten in Basel-Stadt in a way that is reassuring to many foreign parents:

> In my daughter's kindergarten, they can do reading and writing. The teacher spends time on it with them if they are interested. She's very good on the academic side. She also created a

magic kingdom, where the children's imaginations are allowed to find full expression. They do plays of a very high standard. There is an atmosphere of peace as you go in, go up the stairs, along the stairs are games, boxes with puppets, photos of trips. Kindergarten also has lights, colours, pictures, magical things.

The Christmas show: it is an old-fashioned house, with the shutters closed, candlelight, netting, a mirror glitter ball suspended, children could twirl it and it was as if snow was swirling down. The children were dressed as furry animals, Santas, and angels. It was another world. They often make bread together. They are kneading the dough, singing songs in Swiss German. All are focussed doing their thing. All have name cards beside what they are going to do. Their *Fasnacht* (carnival) masks are wonderful. The children are fully involved.

There is less involvement in England where there is very little time for music and art (because of the National Curriculum) as ways for the children to express themselves. They go to school at the age of five and the school has to pass targets. Kids are forced into a more formalised learning from an early age.

The curriculum

A canton's curriculum usually provides learning goals that all teachers adhere to. In the French-speaking cantons and Ticino, the *Plan d'études romand* provides a curriculum for eleven years of school from the ages of 4 to 15.[26] It specifies five main domains of activity: languages; maths and natural sciences; human and social sciences; arts, involving creative and manual activities as well as visual arts and music; and body and movement, which includes physical education and nutritional education.

Five lateral capacities are also outlined: collaboration, communication, learning strategies, creative thinking and reflective activity (see page 82). At kindergarten level in particular, emphasis is also placed on socialisation, construction of knowledge and developing cognitive tools in order to 'learn how to learn'.

Lehrplan 21 is a coordinated curriculum now being developed for the 21 German-speaking cantons.[27] It is likely to be introduced around 2015. In the meantime, many German-speaking cantons refer to the curriculum from Canton Berne to define their learning goals and content at kindergarten level.[28] As an example, the Baselland curriculum states that the subjects taught at kindergarten are:

- language
- people in their environment
- music
- mathematical activity
- art/handwork
- physical movement[29]

Teachers evaluate children's progress in each of these. It is a holistic approach to facilitate the development of the child's social skills, personal competence, and knowledge.

Social competence could also be described as interpersonal skills. They are developed as children learn to make contact, share, listen, empathise, show consideration, play and work together, keep rules and resolve conflicts. Personal competence comes through developing self-awareness and awareness of the environment. Children express themselves and communicate about themselves. They tell and hear stories and extend their vocabulary. They practise listening and watching carefully, and express their observations in words. Feelings are also addressed and expressed via language and creative expression. Children extend their motor skills. They learn to become independent and self-confident. (In pedagogical jargon in English, this would be described as 'self-mastery'.) They learn to manage success and failure and reinforce their concentration and perseverance.

Knowledge is acquired by experimenting with different materials, using tools, equipment and musical instruments. Children process their experience of using different media and practise orientation in the area nearby and in traffic. They learn about relationships, natural laws and principles. They train their memories and extend their experience of the animal and plant world. It is in this knowledge category that cognitive or intellectual skills are developed. These are, however, only part of a broader curriculum.

Any similarities between the curriculum of canton Bern and the *Plan d'études romand* are not coincidental. Niggi Thurnherr is responsible for school harmonisation in Baselland at the level of kindergarten and primary school. He agreed with my observation that the approach to learning seems to be quite similar in practice across the country, although the learning goals and content may be described a bit differently in each canton or linguistic region. Some of the approaches and best practices have been implemented by teachers for decades, but have only recently been formalised in a curriculum. Niggi Thurnherr named the cantonal Departments of Education and what are now known as the Universities of Teacher Education as the two main drivers in developing the approach taken. Experts in both of these institutions exchange views and expertise with their colleagues around the country. The third driver is the strong feedback culture coming from the grass roots of the teaching profession. Practising teachers share activities and methods they have used successfully in the classroom for many years. Their views are highly valued.

If you are familiar with the philosophy of Waldorf or Steiner schools, you may notice that some of the Steiner philosophy has rubbed off on Swiss kindergarten. As in Steiner schools, the focus is on experiential learning through practical activities.[30] There is guided free play in a home-like classroom environment that includes natural elements. Outdoor play periods provide children with experiences of nature, weather and the seasons. Oral language development is addressed through songs, poems and movement games. Exposure to TV, computers and media games are discouraged.

You may also recognise many of Howard Gardner's multiple intelligences threaded through the descriptions above. Gardner described spatial, interpersonal, intrapersonal, logical-mathematical, linguistic, musical intelligence, as well as bodily kinaesthetic intelligence (commonly known as motor skills). Gardner is not mentioned nowadays in Swiss curriculum development but, as far as I can see, his intelligences are still present.

A play-based curriculum

Around 230 British experts on child education and psychology wrote a letter to the *Daily Telegraph* newspaper in 2011 to warn against the erosion of childhood.[31] Among other things, they argued for the establishment of a genuinely play-based curriculum in schools up to the age of six, free from the downward pressure of formal learning, tests and targets. They also defended community-based initiatives to ensure that children's outdoor play and connection to nature are encouraged, supported and resourced within every local neighbourhood. The play-based curriculum is what educators in Switzerland believe early learning should mainly be about. Play theory in Switzerland emphasises that play provides the most important learning environment a child can experience. It is believed that the development of the ability to think is dependent on the intensity and frequency of play in childhood.[32] However, this British call for less formalised early education comes at a time when the Swiss pendulum is at least edging, if not quite swinging, more in the direction of formalised early education for children who are actively seeking it, as will be shown below.

Socialisation and fitting in

Many foreign parents report the emphasis on socialisation and fitting in with the group. The teachers know what kind of behaviour they will and will not accept. Some find this difficult while others welcome it. Tünde is Hungarian and is impressed by her daughter's kindergarten teachers.

> They are so natural. They don't try to over-regulate the children. They are willing to repeat the same thing five times. At the same time, they are very clear on a point, so they don't lose their authority. The children feel comfortable and proud when they can achieve what is expected from them because they are appreciated. It is also a good feeling for them to see that they can do what the others can. Plus there is another beneficial fact: in kindergarten there are two age groups interacting together so the role modelling is there. This is great for kids who have no older siblings.

Kindergarten is a time when your child has the opportunity to integrate into the local community. At the same time, individualisation is emphasised greatly at both kindergarten and primary school levels. In the *Plan d'études romand,* for example, it is stated that the aim of the first two years of schooling (from ages four to six) is to facilitate a harmonious transition from the child's home world to the world of school, taking into consideration the particular child's psychomotor, psychological and affective development. Teachers devote as much time as is needed to meeting and working with each child both as an individual and a group member. The German-speaking curricula also emphasise that the needs and interests of the child are at the centre of kindergarten activity. For example, the Baselland curriculum states that the kindergarten builds its day-to-day activity on the fundamental needs of the child: to self-actualise, be given attention, be valued, to belong, feel loved and feel secure.

A child-centred education

In German-speaking Switzerland, the paediatrician Remo Largo is a child development expert with guru status among parents and teachers alike. He has written several bestsellers, including *Kinderjahre*, (*Childhood Years*), in which he emphasised the individual developmental needs of each child.[33] Largo refers to Pestalozzi, Piaget and Montessori, and many others, emphasising that upbringing and education must be adjusted to the individual needs and characteristics of the child. He also states that a child is not a lump of dough that can be formed at will. Each child develops at his own pace. He cannot make more progress just because he is offered more knowledge and made to practise more skills. True learning is self-directed and independent. Largo argues strongly for the well-being of the child above all, rather than the good of the parents or teachers.

In French-speaking Switzerland, there are many experts who are highly respected. Sarah M recommended the work of the French paediatrician and psychoanalyst, Françoise Dolto. Dolto was very influential from the 1970s in moving away from a patriarchal approach to bringing up children to an emphasis on the individual child's best interests. Her books in French are still being sold in Swiss bookshops. Other current influential experts from France for French-speaking parents include the psychoanalyst Claude Halmos, the child psychologist Marcel Rufo (both of whom have also had TV series), and for professionals, the psychotherapist Maurice Nanchen.

Dolto has been accused of introducing the idea of the *enfant roi*, or child king. In her defence, Dolto's concern for a child's well-being does not mean that she advocated giving the child everything she wants. One of Dolto's key messages is that the child's best interest is not always what will make him or her feel happy. A child's desire is not a need. It should not necessarily be satisfied, but we should listen to it and speak about it.[34] Claude Halmos worked with Dolto and has further developed and adapted her ideas.

Kindergarten teachers also vary the degree of difficulty of a task to suit the cognitive, emotional and developmental ages of the children. Largo shows that a typical group of 20 seven-year-olds may have developmental ages ranging from 5.5 to 8.5 in terms of their height, IQ, and ability to read, count, draw and make music.[35] Only around six of them have a developmental age of 7. One has the age of 5.5, two of 6, four of 6.5, four of 7.5, two of 8 and one of 8.5.[36] These charts are available online.[37]

A system in flux

What happens at your child's kindergarten will of course be influenced by other factors than the official curriculum. The approach can vary greatly, depending on individual teachers and the pedagogical approach they use, as well as the approach a particular canton, municipality or school is now taking. New models are rapidly being introduced around the country. You will not necessarily get up-to-date information about the extent of academic learning in your local kindergarten by talking to people whose children were there ten years ago. Below, I describe three main approaches you are likely to come across, depending on the particular teacher as well as political developments in your canton. This division into three approaches is my own, and not an official distinction.

In what I call the traditional kindergarten approach, systematically learning to read and write is not on the programme at all. Officially, at least, formal learning only starts systematically when children start primary school at six or seven. This is also officially the case in the Italian and French-speaking parts of the country, although they use the word 'school' (*école infantine, scuola dell'infanzia*) from the ages of four and three respectively. It used to be the norm that kindergarten teachers were not allowed to teach reading and writing, and many older teachers have developed a

whole range of other ways to facilitate the cognitive development of all children, including very bright ones. Nevertheless,
some parents report that their children are under-challenged or
bored at kindergarten.

A slightly different approach is taken by some teachers, usually younger, who have been trained to teach children of four to
eight years for the two years of kindergarten and the first two
years of primary school. They are taught to work on formal academic skills with individual children when it is appropriate for
their developmental level, rather than their age. They may teach
basic reading, writing and maths in a fairly informal way to cog-
nitively advanced children while others are doing less academic
activities. They will still keep a focus on a range of skills, and
see cognitive skills development as a small part of a broad programme. When a child is playing or doing handwork, cognitive
learning also takes place.

A third approach is the *Basisstufe* (basic level) model, which is
a very interesting development that has been piloted in German-
speaking Switzerland (in AG, AR, BE, FR, GL, LU, NW, SG, TG,
ZH) in recent years. The curriculum of the kindergarten and the
first two years of primary school are all offered in the same classroom. It is known as the *Grundstufe* in canton Zurich, where it
only lasts for three years, the two kindergarten years and the
first year of primary school. Between 16 and 24 four to eight-
year-olds are in the same class with two teachers, both part-time,
but both present all morning. There is a maximum of 18 pupils
in a class if it includes children who need additional provision
for special needs education. All younger teachers who have been
trained to work with four to eight-year-olds may work in the
Basisstufe or *Grundstufe*. Older teachers who are specialised in
teaching either four to six-year-olds or six years upwards take
an additional certificate course to work with the mixed levels.

There is a saying in German that life ('*Das Ernst des Lebens*')
gets serious when you start primary school. The *Basisstufe* aims
to give children a gentle start to their school life. Each child begins reading, writing and maths when they are ready for it, irrespective of their age. Younger children learn from older children. There is at least one meeting per year between parents or

guardians and teachers to evaluate development in play, learning and achievement. A report card is also provided. The child can stay in the *Basisstufe* for three to five years, or in the *Grundstufe* for two to four years. Gifted children will reach the targets early and may move up a year earlier. Children needing more time can stay a year longer.

You do not need to worry that your child is missing out if they are not in the *Basisstufe*. A study conducted by Swiss pedagogical experts (Urs Moser and Franziska Vogt) in 2004 compared children's progress in reading in the three models.[38] They showed that in the *Basisstufe* and *Grundstufe* children made more progress in phonological awareness, reading, writing and maths than in traditional kindergarten after the first 12 and 24 months. After 48 months, as they entered the second year of primary school, there was no difference any more and all progressed at the same rate. In all three models children's social relations (peer acceptance) and self-confidence were measured to be equally positive.

The *Basisstufe* could provide a vehicle for bilingual early education, which might be of interest to the bilingual cantons. Pius Theiler works for the Education Department in the Canton of Lucerne, and told me about a visit he made to a small primary school in the country. It was not a *Basisstufe* class, but a class teacher worked alongside a remedial teacher, both acting as coaches while the children did either maths or German activities. Pius Theiler noticed that the teacher was speaking in English to one boy during the maths lesson, and asked why. The teacher explained that she had agreed to do this at the boy's request, because he liked English. Pius Theiler believes that with the *Basisstufe* model, it would be possible to have bilingual classes with two teachers, speaking the school language alongside a second language of the canton, such as French or Italian, or even English.

Chapter 7   Examples of kindergarten in practice

The comments below are based on observations and subjective opinions of kindergarten teachers and expatriate parents around the country. They will provide you with some impressions as to what you *might* expect of kindergarten, but practices will vary greatly from teacher to teacher as well as from canton to canton.

A process approach

Whether teachers take a traditional or a progressive approach to teaching, they will adhere, at least loosely, to the kindergarten curriculum of their canton. Teachers with a traditional approach have their own ways of preparing children for reading and maths at school. Yvonne M has been a kindergarten teacher for over 30 years in canton Baselland and is also a teaching practice trainer. She has many foreign children in her class and is aware that expatriate parents are sometimes disappointed that their child is not bringing home maths exercises or writing worksheets. However, she sticks to her guns and emphasises the importance of building a strong foundation, taking the time to promote social and emotional development to strengthen the child's character and prepare him for school.

Yvonne M emphasises that her focus is on the process of learning rather than the end product, and that there may be little concrete output for some of the learning achieved. A child can develop a new skill without it resulting in a work of art. Every week she gives children a task to work on in small groups, and no single child can take the finished product home. There is also no way to evidence the group dynamic processes children go through as they learn to listen to each other, communicate their ideas convincingly and, at times, let go and adopt others' ideas. She advises parents not to judge learning by what the child brings home. I would add that you cannot judge learning by what your child reports having done each morning.

Learning by playing

Like all Swiss kindergarten teachers, Corinne H believes strongly in the value of playing. Didactic approaches make use of games, exercises and pedagogical concepts that support the development of both motor skills and cognitive development, as well as personal competence and social skills. These act as a precursor to learning to read, write and do maths. Through play, the child achieves social, linguistic, musical, mathematical and scientific development.

Children do a lot of role playing at kindergarten, in what is often called the building corner and the dolls' corner. The contents of each reflect a traditional gender division but parents report that boys and girls now play in both. In the building corner children can usually play with building blocks, trains and train tracks, cars and trucks, magnet kits, marble runs and Meccano. In the dolls' corner, beside the dolls, there is usually a shop, toy appliances, dressing-up clothes, cuddly toys, and home-related toys.

Too few girls in the boys' corner

The building corner and the dolls' corner were known in Swiss German as 'the boys' corner' and 'the girls' corner' in playgroups and kindergartens until the late 1990s. This probably reinforced the idea that construction was for boys only. Impressions from early childhood can be long-lasting and this might help to explain why the numbers of girls entering tertiary education in technical domains ('the boy's corner') is still low in Switzerland. Girls who experienced the new terminology will probably not be starting tertiary education until 2015 at the earliest.

Yvonne M finds that some children are not used to taking the initiative in unstructured play sessions and wait to be instructed as to what to do. If she notices they do not know how to engage in role plays, or 'let's pretend', she organises a puppet theatre with them, for example, on the topic of a group of dwarves. After they have made up a story together and performed a play with her, the children then develop the topic further in their own games as they wish.

Better for boys

Karen appreciates the learning taking place at kindergarten, as she sees it as appropriate to her children's ages. She thinks Swiss kindergarten is much better for boys, and quotes Steve Biddolph, the author of *The Secret of Happy Children* and *Raising Boys:*

> Biddolph says that in England, boys start school too early. They are not ready at five. He correlates it with hormone levels. Boys have high levels around the age of five and want to use up their energy. Girls already know how to hold a pencil, and like to spend time colouring. Meanwhile, boys are drawing big things. Their fine motor skills come around the age of six-and-a-half. Swiss kindergarten is perfect for boys. They have days in the woods involving physical activity, walking through the woods, making a fire, cooking sausages, learning the names of trees. It's all very practical.

Special occasions

As well as daily rituals like the circle time, and the celebration of children's birthdays, Swiss kindergartens often celebrate the four seasons. There are also special rituals and musical and artistic activities related to the local autumn fair, Christmas, Easter, the carnival and other special days. The tasks centred round special occasions often have multiple purposes and learning aims. Rituals give children security and a sense of belonging. Development of team work, as well as gross and fine motor skills can all be practised at the same time.

Yvonne M described a ritual in her class every morning as St Nikolaus (Santa Claus) day approached on 6 December. Her class all sat in a circle on a large cloth on the floor every morning in December and she read out a letter from St Nikolaus himself. On the first day, he sent them a bunch of thin sticks (a *Rute,* or birch) and a picture of his house. He gave the class the task of breaking up the sticks into different sizes and laying them out in the middle of the cloth to represent his house. For this exercise they had to work together to decide how long all the pieces of stick needed to be and where they should be laid. The following day, he asked them to draw a picture of their own houses on the cloth and then draw the route from their house to his house. It sounds to me like early lessons in cartography.

Learning perseverance

Kindergarten teacher Corinne H comments that children are very different and she has different expectations of them. She gave me an example of a five-year-old child learning perseverance while organising her play. A did not speak a word of German when she started kindergarten. In the second week she approached Corinne H with a memory game and asked her to play it with her. Corinne H told her to ask the other children to play with her. A worked her way round the room, until she found someone to play with her. Many children said 'no', but she kept going until someone said 'yes'. The two children then spent a long time playing together. Corinne H empathised with A having to take the refusals until she got a 'yes', but felt she had learned something important in persevering until she got results. I commented that if I had been there, I would have intervened, asking the other children to play with her. Corinne H explained that she would have done that with other children, but she recognised that this particular child had a lot of initiative, even courage. She therefore supported her in doing it by herself, saying, "Who would you like to ask?" I would see this as also developing her self-reliance and ability to do things by herself.

Pre-maths

Mathematical activity is very much on the kindergarten curriculum. It could also be described as 'pre-maths' as the aim is to help children develop the skills that will make formal maths easy to learn in primary school. Caz reports that her daughter's kindergarten teacher plays *Uno*, a numerical card game, with children if they arrive early. In 'mathematical activity' children learn to recognise shapes as a preliminary stage to both language and maths at school. Yvonne M describes how she helps individual children develop their observation skills and recognise patterns. She lays a row of wooden shapes in different colours, for example, a yellow circle, followed by two blue squares, a red diamond and a yellow diamond, and so on. In the simple version of the task, the child copies the pattern in a row below. Doing the exercise as a *Wanderdiktat*, or a walking dictation, is more challenging. The child has to study the pattern and then go somewhere else and replicate it from memory alone. Depending on the child's ability, the teacher will provide shape patterns of varying complexity. Shapes may be dotted around a picture of an Easter egg and these have to be copied from memory.

Reading and writing

In Corinne H's kindergarten, children who want to write may do so. They play working at shops and want to know how to write the names of things they are selling. Or they make a telephone out of paper and write the numbers on it. A useful pre-reading skill is putting a story in order. A group of children draw a story line on a long piece of paper, each one drawing a different section. Together they plan how it develops. When formal learning happens, it is sometimes wrapped up as a fun activity. Caz reports how the teacher also uses themes such as dinosaurs and Native Americans to introduce all manner of lessons, from counting the number of arrows fired to following dinosaur footprints round the paper to the right dinosaur.

A certain number of parents report that their children are doing reading and writing at kindergarten, even if they are not in the *Basisstufe*. The teacher spends time on it with them if they are interested. Louise is from England, and describes how her daughter did phonics during her 2nd year (H2) of *école enfantine* (kindergarten) in canton Vaud:

> After following a phonics scheme to learn their letter sounds, the children were encouraged to read simple words and phrases about classroom events, or to work together as a group to write a sentence to accompany a photograph in the class diary. They also brought home early readers which introduced the high frequency words. Each child was able to progress at their own level – at the end-of-term show, when most children were singing or displaying pictures, two boys gave very good reading demonstrations and were warmly applauded for their achievement. All this came as a welcome surprise, as the teacher had told us that reading and writing was not taught until 1st grade in the Swiss curriculum! I'd got the impression that literacy would be almost prohibited at this age, but that was absolutely not the case for us.

Assessment

Increasingly, parents are given a report or assessment of their child's development, although this does not happen everywhere. Caz describes how it happened at her kindergarten in canton Zurich:

> Every *Elterngespräch* (parents' meeting) we have attended has a whole remit of categories that have been looked at and scored. I think the system is well geared up to evaluating children and flagging up any areas which may not be age appropriate or a concern. The gym classes are geared towards developing big motor skills and these too are closely evaluated. Both children did a lot of pre-writing skills work, a lot of logic puzzles, ordering puzzles, dexterity tests, reasoning puzzles and memory games. A lot of this was pitched in such a way that they were barely aware that they were being assessed or working. It was another fun thing to do and that is one thing that has been great. All the children had a folder and their progress and work was kept in this for parents' meetings and given to the child at the end of the year. When my son came home last week, having finished his first year, he was very, very proud of all his work and wanted to sit and show us over and over all the fun things he had done.

Academic learning

Gail describes how, back in the 1990s, when her older daughter S was five, she enrolled her for a private afternoon reading class for native English-speaking children attending Swiss kindergarten. The Australian teacher allowed the children to choose their own activities. Given the choice of learning to read or playing in the sandpit, S usually headed for the sandpit. Gail eventually stopped the classes as S was learning nothing and the sandpit at the local park was free of charge.

Gail assumed that S's lack of interest in learning to read meant that she would not be particularly advanced for her age group and was unlikely to be heading for the academic path. S then started school at seven and learned to read like all the others in her class at that time. She then applied her German reading skills to English children's books, reading them to herself when she was nine. When she was ten, to Gail's surprise, the teacher predicted that S would go to gymnasium, the school stream that is required for university entrance. She duly did her 12 years of school and started studying law at the age of 19. S couldn't read much more than her name on her seventh birthday, but she asked questions about legal matters from a young age. She was developing intellectually rather than academically. Gail's younger daughter, C, on the other hand, was very keen to read when she was five, and would have loved to have done some reading and writing the way it is now sometimes offered in kindergarten.

Teaching your child to read

It used to be taboo to do the teacher's job and send a child to school already able to read. This has changed in recent years and many Swiss children now learn to read at home. Their parents just teach them if they are interested. Foreign parents also report teaching their children to read in their first language at home. They see it as a good way to complement the play-based learning at kindergarten. Wendi is an English teacher in canton Thurgau, who teaches children to read in English. She uses the *Jolly Phonics* programme, which is used in many British primary schools. She taught her daughter N to read at the age of four. Wendi was quite happy that N was having fun at kindergarten because she could then spend time concentrating on learning to read in English at home. She comments:

> It's probably best not to learn to read in both languages simultaneously. It's too confusing. It makes sense to me to learn to read in English first because German is so easy afterwards. English spelling is around 65% phonetic and German at least 95%. N just transferred her reading skills from English to German. She never actually had to learn to read in German and I think that's the case with most children who learn to read in English first.

Chapter 8   The primary school curriculum

This chapter briefly outlines the curriculum in primary school around Switzerland and Chapter 9 provides a range of examples from parents and teachers as to what is taught in practice around the country. You might like to go to Chapter 9 first to read some examples, and then come back to this more factual chapter later.

French and Italian-speaking Switzerland

As mentioned in Chapter 6 on kindergarten, the *Plan d'études romand* of the French-speaking cantons and Ticino[39] specifies five main domains of activity for 4 to 15 year olds: languages, which includes two foreign languages; maths and natural sciences; human and social sciences; arts, involving creative and manual activities as well as visual arts and music; and body and movement, which includes physical education and nutritional education. The first foreign language in the French-speaking schools is German and in Italian-speaking Ticino it is French. Five skill areas (*capacités transversales*) are also outlined: collaboration, communication, learning strategies, creative thinking and reflective activity (*démarche réflexive*).

German-speaking Switzerland

In the German-speaking cantons, the definitive curriculum, the *Lehrplan 21* should be implemented around the year 2015. Here I describe the current curriculum. There are different ways to express the subject groupings, but the subject areas with the most hours tend to be defined as follows: people and the environment; German and maths. Around five or six hours per week is spent on each of these. In addition, around two or three hours are spent weekly on handicrafts, music and physical education. Two to three hours weekly are added later for the first foreign language, introduced in the 3rd (H5) class, and the second foreign language, introduced in the 5th (H7) class. Some bilingual cantons or German-speaking cantons near a French-speaking canton (BS, BL, SO, BE,

FR and VS) decided to coordinate their language teaching and have French from the 3rd (H5) class and English from the 5th (H7) class. This is known as the *Passepartout*. In other German-speaking cantons English is the first foreign language. In Graubünden, Italian or Romansh is the first foreign language taught in German-speaking schools, while German is the first foreign language in Italian and Romansh-speaking schools. From 2012 English is taught as the second foreign language from the 5th (H7) class.

The Geneva example

Each canton has its own description of its curriculum, which may be available online. As an example, the canton of Geneva school record book of 2011 listed the primary school subjects in English as shown in the table below.[40]

French I	Reading and writing texts of different genres, oral expression and understanding oral texts
French II	Studying elements of the language: spelling, vocabulary, conjugation, grammar
Writing, handwriting	Writing legibly and following the conventions of joined-up writing
German	Understanding oral and written texts, oral expression, writing brief texts
Maths	Resolving mathematical problems relating to number and space
Environment and Natural Sciences	Discovering the surrounding world through observation and experimentation
Human sciences: - Time - History	Placing oneself in time, discovering lifestyles past and present
- Space - Geography	Situating and describing landmarks, describing the organisation and layout of near and/or faraway places
Artistic Education: - Visual Arts	Producing a concrete work (drawing, painting, object, etc) in different materials based on an idea, a visual concept, a technique
- Musical Education	Listening to music and self-expression through music
Physical Education	Coordination of body movements and developing physical strength

Table 2   Primary school subjects in canton Geneva.

National standards

The Conference of Cantonal Ministers of Education (*EDK, CDIP, CDPE*), www.edk.ch, (referred to as EDK in English) has published national educational minimum standards with the aim of harmonising the areas of the school language, foreign languages, maths and natural sciences across the country by 2015.[41] The standards were defined by experts and practitioners around the country and should be implemented by the end of the 2nd, 6th and 9th class (H4, H8 and H11). These specific topics or other topics of a similar nature may already be taught in your child's school. They are not intended as a classroom guide for teachers, but rather as an instrument of reference for curriculum design and assessment. Below I highlight aspects of the skills areas defined for the end of primary school, that is, the 6th (H8) class. Please see the EDK website (written in French and German) for a more detailed description of the national standards.

School language

The skills areas defined by the EDK for the school language by the end of the 6th (H8) class are listening, reading, speaking, and writing, as well as spelling and grammar.[42] The following is my summary and translation of key aspects of the skills:

Comprehension skills: Pupils will develop the ability to understand different kinds of listening and reading texts (from spoken instructions to debates and from literary texts to factual written information) and perceive them as the expression of a culture. They should be able to reflect on them and exchange views on them with others.

Production skills: Pupils will learn to take part in a conversation, following social and linguistic rules and norms, to ask questions and to reflect on what is said. They should also be able to make a presentation, give an oral account and summarise information. They will learn to write aesthetically and culturally appropriate texts of different genres, such as science-fiction, an account of events, instructions, and readers' letters.

There is a solid grounding in grammar, grammatical categories and analytical competence in grammar at word and sentence level.

This will also provide pupils with a foundation for learning foreign languages. Given that entrance to a Swiss university requires having taken two foreign languages up to Gymnasial Maturity level, this foundation in grammar is very important.

Natural sciences

What is defined as natural sciences in the EDK national standards (and in the *Plan d'études romand*) is more traditionally known as 'people and the environment' in the German language curriculum. It is normally taught via project work. Some parents may not have been aware that their child was learning about science at all. Below is my translation of the topic areas the EDK define for natural sciences by the end of the 6th (H8) class and provide an example of each:[43]

- Movement, power and energy, e.g. measuring volume or speed
- Perception and regulation, e.g. use of electricity
- Materials and transformation, e.g. expanding, changing temperature
- Living organisms, e.g. how they need light, air, water, nutrition
- Habitat of plants and animals, e.g. ecological systems
- People and health, e.g. nutrition, physical education, risk factors (related to traffic, water and electricity)
- Nature, society and technology, e.g. sustainable development, technology in everyday use

Maths

The content areas defined by the EDK for maths up to the end of the 6th (H8) class are shapes and space; numbers and variables; functional relationships; and quantities and measures.[44] The competence areas that are developed are knowledge, cognition, and description; operation and calculation; use of tools and instruments; representing and communicating; modelling and transforming into mathematics; reasoning and justifying; interpretation and reflection of results; and investigation and exploration.

Chapter 9   Examples of primary school in practice

In this chapter I provide examples of parents' observations and subjective opinions as to what and how their children were taught in the first six years of school around the country. Some examples are taken from cantons where the 6th (H8) year (or even the 5th (H7) year in the case of Basel-Stadt) was not part of primary school, but I still include them here. In future all cantons except Ticino will have six years of primary school. Some teachers also talk about how and what they teach. The chapter aims to give you a general idea of what you *might* expect, but it is no guarantee as to how a subject is taught by a particular teacher in a specific canton or municipality. It seems to be that the greatest variation is from teacher to teacher.

An important initial point related to primary schools around the country is that pupils tend to have the same teacher for two to four years, possibly with three years as the average. The ten and eleven-year-old girls I interviewed in canton Baselland generally liked this. R commented, "If you keep changing teachers every year, you have to get used to them and what their rules are. It's fun here because you know them and what they expect you to do. You know how they want your homework to be so it's better." A found it helpful that the teacher knew what she could and couldn't do in German. D thought it was helpful for the teachers to know you well as they have to decide which level of lower-secondary school you would go to afterwards.

Increasing pressure

Primary school is when it all starts to happen. As I mentioned earlier, expatriates who get to know the Swiss school system tend to comment on how things gear up or ramp up when children finally start school. Karen observes that in England there is pressure very early on for the children to achieve, while in Switzerland, the pressure is later. "For a nine-year-old, the level of schooling is not much different." Nicole J is a teacher in canton Ticino who commented that it is a shock for children when they start first grade, and have to sit all day long: "It is quite a big change. My younger son turned

6 in November. In Ticino, you start school in the September of the year you become six years old. He was a bit young, but he was fine in the end." She also sees the pressure increasing again in the 3rd (H5) class. "They have the same teacher for two years, then the next one for three years. My younger son's new third grade teacher gives them a lot more work. There is so much homework, even during the holidays. He can barely keep up. She expects students to memorise times tables."

Hazel in canton Aargau realised that the slow start at kindergarten was deceptive. "They keep them younger a bit longer. But by the time they reach eight or nine, the level of maturity and personal responsibility expected of them is very high." Rachel in canton Basel-Stadt comments:

> It ramps up quickly after the fourth class. There is a lot more homework. This may be influenced by the fact that they are not in school every afternoon and are given homework to do in their free time. They also have to exercise a lot of personal responsibility in organising themselves and this is dependent on personal maturity rather than academic brilliance. Being a year older than the others, rather than a year younger can often be an advantage.

Maths

Maths may be taught from a book, or from worksheets alone. Some teachers (or possibly whole cantons) use a series of follow-on books, for example, the *Schweizer Zahlenbuch* series is used widely in German-speaking Switzerland.[45] It offers a whole range of additional workbooks, etc., including a supplementary reference book to guide the teacher in adapting the material for children with learning difficulties. Other teachers use worksheets only for the first few years.

With regard to the approach to maths, English-speaking parents often describe the way of teaching it as quite traditional, as slow and thorough, in effect a 'no child left behind' approach. Karen emphasises that everyone does the calculations until they've all got it:

> They make sure the basics are in place, and that they are reinforced. There is a smaller tail of low attainment. Then they move on to the practical application in their workbooks, like adding things up, using money to buy things. They do not follow

fashions readily, for example, doing Venn diagrams. My kids are more confident about using numbers here, playing with them, doing things in their heads. In England one of my children was written off in maths at the age of seven. In the Swiss system she gained confidence. She learned the multiplication tables and can now do things with numbers she couldn't do before.

In spite of 'no child left behind', there is still the possibility with many teachers that individual children can zoom ahead. Nicole J described how her older son had a teacher who let them all do maths at their own rate. He was flying through the programme, and others could take their time. Myriam K, a trainee teacher, reports how children work with a numbers wall (see the illustration below), where they have to add up and fill in missing numbers. Children who need more of a challenge can create their own walls, of any size they like.

Figure 3   Numbers wall

Some parents report needing to help their child with maths homework, although this tends to be discouraged by teachers. Kate in canton Zurich describes how her son had mental arithmetic exercises three to four times a week in the 4th (H6) class. He brought home a double-sided laminated sheet of 90 multiplication sums to do per side, using washable marker pens, several times per week:

> They had also been given a marking sheet for the parents to sign, stating the date, time taken over the sheet, and number of sums incorrectly calculated. There are 90 sums per side, and the aim is for them to be able to work the whole side, accurately, in less than three minutes. So that's a work in progress, which we do three to four times per week and continued with during the holidays. Needless to say, my own mental arithmetic has also improved as a result! Since the holidays he has now come home with a third sheet, which is division – but the same idea. The results are incredible and very obvious: in September, the first time he did the first side, it took about 15 minutes. After two months the first side took 4 minutes.

Kate was then surprised that her younger son C's teacher did not give them extensive mental arithmetic exercises. Describing herself as a 'tyrant mother', she commented: "I have got C to do it himself anyway, as he is a lot weaker in maths than J."

Angela in canton Vaud found that the basics were taught in a fairly dry fashion:

> In England teachers jump through hoops to make it more interesting. Children learn the multiplication tables using grids and games and songs. In the village school here they just recite them, chanting in pairs. Each pair recites a table (like the four times table) in turn to the teacher and the whole class. Then the teacher tests the pair by asking each one a specific question, such as, "What's four times six?" It is mildly competitive. I think it makes things easy for the rest of your life if you know these. They just wouldn't chant the tables in England.

As well as learning the multiplication tables, children learn to do mental maths, where the only thing they write down is the answer. The way they go about this is part of their training in thinking. If a child in 2nd (H4) class has to add 67 and 14 in her head, she is taught three different ways to do this and can then decide which way works best for her. There are many permutations of this approach over the years, applied to addition, subtraction, multiplication and division. Mental maths is valued for teaching children to concentrate.

Writing numbers backwards

One of the challenges for a child who starts learning maths through German is the fact that the numbers are 'back to front'. In English you say 'seventy-nine' for '79'. In German you say 'nine-and-seventy'. It comes automatically to German speakers to think of the second number first, as can be seen in the way they write telephone numbers. In English the listener writes '0-7-9' in the order in which it is spoken. In German you say 'null, neun-und-siebzig', so the listener writes the 0, leaves a space, writes the 9, and then goes back and fills in the 7 in the space before the 9. It could be a good exercise for your child to practice reading and writing telephone numbers before he or she starts Swiss schooling.

Learning to read

Myriam K explained that one method of learning to read is 'reading by writing' while another is phonetic, using a mirror to see how you make the sound, and then identifying the letter. Natalie M is a primary school teacher and explains how this works:

> With this method the children will also learn how to 'write' using small pictograms of faces 'saying a letter'. This is often a little confusing for the parents, but if you let your child teach you the 'sounds', it's easy to follow and well worth it. Once the children can 'read and write' with these faces, the 'real letters' are added and the children can often read and write with 'normal' letters within a few weeks.

Angela comments that children start to read and write two years later than in the UK, and one year later than in the US. Some parents find it a bit awkward to go back to visit their families and friends in countries where seven-year-olds are reading books if their own children are not reading yet.

When we first spoke, Karen's six-year-old son had just started to read in both English and German. "If someone had told me that my near seven-year-old would only be starting to read simple books now, I'd imagine that I would have to refer him to a child psychologist." she reflected. "He's not dyslexic, as I thought he was. He is now reading both languages in tandem because he is ready to read." At the ages of nine and ten, Rachel's children experienced learning to read in German as very straightforward: "Both kids could read well in English, and once the rules were explained, it didn't seem to be a problem. German pronunciation has very few exceptions as far as I can see, unlike English which is full of them!"

My daughter's primary school teacher explained to me that when the children were learning to read, she and her partner teacher did the same work with all the pupils for a few weeks. Then they had a more individualised programme after that (see the 'plan for the week', page 97). "Those who could read told us stories that we wrote down for them on cards. Then they read through their own story texts while others kept with working with the letters." I was intrigued to hear this. At home, my daughter used to ask me to write down a story she told me, but she never told me it was something she had experienced at school. There was probably a lot I never heard about.

Wendi, in canton Thurgau, describes how her daughter has been encouraged to use the Antolin reading system during her second year of school. Antolin is a German reading programme of 30,000 books for 1st (H3) to 10th (H12) class. There are also some English books and other foreign languages. Antolin was mentioned by several mothers and is used from either first or second class. The teacher or school obtains the licence and takes pupils to the library to choose books that are marked 'Antolin'. They can also download books to read. They can read as many books as they like at home and answer reading comprehension questions on them for points.

Natalie M explains that teachers have access to the computer accounts of their pupils and can (and often will) go and check on their progress. In some schools, individuals compete with each other, while in others, whole classes are in competition. This is the case in Kate's younger son's school in canton Zurich, where the teacher gives a prize to the child with the most points at the end of the school year. The Antolin scheme functions throughout this school, to the 6th class (H8), and has very effectively helped Kate's son improve his German language skills.

Foreign languages

Angela's son began German in the third class in canton Vaud. However, he missed a little of it as he was taken out of class for extra French lessons. It is important to keep an eye on this, and, if possible, help your child catch up on the classwork missed. Languages and maths both build on a strong foundation, and are worth keeping up.

The first foreign language may get less attention if the child is learning the school language at the same time. The school language obviously has priority. However, the foreign language will remain an important subject for many years, and it is important to get the basics in place in the first few years. In some cantons, all languages are added together to give a combined grade that is considered in the selection process. Depending on the canton, the weighting of each language will vary. It could be that the school language makes up half of the grade and the two foreign languages combined make up the other half.

Parents report that grammar is a bit of a dirty word in some language classes in English-speaking countries. Teachers have to try to organise fun activities for their pupils and sneak the grammar in when they are not looking. In Switzerland grammar is a *duty*. It is boring, but it is clearly the backbone of language teaching at school. Pupils cannot stop learning grammar or vocabulary after a couple of years.

In both lower and upper-secondary school, pupils expect a lot of hard work and have to be prepared for little surprise tests (for crucial end-of-year marks) to check that they've been keeping up and learning it properly. Gymnasium pupils (and applicants from abroad) need to have studied two foreign languages at school to gain entrance to a Swiss university.

Sarah in canton Zurich commented that bilingual kids may get a shock that they have to actually *learn* a foreign language. "They underestimate the work involved because learning the language that's spoken around them is relatively easy in comparison. That's the trap my daughter fell into." Tracey from Canada observed something similar with her daughter S:

> She grew up bilingual in German and English and was praised for that by many people. Of course there is actually no 'studying' involved. She then seemed to imagine that when she started learning French, she would find all the words in her brain readily available for use, just like with English and German. It was quite a shock to realise that every word that you wish to 'retrieve' has to have been entered into the 'system' at some point. In retrospect, I regret that I did not offer to support her by checking her vocabulary with her before tests. It would have been good if she had developed more confidence in French.

Creative writing

Generally speaking, creative writing does not seem to be a priority in Swiss primary schools. Angela noticed that there was no creative, free writing at her school in canton Vaud. "They don't do that here at all," she said. "My children don't miss it, as they didn't like it." Barbara thought the focus on reflective writing was very toned down in Swiss school. "It is a case of 'Today we did this and that.' Not how I feel about it."

Tara is Indian and describes how one of her children's primary school teachers in canton Aargau had the children writing stories and poems every week. It was very creative. Her other child did not have this. Natalie M confirmed that, as with nearly everything in Swiss schools, it depends largely on the teacher. Teachers can choose freely what kind of writing exercises they want to do and how frequently. They can also decide whether to focus more on grammar, writing or something else.

Art and music

Art and music seem to be areas where the curriculum varies greatly from canton to canton. While all cantons report having a strong emphasis on handwork, not all focus on the fine arts.

Angela observes that the children do a lot more *bricolage* (handwork) or creative things around the ages of seven to nine. In England this takes place more in infant school, from ages four to seven. They do many more artistic things than in the UK – for example, works of art, like a picture frame they spend a long time on. She compares this with England, where she says there is so much to fit into the curriculum, they just do half an hour of 'this and that'.

Sarah in canton Zurich commented that her daughter never went to a museum or art gallery in Zurich. Karen's eight-year-old had an art project on Paul Klee in canton Basel-Stadt. They drew in the style of Klee, went to a museum to see his work, and had a workshop there. Then they focused on Vivaldi and Mozart. The teachers played instruments and asked the children to bring in their favourite music. They had a show for the parents, with songs, pictures and presentations. Anne in canton Neuchâtel commented that the teacher has the freedom to deviate from the curriculum for some subjects, depending on the interests of the class and their teacher. "One teacher may be interested in music," she explained, "and then the class all get a recorder. It's a matter of luck."

People and the environment

This subject may include natural sciences, geography and history. Natalie M says that it is up to the teacher to choose the topics to be covered. "This could mean that not all the areas are covered equally – or even at all," she comments. "But most teachers do try to fit a topic in from every area of it."

One comment I often heard was that there is a strong focus on children's immediate environment in the early years of primary school. Lise describes how her son's class focused on the geography and history of their village for the whole year in third grade as part of the Ticino curriculum. In the 4th year they focused on Ticino, so that he knew everything about the local mountains and rivers.

In the 6th (H8) grade, in the *scuola media*, they move on to learning about Switzerland.

A project-based curriculum

'People and the environment' may be covered to a large extent in project work. Karen describes how learning is less formalised at Swiss school. There is an acceptance of the whole person in the children's early years. They are fully involved in their school activities and gain experience developing different types of skills. They will later be adaptable in many fields and able to turn their hands to different kinds of jobs. This may produce a more flexible workforce who is taught to think and act. At the age of ten, Karen's daughter, D, was learning through doing:

> Things are very tactile here for children. Take 'Farming' in D's class. The teacher took them to the farm. They planted the corn, using a lot of maths. How much corn to fill this field? They measured how it grew in the timespan. They went back and helped the farmer harvest it and ground it into bread. Then they learned the biology of the cow, the stomach chambers, with diagrams labelling them all. How does the cow process food? How does it produce milk? In cities in Britain, a lot of children think eggs come from Sainsbury's. There was also a project here in D's class on the human body, where the teacher brought a skeleton into class, to see the bone structure, looking at all the parts of the human body.

Melanie G is a primary school teacher in canton St Gallen. She keeps her own horse in a stable on a farm. She conducted a project week in the form of a field trip with the 20 pupils in her combined 5th/6th (H7/8) year class. Melanie G showed me her documentation detailing the 14 main goals for the week which came under the categories space and time; individual and society; and nature and technology. There were a further 11 detailed goals related to knowing about horses. Melanie G and her pupils put up their tents beside the stable and slept there for two nights. The children then spent the week helping out at the stable where they were mucking out, feeding, exercising, grooming and riding the horses. They organised a *gymkhana* (a riding competition). They learned the biology of the horse and how it behaves, and also about what it takes to run a farm. There was an emphasis on the children's interactions with each other and finding out more about their individual abilities. In addition there was a focus on how to live healthily.

Some parents report that there is not much project work done, while others experience it the way Karen and Melanie G describe it.

Handwriting

Parents around the country all seem to be in agreement regarding the importance of penmanship in primary school. They are taught cursive, or joined-up writing, known as *Schnurlischrift*, or *verbunden* in German. Barbara in canton Schwyz was surprised that children had to learn this. "They didn't do *Schnurlischrift* at the international school," she explained. "As long as my daughter could make herself understood, it was fine how she wrote. This was absolutely not acceptable in the Swiss system."

Angela in canton Vaud reported that her children had to relearn how to write with ink pens, using Swiss-French cursive writing. Joined-up writing in England is a different style. In Switzerland, if they haven't written something neatly, the teacher makes a critical comment. Nicole in canton Ticino describes the approach to handwriting as very old-fashioned compared with the USA:

> They have to learn to write with a fountain pen in the second half of the first grade. They learn old-fashioned letters, almost like calligraphy. They focus on perfect handwriting, using graph paper, and getting the letters inside the boxes.

Kate describes how, on moving to Swiss school in Grade 4 (H6) her elder, left-handed, son was given the canton Zurich *Schnurlischrift* exercise books to work through, along with a left-handed fountain pen, so that he could catch up with his peers. His younger brother, in Grade 2 (H4) missed out on most of the handwriting lessons due to his extra German lessons, but later caught up at home by doing a page a day out of additional copies of the same exercise books.

Natalie M told me about the *Basisschrift* (basic writing), which is easier to learn and faster to write.[46] This is now being introduced in many cantons.

Homework

I spoke to Hannah in canton Basel-Stadt when she was in 6th</br>(H8) class at the age of 11. She described the *Orientierungsschule* (a school level now being phased out) as a really good school:

> Here we study much more intensively and I've come on much more. There is more homework from different teachers – history once a week, German three times a week. I need to be more disciplined. It is a big step for me. I don't like homework but I have to do it. In England, if you don't do it by Friday, they just say, "Bring it on Monday." Here you get a *Strich* (a black mark). If you get 3 *Striche*, you get a letter sent home. One girl doesn't pay attention in class and therefore doesn't always do the homework. They're really disappointed. They make you feel really bad. Most people do it. Two boys forget it a lot, class troublemakers. They have to stand outside a lot too, as they disrupt the class.

Homework is taken very seriously in Swiss primary schools. Pupils have a lot of free time, and their homework is an integral part of the syllabus. There is, however, a maximum recommended time to be spent on homework that varies from canton to canton, and in most cantons there should be no homework during school holidays. As an example, the curriculum of the canton St Gallen recommends 60 minutes of homework per week in the 1st (H3) and 2nd (H4) classes increasing to two hours in the 5th (H7) and 6th (H8) classes and 4 hours in the 9th (H11) class.[47]

The plan for the week

The 'plan for the week' in German (*Wochenplan* or *Arbeitsplan*), known as the 'plan of work' in French (*plan du travail*), is commonly used by teachers to let children organise their own classwork, homework or both. It takes one or two weeks. The Swiss *Wir Eltern* parents' magazine website describes it as an approach designed to tailor learning tasks to individual abilities, needs and interests.[48] Some tasks are compulsory while others are optional, if the child is keen and able to do more. The teacher may stipulate the tasks and the time frame, or else state the goal and plan the tasks required to reach the goal together with the children.

Melanie G has a mixed-age class of 5th (H7) and 6th (H8) year pupils and describes how she works with the *Wochenplan:*

> I have an open programme of classwork for the week. I hang it up on a poster on the blackboard. Each child has their own individual plan too. On Monday morning they can choose whether to do music, maths or German for two lessons. They can choose from a range of exercises from the coursebook and additional worksheets, from very easy to very difficult, according to what they think they can manage. I give them homework from day to day and other work in advance for the whole week, and support them in doing this.

Myriam K is a trainee teacher in canton Basel-Stadt and describes how exercises can be graded into one star (the easiest) two stars (medium) and three stars (the hardest). Pupils can assess their own ability and choose what they think they can manage. One child may choose a one star activity, but then decide to try something harder the next time. For that child, two stars is an achievement. In the course of the week, some pupils may only do three exercises in total, others do five, and very able pupils do the five, plus three more. It is part of Myriam K's job to encourage the minimalists to do a bit more to extend their skills.

Joanne lives in canton Thurgau and would have welcomed a flexible plan for the week. She explains that she asked her son's class teacher to make the work more challenging for him or give him extension activities but that it did not happen. "He is way ahead of the class in maths and is given the same work as the others," she said. "He takes five minutes to do his maths then often waits for up to 30 minutes until the others finish." The plan for the week seems to have trickled down to kindergarten level in some places. Claire, in canton Vaud, describes how her daughter had it in *enfantine* (kindergarten). Tasks were colour-coded and the children had to wear the appropriately coloured bead necklace to show what task they were working on.

The plan for the week may affect how much homework the child has to do. Angela in canton Vaud comments that if the plan isn't completed in the time period, it is sent home to be finished. Sarah in canton Zurich described how she had to sign a form if her daughter did not manage to complete it. "This upset all of us very much, particularly since there was nothing we could do to help," she explained. "In the end, I started to treat it as a joke, which helped us not to worry too much about it."

Chapter 10   Individualisation and comparisons with others

Cultural values are woven throughout a school system and are also referred to throughout this book. The next two chapters draw your attention to specific issues that may be culturally challenging at kindergarten and primary school levels and beyond. It is important to be aware of them in order to be better prepared for the selection process that is outlined in Chapter 14.

Understated appreciation

As was discussed in Chapter 6, the gurus on child development in Switzerland emphasise individualised education at Swiss kindergarten and school. However, some parents report that they are not aware of this. Lidia in canton Zurich comments, "Pupils are not encouraged to be proud of their achievements and themselves but their shortcomings are pointed out to them instead. This might be a cultural thing as understatement is considered a virtue here."

It is indeed a tendency in Switzerland that children are not singled out for praise and for this reason many parents do not realise their child's uniqueness is being noticed or appreciated. This fits with the view of Largo, who states that children want adults to notice what they are doing but that they do not primarily initiate or continue their activities in order to get praise and attention.[49] A child is satisfied with himself and his self-esteem is developed when his achievements are in accordance with his stage of development and should be recognised for this. Adults should give him the feeling that he can develop his abilities and learn to solve problems. Adults should also give him the feeling that what he does is meaningful, and that he is appreciated by the important people in his life.

The American author Carl Honoré explains how, in the USA, his son's teacher described his son as gifted. It was this incident that led him to write the book *Under Pressure*.[50]

> It all started at a parent-teacher evening. The feedback on my seven-year-old son was good but the art teacher really hit the sweet spot. "He stands out in the class," she gushed. "Your son

is a gifted young artist." And there it was, that six-letter word that gets the heart of every parent racing. Gifted. That night, I trawled Google, hunting down art courses and tutors to nurture my son's gift. Visions of raising the next Picasso swam through my mind until the next morning. "Daddy, I don't want a tutor, I just want to draw," my son announced on the way to school. "Why do grown-ups always have to take over everything?"

You are unlikely to hear this type of gushing in Switzerland. The teacher in Honoré's story was using superlatives that would be seen by Swiss educators as detrimental to the child's development and mainly serving to inflate the ego of the parent. If the child's performance is too much the focus of attention, he will become self-conscious in the future, thinking about what people think of him rather than focusing on the task at hand for his own enjoyment and satisfaction as he draws. Yvonne M, the kindergarten teacher mentioned earlier, explains that she does not like to emphasise the difference between the children or even say to a child or her parents that she is 'very clever'. She is more likely to describe her to her parents as *aufgeweckt* or 'bright'. She does not want to create high expectations at such an early age.

Sarah M comments that in her work with primary school children in canton Geneva, she has met children who know an unbelievable amount about something, for example, dinosaurs or ants. It is important to recognise (*valider*) them for this and show appreciation of their knowledge. However, if the child is disruptive in class, the teacher will talk to the parents about this as something that needs to be addressed, and the child's abilities may not be mentioned. At the same time she emphasises that teachers in Geneva will show an interest in the language and culture of origin of incoming children, and validate these.

It is also important to keep in mind that parents are not always informed if the teacher considers their child to be excelling. They are more likely to be told if their child is not keeping up. Parents of bright children often do not realise that they are getting more challenging work at school. I did not know that my daughter was getting more advanced maths, or that she was telling her primary teacher stories, which the teacher wrote down so that my daughter could practise reading her own stories. I only discovered this years later when I interviewed this teacher for my first book.

The formal assessment controversy

It varies from canton to canton whether marks are given for academic achievement at primary school and, if so, what form they take. In some cantons the traditional range of marks from one to six will be applied. Four is the pass mark and six is the top mark. There are different philosophies regarding whether it is good for children to be formally assessed with marks at a young age. In some cantons, there will be a qualitative form of assessment instead. As an example, in the canton of Geneva, the child's 2nd year (H4) report card will state whether the child's level of acquisition of knowledge and skills was attained comfortably, attained, almost attained or not attained. From the 3rd (H5) to 6th (H8) year, these four criteria are still used and a mark from six down to three is added. Marks and other forms of qualitative assessment become more important in the 5th (H7) and 6th (H8) years, when children are being selected for different paths of lower-secondary school, which is discussed in Chapter 14.

In some cantons, parents are almost unaware that their children are being marked or assessed. In others, parents find it happens more extensively than in their home country. Angela in canton Vaud finds that her children are tested on nearly everything and anything.

> It is just part and parcel of school life. My children haven't been fazed by it. They get one of five grades, three of which are pass grades, and two others which are fail grades. They get marks for poems, for French, for songs they sing, for art work, gym, swimming. Foreign children have a two year cushion period where their marks for French do not have to count. They are assessed on a regular basis and the teachers are not afraid to say if someone hasn't made the grade. In England everything is wonderful and teachers can't give negative comments or marks. You don't know how your child is really doing.

Marks play a greater role from lower-secondary level onwards. Children often spend more energy on attaining a minimum level across the board, rather than on shining at something. As Sarah in canton Zurich comments about marks at gymnasium level, "It is amazing how many subjects they have to keep topped up. Some kids and their parents get scared. If marks drop below a four, they have to repeat the year. In the UK, you're as good as your best subject. In Switzerland you're as good as your average. They don't bother about your strong subjects." In gymnasium, each pupil just needs to obtain a pass mark in order to gain access to almost all traditional Swiss universities to study almost anything. This means that pupils are not in competition with each other.

Repeating a year

As competition is played down, repeating a year is also no big deal. It is also a way to ensure that each 'floor of the house' is being built properly. Angela describes it as considered 'utterly shameful' in the UK if a child is held back a year. In Switzerland it is different as there is no stigma associated with repeating a year. "Here a very highly educated mother chose to place her child in the year below," she comments. "She will be old for her year. Some even hold them back for two years so that their child might have an easier time at school."

No comparisons

Parents are not informed how their child is doing in comparison with other children. A mother once told me that she asked the primary teacher: "Where are my children in the class? I know you know. Tell me." The teacher was shocked at being put under pressure to reveal this. It was a taboo topic. Allan Guggenbühl is a Swiss child psychologist who is against competition. He explains that Swiss pedagogical practice aims to motivate the child to work independently and reach individual goals at his own pace.[51] A child should not have to experience fear or criticism from fellow pupils due to not achieving what others achieve. The path to the goal becomes more important than the goal itself. This is supposed to reduce competitiveness and comparisons.

However, Guggenbühl notices that children may perceive learning as a dimension of social interaction that can be very competitive. A child may wonder, "How am I positioned in the class as a result of my effort or knowledge?" or think, "I jumped further than Barbara in the sports lesson." He argues for considering children's perspectives, which may be less than ideal, but reflects aspects of Swiss society. "I'm faster at counting than Victor" shows that, for some, learning is about working better than others. He argues that the art of good teaching is to make use of this competitive spirit without orienting one's teaching to it completely. Incoming parents often see Swiss pupils as uncompetitive in comparison to children back home.

Charles is from Canada and has two children in school in Basel-Stadt. He comments on the difference in competitive focus and the extent of extra-curricular activities that children in North America often have from a very early age.

> Children in North America tend to be involved in a broad number of activities offered through the school or local community. There's also a higher expectation to perform and to win. You are expected to push beyond your limits since you want to win. In Switzerland there is a stronger sense of reservation and less expectation that you're going to win. The social expectation to fit the norm is greater in Switzerland and there can be a tendency to malign winners and people who stand out. In Canada it's expected that you'll stand out and hence also encouraged.

Charles believes this is also reflected in the approach pupils take in their interactions at school. Each child is keen not to be seen as trying to be better than the others. In German-speaking Switzerland, a *Streber* is literally a 'striver' or someone who is overly ambitious.

Tara is an Indian mother in canton Aargau. She explained how she sees the world as a competitive place:

> When one looks around the world, one realizes quite quickly that for every chair in the world (speaking academically and professionally) there is a queue behind the person occupying it. Just look at the population of the world! There just are too many people vying for each place. I attended a government-run school until I was 15 in the town where I grew up in India. My parents believed that you send your child to school, but learning is done at home. Here in Switzerland, I was not happy with the pieces of paper or the maths books my children brought home that consisted only of pages of exercises. I kept buying extra text books that explained the theory in more detail. I grew up reading from parallel textbooks and wanted them to have the same opportunity as I had had, to understand the theory in different ways.

So I supported my sons with science books I bought. I also sub-
scribed to magazines like the American Chemical Society magazine, and chemistry home experiment magazines. The kids did
experiments with me for a while until they were around eight
years old.

Tara was not only helping her children to become excellent scientists. She also got her younger son extra lessons (*Nachhilfe*) for his
French, as neither she nor her husband could speak French. She is
aware that her approach was not always well accepted by others:

> I struggle in this culture. Anyone who does more is a *Streber*. As if
> it's wrong to work hard. I have my Swiss friends who do not feel
> that they should teach their child at home. They said, "It's the
> school's job to teach my kid, not my job." I said, "School shows
> what they should learn, and I have to make sure they learn it." I
> didn't discuss with the teachers that I was doing stuff at home. I
> didn't see any necessity to do so. The 'Tiger Mother' book makes
> the *Streber* thing positive.[52] It's extreme of course, but very inter-
> esting. A weakness of Swiss schools is that they avoid all com-
> petition. But the world is very competitive. We never know who
> has the best marks. But to win a prize is nice too. It could be
> motivating for kids.

Competition is not just played down in primary school but
this attitude may continue all through your child's school life in
Switzerland. Please see Cathy's comments in Chapter 15 for an
example of playing down differences in gymnasium. At the same
time, I find it interesting in this regard that the Antolin reading
system, mentioned in Chapter 9, is now encouraging competition
between children and/or between classes. It may be that things
are now changing slightly.

Chapter 11 Training in responsibility

Another key cultural theme in Swiss school is that children are expected to take responsibility for themselves from a young age. It is important not to underestimate the psychological value of this training process. It begins at kindergarten. Karen in canton Basel-Stadt found it quite tough at first to let her children walk there on their own: "Your heart goes out to this tiny little dot of a child walking down the street and crossing the road," she commented. "You imagine all kinds of things. Some Swiss mothers wait at the halfway point. Others take their children by car." The school psychologists and even the police discourage this. Daniela, a Swiss mother, describes driving primary school children to school as a topic that creates heated discussions these days. "The teachers and the psychologists are against it, because it isn't good for the child," she explains. "The neighbours feel disturbed by the extra traffic in what is possibly a residential area and the parents whose children walk to school are upset about all the cars that make the streets more dangerous for their children. Then it is a vicious circle. You have to drive your kids to school because other parents are making the streets unsafe by driving their kids to school."

In lower-secondary school, children start cycling to school. Daniela showed me guidelines she uses, published by the Zurich police, advising parents to teach their children how to cycle on the road safely.[53] They emphasise that parents should consider how well their child can concentrate and how responsible the child is. They suggest practising cycling on the road, but state that there are limits. For example, turning left is considered to be a difficult ma-noeuvre, so they recommend that children push their bikes across the pedestrian crossing instead of turning left. Even if the school is too far for children to walk, they still learn to get about on their own. Angela in canton Vaud noticed how small children using buses have to pay attention to getting on and off the right buses at the right place:

> School buses are provided to get the kids to school. In England the driver has a list of who should be on the bus and the teacher meets the bus and accompanies the children into the school play-

ground. In Vaud no one is helping the kids get on the right bus. Some days they go on different buses to their friends' houses. Five and six-year-olds manage this by themselves. The bus is parked outside the school. Mine got on the wrong bus once when we first got here. I was standing at the bus stop waiting and they didn't get off. I was quite chilled by it. I was meeting them off the bus for a while, until my son said, "Would you stop doing that? No one else does it."

Children doing their own risk assessment

Children also tend to be very well-behaved when out as a group. Angela also told me how surprised she was at how little supervision Swiss children need:

> On a school trip recently, I dropped my nine-year-old son off at the railway station platform. The other parents just dropped off their kids and left. The children congregated near the teacher. The train arrived and all the children just got on, without the teacher's saying anything. They didn't have to round them up or 'stop the escape artist'. In England it would be guaranteed that at least one child would be legging it across the platform. They wouldn't have been standing still waiting like that.

This reminds me of the time I told my 13 year-old nephew in Scotland that my 11 year-old daughter had been on a school trip to a sewage treatment plant and that they had been given a guided tour of the facilities. He found the idea very entertaining and said that his class would never be allowed to go on a trip like that because they would all be pushing each other in.

So why do Swiss children not push each other in? In my first book *Beyond Chocolate – understanding Swiss culture*, I describe how children in Switzerland are educated from an early age to do their own risk assessment.[54] A Swiss child will be trained to see the world as a place with limits and will of her own accord look around more, anticipate and assess potential dangers and then avoid them. New residents from abroad are surprised to hear about their young children using saws, drills and knives at the local school and making fires on trips.

School trips are more adventurous than in countries with a very proactive health and safety culture. Rachel appreciates this aspect of *Lager*, or school camp, organised by teachers for their class. It would not happen so much in UK because of the risks and especially the liabilities involved. "It is an individual school's decision in the UK," she explains, "and there is a lot of paperwork for risk assessment. My daughter has been all over Switzerland, catching trains, walking, staying with her class in different places every night."

Getting organised

Another strand in the theme of children taking responsibility for themselves is the topic of organisational skills. This will also be addressed in Chapters 14 and 22 in connection with homework. In some schools extra classes are available to help pupils get organised, but the emphasis is still on them learning to do it for themselves. When my daughter was eight, she told me her teacher was annoyed that when a boy in her class had forgotten to clean his little blackboard they used to practise their maths on, he blamed it on his mum. Saying 'My mum forgot to clean it,' is not an acceptable excuse. At the same time, parents also need to get organised. Jo in canton Basel-Stadt describes how she had to make sure she always knew what the school had communicated:

> I always had the fear I was going to miss something. The girls brought notes home but I didn't understand them all and then my daughter would turn up at school for an excursion I didn't realise was on, without the required packed lunch. I had missed that. It is a bit tricky. As I worked full-time, I relied heavily on the nanny to ensure we didn't miss anything. Teachers can interpret it as lack of interest on my part if they turn up without things. Now, every night I ask, "What notes have you got from the teacher? What do I need to sign?" One of my daughters is forgetful and she sometimes says she has nothing to sign. I then look in her school bag and, sure enough, I find something there.

Cathy reports how her son Y always got comments on his writing and organisational skills in primary school in canton Geneva. Her daughter got comments that her desk was not tidy. There were, however, no sanctions and no undue comments. There would only be sanctions if they forgot to do a piece of work.

Sharp pencils

My daughter was keen to have very sharp pencils for her primary school pencil inspection on Monday mornings. My little plastic pencil sharpener was not really up to the job, so I went to the stationer's and bought a very expensive Caran d'Ache desk pencil sharpener for nearly 40 francs. I did not find this very important, but she did. Her pencils had to be 'really *spitzig*' (meaning sharp).

French psychologist and advertising consultant Clotaire Rapaille talks about the significance of quality and perfection.[55] The Americans he asked associated the notion of quality with functionality. He concluded that the Culture Code for quality in American is 'It Works'. I would suggest that in Switzerland the Culture Code would be 'It Works Perfectly'. Moving on to the subject of perfection, Rapaille found that it was experienced as something abstract, distant and maybe even undesirable in the US. He concluded that the Culture Code for perfection in America is 'Death'. It is not something we expect in this life. I would suggest that in Switzerland, perfection is seen as the prelude to starting work.

I discussed this topic with Stefan Philippi, a Swiss sociology researcher. I explained how some incomers argue that they instinctively feel that their children should not have to focus on their tools for work being 'too perfect', as it could put a damper on their creativity. Stefan did not see why it was an issue. He replied that a good workman needs well-organised, clean tools. Once everything is arranged in its place, the work can begin. "Picasso needed his paint brushes to be clean in order to get the exact colour he wants," he pointed out. "He also needed to be able to find the exact colour he wanted. Scientists have to submit research proposals in order to obtain funding. It helps if there are no coffee stains on the page."

Most Swiss people I spoke to viewed the neatness topic, be it sharpened pencils, tidy notebooks and pencil cases or handwriting as a non-topic. Having sharp pencils and pencil boxes with the pencils arranged in order of the rainbow and keeping perfectly neat notebooks was second nature to them. I see it as partly practical and partly culturally conditioned, a bit like laying a clean knife, fork and spoon in a specific position on the table before you eat, and then washing them and putting them away again afterwards for the next time. I have to admit that in my house, paint brushes did not necessarily get the same treatment as cutlery.

Sarah M explains the importance of putting the child at the centre in canton Geneva, and that this involves an emphasis on autonomy. The child should take charge of his or her own tasks. Three criteria are evaluated: progress in taking charge of his or her own work, developing relations with others children and adults, and respecting the rules of community life. In accordance with this, learning to keep a notebook tidy is important at school. Mastering this and paying attention to these little things is a sign that he has understood the customs and is integrating well. Agnes, an American mother, told me how she experienced the increase in expectations in relation to the age of the child:

> Kindergarten children need to be able to take care of themselves bodily, but they don't need to remember any kind of dates or notes home or any important stuff. Either a stamp on the hand tells you it's *Wald* day (a day in the woods) or a note is hung around the neck of the child. In primary school years, some teachers expect even first graders to remember what book needs to be taken on what day and what homework is needed when. This is far more than my son's school in England would expect. My middle son's teacher is far more relaxed but he is still expected to know what he needs, where he is supposed to be and when, which is much harder for foreign kids because they have special classes during the course of the day so they can't just go with the flow. I found that discussing the situation at the start of the school year with the teacher is very helpful. If you think your child will struggle, talk to the teacher and have her, in a sense, 'own' the problem.

Natalie M says her seven-year-old son brings bits of paper home that are screwed up in a ball, or slightly torn. "As a teacher I would not accept it," she comments, "but his teacher is okay with it. When I taught six to eight year olds, I insisted on neatness because I knew they were going on afterwards to a teacher who tore up pupils' work if it was not neatly written."

Kevin noticed the difference in the degree of organisation expected of the children in the French school he visited, compared with his Swiss school. His new French friend Brian often forgot his school books and the teacher was never cross with him. "In

Switzerland," he says, "while you are not immediately in trouble if you forgot something, the teacher will roll his eyes and say 'What am I supposed to do about it?'" Kevin sees the mark they get for *Heftführung* (keeping your notebook nice) as playing a role if they are borderline for being recommended for gymnasium (please see Chapter 14 for more on this topic). I asked him why this is so important. "You always have to have glue, scissors, a pencil and an eraser with you at school," he told me. "When a teacher gives you a new piece of paper, you cut it to size and glue it in your notebook. The day before a test, you read everything through. If you haven't stuck in the bits of paper, you will have things missing and will not be able to learn properly for the test."

Boys and being organised

As a mother of three boys and three girls between four and 15, Karen suspects that the emphasis on independence in learning in Switzerland suits girls better than boys. "Girls plod on in a more consistent fashion," she says, "while boys have spurts of action, living close to the line." Rachel is concerned that parents are meant to step back somewhat from organisational matters related to school work:

> I see a dichotomy between the Swiss schools wanting all children to be very organised and so penalising forgetfulness and lack of organisation, yet at the same time discouraging parents from helping in what is clearly a valued aspect of behaviour. I think this is to try to get children to adopt the behaviour for themselves and not rely on others. The schools seem to expect all of the children to do this at the same time, which seems to favour girls, as most of them do get this for themselves at an earlier age.

The extent to which teachers help pupils get organised can vary. Eugene reports that he and his wife Victoria struggled for a long time in dialogue with their 13-year-old son L's school teacher and headmaster before taking him out of the local school and sending him to Swiss private school. L was seriously underperforming at school. He often appeared to have no homework, but in fact he was forgetting to write it down in his homework notebook, and was therefore missing important work. Eugene and Victoria asked the teacher to just check every day that L had written it down. The teacher refused to do this. Other teachers look more kindly on disorganised pupils. In Kevin's class, if pupils don't do their homework, the teacher starts to check whether they had written it down in their homework notebooks. One boy not only didn't write it down, he also kept forgetting his homework notebook. "The teacher punched a hole in the notebook," said Kevin, "and tied it to his school rucksack, so that it would always be there. They're very good like that in my school. They do check."

Maturity levels of boys and girls

The level of maturity of boys and girls in early puberty could be decisive for the school they are allowed to attend at lower and upper-secondary level. As the school path is influenced by the child's level of maturity, boys may be at a disadvantage. In a dialogue with Martin Begliner, Remo Largo reports that in canton Zurich, 60% of gymnasium pupils are girls while two thirds of pupils in special schools are boys.[56] Largo sees three reasons for this. Firstly, at the age of 12 ½ years, girls are 1 ½ years ahead of boys in maturity and therefore in performance. Secondly, schools have placed more emphasis on languages in the last two decades, which is something girls are better at.

It is, however, the third point that is particularly important according to Largo, and that is girls' attitude to work. They are more responsible, more industrious and better at fitting in. He argues that the more the secondary virtues of orderliness, hard work and punctuality are emphasised, the worse the boys' chances are of getting into gymnasium.

Marcel Lüthi has worked for many years as the head of the bachelor's programme Business Economics at the School of Business, University of Applied Sciences of Northwestern Switzerland. He sees organisation as a key to success:

> When students do not succeed it appears to be due to a lack of planning, organisation, time management. They underestimate the work required for exam preparation and plan inadequately. Also during the semester, they neglect these aspects, overestimate their ability and underestimate the planning and organisation needed to carry out the course assignments. We now offer a course in the first semester called Work and Learning Techniques.

Your zone of control

You might feel you are losing control by letting your child take responsibility for getting organised. However, from the Swiss point of view, by taking a back seat, you are helping your child increase his or her sense of self-mastery. It is good to start practising early. Liz comments that it is a reciprocal or inverse relationship: as you relinquish control your child gains control, and for the Swiss this is a pillar of parenting. She is Irish and came to Switzerland with her husband and two daughters, aged four and six. She told me how she was already mentally focusing on their future careers in their early years. Metaphorically speaking, she was focusing on differential calculus, when she should have been making sure they had sharpened their pencils (by themselves) for the Monday morning pencil inspection. She refers to Stephen Covey's *7 Habits of Highly Effective People* in explaining why she now thinks the Swiss way is a good approach:

> Stephen Covey's first habit 'Be proactive' can be applied when you feel powerless against life's forces. He recommends examining where you *can* be proactive, taking action, instead of focusing on worries over which you have no control, like your children's careers. The Swiss education system concentrates on giving children control of the things over which the children themselves have influence and so instils confidence and independence. Like the way they get to school. Schools are small, built nearby. The children can get there by themselves because of the proximity. The school seems to stay within the zone where the child can take control.

Liz believes that, if both parent and child can embrace this philosophy, there may be a smooth journey as the child's circle of influence increases. Eventually the child can do differential calculus on their own – with the sharpened pencil, of course. As a parent, one strategy to support this Swiss parenting pillar could be to think of ways to be more proactive, not aggressive, to enlarge your circle of influence and reduce your circle of concern, for example by volunteering to join the parent's committee in the school. See Chapters 21 and 22 for more on working together with the school.

Section three

Lower-secondary school

Chapter 12   The lower-secondary curriculum and school models

As stated in the introduction, the content of this book is driven by the aspects of the Swiss school system that were experienced as the most challenging by the people I interviewed. While parents expressed concern about the curriculum at primary school level, their concern at lower-secondary level focused on the difficulties of understanding the selection process and supporting their child through it. In this chapter I briefly outline the lower-secondary curriculum and the different school models to be found. In Chapter 13 I provide a brief overview of the pathways through upper-secondary school and how they may lead to tertiary education. In Chapter 14 I summarise the selection criteria, or the key factors influencing the decision process regarding which type of lower and upper-secondary schools your child may attend. I then go on to give examples of how parents and their children have experienced the selection process. If you find this section a bit complicated, you might like to turn to Chapter 14 first to read about parents' experiences of the system and then come back to the more factual material here.

As with the rest of this book, no guarantee can be given for the information provided here. I am trying to describe a moving object, or rather, 26 moving objects, whose school models overlap, intersect and diverge again along the way. This overview is intended as a starting point to be complemented by the information provided by your local school. It should help you to know what questions to ask. The EDK provides flow charts of the school system nationwide in four languages (English,[57] German,[58] French[59] and Italian[60] as well as the system for each canton for the current year.[61] It is well worth getting hold of the specific diagram of the education system for your canton with all the different names of stages and school types. For some cantons you will need two diagrams if the number of years of each school type is changing due to HarmoS (see pages 14 – 15, 253).

If you cannot find the diagram(s) you need online, try phoning the Department of Education for your canton. There is a list of telephone numbers in Appendix 1 (pages 258 – 259). School administrations are very approachable and are happy to fulfil requests for information about the system. They will pass you on to someone who can guide you through the website until you come to the document you need. Information in English is sometimes buried somewhere and this is when you may need someone at the other end of the phone to guide you through the maze. Some cantons may also be willing to put you on their mailing list to receive updates about different stages of school, even if you are not yet in the local system.

The lower-secondary curriculum

The main purpose of lower-secondary school is to prepare pupils either for an apprenticeship or for the continuation of their general education. As outlined in Chapter 8, on primary school, the *Plan d'études romand* of the French-speaking cantons and Ticino specifies five main domains of activity for all levels up to 9th (H11) class.[62] At lower-secondary level the subjects defined are as follows: languages (French, German and English); maths and natural sciences (physics and biology); human and social sciences (history, geography and responsible citizenship); creative and manual arts; and physical education. In the German-speaking cantons, a curriculum is being designed in accordance with the *Lehrplan 21*.[63] The names of subject areas are similar to those used for the *Plan d'études romand*. Subjects and the time spent on them will not vary greatly from current curricula, which tend to include the school language (15%), foreign languages (15%), maths (15%), natural and social sciences, including history and geography (26%); art (17%), physical education (5%), and other subjects, such as ethics, religion or citizenship education (7%).[64] Please also see the EDK website for details of the national educational minimum standards in the school language, foreign languages, maths and natural sciences for the end of the 9th (H11) class to be implemented by 2015.[65]

The academic standard of Swiss 15 year olds

The OECD PISA survey regularly tests the abilities of a national sample of 15-year-olds in reading, maths and science in 70 countries. It is designed to see how well students can apply their learning to real problems and situations. In 2009, Switzerland was 8th in rank in mathematics.[66] Shanghai-China, Singapore, Hong Kong-China, Chinese Taipei, Finland, Japan and Belgium all did better. It is rather surprising that Swiss pupils do so well in an international comparison, given that in Switzerland both academia and industry complain regularly about the poor level of mathematics of students. It may be that Switzerland just needs a particularly large percentage of students with excellent maths skills to fill the jobs in the banking, insurance, engineering and pharmaceutical sectors. At tertiary level, if you want to study business subjects, you almost cannot avoid taking economics too. For comparison, in some other countries it is easy to find a university bachelor's degree course in marketing or human resources where you do not have to study economics too.

Switzerland comes in 15th in science and 14th in reading in the PISA survey. The reading subscales included:

- accessing and retrieving information
- integrating and interpreting (making internal sense of a text)
- reflecting on and evaluating the form of a text

The EDK, the Swiss cantonal directors of education, have been monitoring the lowest reading scores in particular,[67] as 20.4% of pupils did not reach level 2 (of the six possible levels) in 2000. In 2009 this figure was down to 16.8%. They hope that it will decrease further. This score is influenced by the percentage of young people with a migrant background, which increased from 20.7% in 2000 to 23.5% in 2009. Across the OECD countries, only 10% of the population have a migrant background. The canton of Zurich is working on this issue with its own tests that reveal the correlation between migration status and school performance.[68]

The lower-secondary school models

Pupils are in mixed ability classes throughout primary school. At the end of the 6th (H8) class of primary school (see Section seven on Cantonal Variations, for exceptions) they are selected for lower-secondary school paths according to their ability. (In 11 German-speaking cantons, a small percentage of high ability pupils may go straight to six-year gymnasium.)[69] Teachers working at lower-secondary level are the most amazed of all that I am writing a book about the rich tapestry of Swiss schools. They find the variations between cantons incredibly complicated.

I approach the topic from two angles. Here I provide a broad overview of the range of school types in the whole country (possibly overlooking some exotic specimens). I provide specific information for each canton separately in the charts in Chapter 27, including the names of the levels of lower-secondary school in the particular canton. The number of levels may vary from one to four, according to the canton. Three levels is the most typical, where the highest level is usually the one that is preparing pupils for the academic demands of gymnasium. The middle level prepares them for demanding apprenticeships and the basic level prepares them for more basic, practically-focused apprenticeships. In some cantons there is also a fourth, even more basic level, which has a stronger 'workshop' or focus on practical skills.

As well as having different numbers of levels with different names, the types of models of schools may also vary from town to town and most cantons use more than one model. Below I refer to the Swiss Education Report[70] to describe the three different models: (a) the streamed model, (b) the cooperative model and (c) the integrated model.

(a) The streamed model

In the streamed model, pupils are allocated to different types of schools, all for different ability levels, which function quite separately. This model is decreasing as the sole model used in favour of a mix, or one of the other two. In most of the cantons with this model there are three different types of school. In the streamed model, pupils who are either not managing the level, or are doing particularly well, tend to change school at the end of the school year.

(b) The cooperative model

In the cooperative model, there are different classes or home rooms based on different ability levels for certain subjects, all taught in the same school. Pupils are further divided, for example into four level groups, for at least two subjects. This model makes it easier to move pupils up and down from one level group to another during the year for particular subjects without having to change their home room. A certain amount of criss-crossing is likely to take place as pupils change level groups. Home room changes are more likely to happen at the end of a year.

(c) The integrated model

The integrated model is the closest to what is known as the 'comprehensive system' in English. All pupils go to the same school and have non-selective, mixed ability home rooms. At some point they are allocated to different ability level groups for two or three subjects, usually maths and a language. This is the most porous approach, as pupils can move up and down from one level group to another during the year, as with the cooperative model. There is no need to change their mixed ability home rooms at all. This is the only model used in the cantons of Jura and Ticino, but it can also be found within many other cantons, especially in rural areas.

The cooperative and integrated models are on the increase in Switzerland. This development addresses two issues. First, it allows pupils the opportunity to change level group more easily if their performance improves or if they are finding a level too difficult during their lower-secondary education. I discuss the pathways concept in the next chapter. The second issue is that, nationwide, lower-secondary pupil numbers are expected to decline, with rural areas most affected.[71] As a result, there is a trend towards fewer separate schools, and fewer different ability classes. Class sizes may be reduced in some places and some classes need to be amalgamated or closed down. To meet differing local requirements, many cantons combine all three models, or two of the three. A fourth, mixed-age model was considered in canton Lucerne, similar to the Basisstufe. It met with political opposition and was stopped by parliament. It has, however, been introduced in canton Appenzell Ausserrhoden and may start to appear elsewhere too.

Six-year gymnasium

Not all pupils attend a lower-secondary school. In 11 German-speaking cantons, high-achieving pupils have the opportunity to go to straight from primary school to a six-year gymnasium programme (*Langzeitgymnasium*), starting in the 7th (H9) class.[72] (In Basel-Stadt, gymnasium lasts five years for all pupils in the old system which is being phased out.)[73] In 5 of the 11 cantons (GL, GR, SG, SO, ZH) selection is based on an entrance exam and in the other six cantons (AI, LU, OW, NW, UR and ZG) it is based on marks or the teachers' assessment. Once pupils are in gymnasium they may have provisional status until they have proven they can manage the level. Otherwise they need to change over to a lower-secondary school.

Chapter 13   Pathways to the future

As the time to change over to lower-secondary school approaches, you and your child may be nearing a crossroads. This stage is where different pathways begin in most cantons and there are many different school models around the country. As many parents do not realise the longer term potential of all the paths, I outline them all briefly. I prefer the term 'paths' or 'pathways' rather than 'tracks', due to the degree of flexibility now being built in to the Swiss education system. In the education literature, a pathway can be defined as 'the individual patterning of education-related transitions through the life course'.[74] I imagine this to be like going hiking rather than taking a train. It is easier to change your path while out for a hike than to change track while travelling on a train. 'Route' may be another useful word, suggesting a certain amount of flexibility.

Lower-secondary school finishes in the 9th (H11) year in all cantons[75] and upper-secondary school begins in the 10th (H12) year and lasts three to four years. Broadly speaking, lower-secondary pupils are being prepared for the specific demands of a type of school at upper-secondary level, either (a) gymnasium, (b) an apprenticeship, (c) a commercial or IT school, or (d) a specialised school. (The names of these school types in the local languages can be found in Appendix 2 as well as in later chapters, where they are described in more detail.) Pupils' marks, the teachers' evaluations and/or external exam results are the main factors in deciding which upper-secondary school they may attend.

(a)   Nationwide, around 20% of pupils complete gymnasium, the academic path. It is the most academically demanding school and offers a direct route to traditional university. Pupils who obtain the Gymnasial Maturity (or Baccalaureate), even with a mere pass mark, may enrol at any of the traditional Swiss universities for any course they choose, with the exception of a few subjects, for which there are entrance exams.

(b)   Around 65% of pupils choose a two, three or four-year apprenticeship, officially known as a Federal Vocational Education and Training (VET) programme. When they have completed their apprenticeships, around the age of 19, they can start work for a reasonable salary. If they also obtain the Vocational Maturity (or Baccalaureate), they can study for a bachelor's degree at a University of Applied Sciences and Arts. Alternatively, they may go on to obtain a Professional Education and Training (PET) qualification at tertiary level.

(c)   A smaller number of pupils nationwide enrol for a three year VET school-based course at a commercial or IT school. If they also obtain the Vocational Maturity (or Baccalaureate), they can go on to take a bachelor's degree at a University of Applied Sciences and Arts.

(d)   The three or four-year specialised upper-secondary school is chosen by around 3%, the small percentage of pupils who have a definite interest in health/natural sciences, social work, education, design/art, communication/information and music/dance/theatre. Depending on the specialism chosen, pupils may need to obtain a Specialised Maturity (or Baccalaureate) to gain entry to a University of Applied Sciences and Arts or University of Teacher Education to study physiotherapy, social work, teacher training at primary level, or art.

No dead ends

The information above may be rather surprising. If you understand it to mean that the non-gymnasium pathways may all lead to a Vocational or Specialised Maturity, qualifying pupils for entrance to a University of Applied Sciences and Arts, you have understood correctly. Going to one type of school rather than another does not close doors. As Tony, an English father of teenagers commented, there are no dead ends in the Swiss school system. All types of lower-secondary school may ultimately lead to tertiary education, even to traditional university, if a keen pupil is willing to invest the time and makes use of the passageways connecting the different paths. This is exemplified by the practice of some cantons allowing pupils to sit an entrance exam for gymnasium on several different occasions – for example, after the 6th, 8th, 9th and even 10th year of school.

Patrick Langloh, rector of the *Wirtschaftsgymnasium* in Basel-Stadt, gives the example of a pupil in the lowest level of secondary school at the age of 12 who ended up at university. She was very bright, but had not worked much at primary school due to her family situation. She was therefore put in the lowest stream at secondary level at the age of 12. There she worked hard and after her nine years of compulsory education was allowed to enter a one-year bridging school of commerce (*Kaufmännische Vorbereitungsschule*) that gave her access to a three year commercial school course (*Wirtschaftsmittelschule*). She could then have worked for a year and gone on to sit a Vocational Maturity exam, but instead she spent one year in a *passerelle*, another bridging school, this time giving her access to university.

Another possibility would have been to spend a year in another bridge course (*Übergangsklasse*) after the nine compulsory years, which would have given her entrance to gymnasium, and led direct to university. The bridges and *passerelles* usually involve spending an extra year somewhere, so it takes time. Patrick Langloh emphasises that no one asks you why you took so long. They are more interested in the fact that you achieved this against the odds and what you learned from the experience.

Chapter 14   Selection criteria

"Most of us can still remember the first time we looked into our newborn's face and imagined infinite possibilities. That tiny baby might someday discover a cure for cancer, become president, write the Great American Novel, or invent something to eliminate world hunger. The potential was thrilling, but also scary. What if we, as parents, screwed up, and deprived the world of a great scientist / leader / artist / inventor?"[76]

These comments were made by Barbara Kantrowitz, writing for a *Newsweek* guide to US colleges. She suggests that if you drew a graph of modern parenting's most anxious periods, the peak would probably be that newborn moment, followed by the final years of high school. She goes on to describe the race for college as a very 21st century obsession. In the middle of the last century most parents felt lucky if their kids were healthy.

For parents with children in local Swiss schools, the most anxious period in their children's school years may come a bit earlier and can be split in two, namely the first selection process around the 5th (H7) to 6th (H8) class (depending on the canton), and then again during the 8th (H10) or 9th (H11) class where a second round of selection is taking place. In this chapter I outline a range of selection criteria and present the views of parents and children on the subject. It is important to keep in mind that this is a discussion about the initial selection for one school type or another. As was mentioned in Chapter 12, there can be quite a lot of movement between the different levels during the three years or so that the pupil is in lower-secondary school.

Selection criteria

Selection takes place twice in most cantons, typically during the final year of primary school and again during the final year of lower-secondary school. Each canton has a legal basis (*Rechtliche Grundlage, base juridique*) for the form of selection used, and the legal documents providing the details should be available online. If you cannot find them, you can ask the school to send you the link to them. Please also see Chapter 26 for information on how to appeal a decision made by the school.

There are three main types of criteria used to assess a child's suitability for a particular school, class or group. These are (1) marks from continual assessment, class tests and cantonal exams; (2) external exams and (3) the teacher's all-round assessment of the pupil's attitude to learning and to school work, and potential for development, personal competence and social competence. A fourth aspect in some cantons is the wish of the child and parents. For more detailed information, please see the tables in Chapter 27.

A national custom

Although there are many differences in the school systems around the country, one common feature foreign parents may not be familiar with is the 'rounding up' of borderline marks at the end of the year. This takes place at a teachers' conference. The marks range from 1 to 6, and the pass mark is 4. Final pass marks are generally rounded up and down to the nearest half mark. If a mark is 3.7, it will go down to 3.5 and if it is 3.75, it will go up to 4. However, if a pupil is in danger of having to repeat a year, a borderline mark like a 3.7 may be discussed and rounded up to 3.75 at the teachers' conference held at the end of the year to finalise the marks. This will then give them a 4, the pass mark.

Each canton has its own process of decision making and communicating the decision as to which lower-secondary school the child is to attend. It is very thorough. In some cantons parents are not asked their opinion, while in others they are. An example of this is provided by Melanie G, a primary school teacher in canton St Gallen. She describes how she starts to observe children from the 4th (H6) class onwards. She then makes a recommendation to the head teacher of the lower-secondary school during the 6th (H8) class. Parents receive a form from her in the 6th (H8) class informing them as to what she recommends. They can state their opinion regarding which level they think would suit their child. The form is then sent to the head teacher, who makes the decision, based mainly on what the teacher recommends.

Entrance exams

If an entrance exam is a pre-requisite for getting into gymnasium or other schools, parents have to consider how far they wish to go in preparing their child for this. Barbara describes how this worked for her 11-year-old daughter in canton Schwyz. "There is a whole market of companies supplying exam preparation," she explains. "They also do preparation at school. You need to do extra work to pass. You have to prove that you can sit down and study. They are testing whether you are academically oriented."

In canton Zurich, there is an entrance exam that can be taken at the end of the 6th, 8th and 9th classes (H8, 10 and 11). Kate's son, J was 12, near the end of the 6th (H8) class when he took the first of these, the exam to enter *Langzeitgymnasium* (six-year gymnasium). A neighbour, a gymnasium headmaster, had encouraged Kate to let him have the experience of sitting the exam. J stayed at school over lunchtime on Thursdays and did past papers. There was also a short preparation course on offer at a *Lernstudio* (tutoring studio) for 600 francs in the spring holidays. J's friends had been attending classes at *Lernstudios* from 5th (H7) class. Kate was adamant that J should not have to attend classes regularly at that stage, as he had already had a lot of extra work learning German.

J did not pass the exam. He would have needed to obtain a 4.5. If their marks are borderline, between 4.25 and 4.5, pupils have an oral exam to see if they can manage it. Kate is optimistic about his chances of getting into *Kurzzeitgymnasium* (which starts after the 8th (H10) or 9th (H11) year): "He stands a chance to get in later as he will have more German by that time, and a better command of writing. He's only 12 years old and has never sat a serious exam in his life. He did really well just sitting it. We didn't want to put him under pressure. We don't speak German at home. He needed to do it without the pressure." As Kate explained, "Once pupils get a place in gymnasium in canton Zurich, there is still a trial period from August until January. Everyone has this. There is an intake of 125% and 25% of the pupils don't make it. There is continuous testing for 3 or 4 months. It is very stressful for them."

The tough entrance exam in canton Zurich is often a source of controversy, and much discussed in the Swiss press. Lidia lives in Zurich and considers the competition to get into gymnasium to be unfair: "There are lots of really bright children in my daughter's class but it ends up that only the children of highly educated and financially privileged parents get in." She sees the reason as the amount of preparation these children receive. "Their parents either do extra work at home with them, and if they don't have the knowledge (also knowledge of the language), or the time, they will need the finances to pay for Lernstudios." Lidia herself went to school in Canton Aargau and passed the exam without her (immigrant) parents' help. She comments that the exams have got tougher since then.

Rudolf A is a retired lower-secondary teacher from St Gallen, where there are also entrance exams. He comments from the school's perspective that it is indeed a problem that children are being prepared more intensively for external exams. The negative effect is that if the children are better prepared, the exam has to be made harder to make selection possible. However, some very bright children will pass the exam without extra tuition.

Selection based on marks

In many cantons there is no external entrance exam for gymnasium and marks play the most important role in the selection process. These may be marks from tests, continual assessment, or cantonal tests that are increasingly being introduced around the country.

Andy is a Swiss father in canton Solothurn who explained that all pupils in the canton have the same *Vergleichstests* (comparison tests) in German and maths and that the results count for 40% of the final mark that is the main consideration in the selection process. (This arrangement was agreed by the people by cantonal vote.) "Some teachers do practice tests with the pupils before the external tests," he commented. "My son's teacher didn't practise with them, so I dug out sample tests on the cantonal web page and practised them with him at home."

Nicole J describes the pupils' first experience of selection in canton Ticino. Unlike most cantons, they are in mixed ability classes all through lower-secondary level. They just need good marks to qualify for the *Liceo* (gymnasium) after nine years of school:

> They need an average mark of around 4.75 in the core subjects of Italian, French, maths, science, history and geography and English. They should have a 5 in Italian, and should be in the 'A' level, the best group for German and maths. A teachers' conference decides about the borderline cases. The *Liceo* is very competitive. Many fail the first year or drop out and change schools. Some repeat the first year of *Liceo* while others go to other specialised upper-secondary schools or commercial schools.

Ben did not realise that his daughters were being judged regarding their level for the next school. Officially there were no marks (in the sense of numbers from 1 to 6) in the *Orientierungsschule* (Orientation School) in canton Basel-Stadt, but there were in fact four types of grades: H (high), M (medium), G (basic) and GT (basic, partially achieved). "We learned the hard way that they were being assessed and were more careful with our third child." By that time they knew from experience that a child needed high and medium results in maths, French and German to get into gymnasium after the 7th (H9) year. Ben's wife Pat invited their third child, F, to take part in a system of rewards for good marks in the 5th (H7) to 7th (H9) years of school.

> I offered to pay him for good results and he would have to pay me for bad ones. I gave him ten francs for a 'high' result and five francs for a 'medium' result in seven of his subjects. If he got a 'basic' mark or the lowest mark, he had to pay me five francs and ten francs respectively. So he might go into minus. The results were written up on an Excel sheet and there was then a payout every quarter. He enjoyed working hard and cashing in. At the end of his three years he was recommended by the teachers for gymnasium.

Changes in the system

It is important to stay on your toes and keep informing yourself about developments in the school landscape. I was reminded by Carol in canton Geneva that I am trying to describe a moving object. Improvements to the system are being made continually. I wrote up an interview comment she made in the summer of 2011 and sent it to her to read a few months later. She told me it was already out of date:

In the old system which changed in 2011, my daughter was missing 0.2 marks in her French language course to get into the top group in the first year of the cycle in Geneva. Only after a long interview with the director and a psychologist did they agree to let her in. In the new system post-2011 entry, they state that there are no exceptions to the minimum requirements. However, they now have many more opportunities for students to pass between the levels, using passerelles or bridges once the term begins. There is also a budget for ongoing support for students with slight weaknesses.

Teacher's assessment

In some cantons, selection may be based on academic performance as well as the teacher's assessment of the pupil's attitude to school work and general behaviour.

Swiss teachers are very focused on the present at this stage. Ben was surprised that his eleven-year-old daughter's teacher was not searching for her potential. "We thought her potential had to be drawn out. He did nothing to draw it out. She was not recommended for gymnasium." Most teachers base their assessment on a pupil's current academic performance and current level of independence, organisation, motivation and maturity. They do not focus on potential for which there is currently no evidence. Neither past brilliance (reading Harry Potter at the age of six) nor parents' hopes and dreams will move the teacher if the child is not demonstrating a proactive attitude to learning at this crucial time. This is in accordance with the German proverb, "Do not praise the day before the evening."

Rudolf A comments that a critical point is that teachers do their best to assess their pupils' abilities, but that their interpretation is strongly influenced by how they learn at the time in question. Even if children have plenty of ability, their willingness to learn is strongly influenced by external factors, and these can change in a short space of time. Rudolf A had pupils in the 7th (H9) and 8th (H10) classes he thought would never be suited to gymnasium in canton St Gallen. They later surprised him by doing well in the entrance exam after the 10th (H12) class. It is important to note that they were not doing well enough to pass it after the 8th (H10) class.

Soft factors

Stating what you want for your child may not impress the teacher. The pupil's own beliefs and expectations about succeeding at school (known in English as 'academic self-efficacy expectations') are considered to be more important than those of their parents. The value the young person places on academic, professional and financial success is expected to be a motivating factor for achieving it.[77] The child's attitude and behaviour are also factors that are considered in the teacher's assessment. It is also important to keep in mind that, if the teacher is giving you feedback on poor behaviour, this may have an impact on the path they recommend for your child. Rachel compares this with her experience of schools in England, emphasising her concern that the focus on behaviour is more of a problem for boys:

> Poor behaviour will influence an individual's results in the UK, but unless it is extreme, it won't have an impact on which school they go to. Their first real test in England comes with exams at 16 and, by then, more boys have achieved enough maturity to start doing some work for their qualifications. In Switzerland, the decision about what a child is capable of tends to come earlier and is based on academic results as well as being influenced by a child's attitude and behaviour. In schools with a separated model,

if you miss the entry to the preparatory school for gymnasium, it is harder to make the crossover later. While parents and teacher are waiting for the child to blossom, he will be in a class that reflects the lesser effort he is making at that time. He then has to prove himself academically to move up.

Moving up (or down) is difficult in cantons where pupils are in completely separate lower-secondary schools. The trend now is to change over to a form of school where different level classes are within the same school building. The move between levels is to be made easier so that pupils who start to make more effort can be moved up. With integrated school models such as in Ticino or Jura, there is no crossing over as the home room for most of the subjects stays the same.

Talking about school performance

If the teacher's assessment is taken into consideration in your canton, you will wish to know about your child's performance level. According to the Swiss youth psychologist, Allan Güggenbühl, parents often only hear about their child's academic limitations or weaknesses when it is too late.[78] Many Swiss parents assume that the goal is for their child to get into gymnasium and want to hear how their child is doing compared to the rest of the class or in relation to gymnasium entry requirements. However, they do not specifically mention this expectation. The teacher in turn judges the pupil's performance by the individual goals they have identified for the child according to his or her ability. They may report that a child is a 'good pupil', taking his proven ability level into account. 'He is making great progress' may therefore mean he is no longer the worst at maths, while parents interpret it as meaning that he is now above the class average or has even risen to the top of the class.

Parents may have no comparison with the performance of other children as marks are generally not made available. A good question to ask is where the teacher sees the child in relation to the rest of the class and, as a follow-up question, how many of the class are likely to go to the different types of schools at the next stage.

Children's experience of assessment

The group of 10 and 11-year-old girls I interviewed (see Chapter 2) talked about the pressure of their last year in primary school because they were being selected for different levels of lower-secondary school. Both they and their parents were keen for them to be able to go to gymnasium. They frequently had tests and felt under pressure to get high marks, as well as to be organised and well-behaved. They thought this would be a particularly difficult experience for someone who was new in a Swiss school and couldn't yet speak the language. E explained how her parents put her into Swiss school one year before the selection was made so that the teachers had time to get to know her. R describes how she experienced the pressure:

> These last months, we've had two tests a week and they've all been counting for what you're going to do. They see how you work in class and all the marks you have are put together. It's also the little things that mostly count, how you cut something out, or glue it, or how you colour it in and they also give you marks for how you keep your books and everything. And that's why you always should be organised and have everything so neat – because it counts. In Britain, if you don't understand something, you'll just pick it up later. In Swiss school you have to understand it that day because a week later they'll give you a test on that. So you should always be 100% sure that you know what you're learning. And at the end of the year they talk with your parents and see where you're going. Sometimes you worry a bit when you're getting your tests back because they do mark it really strictly but you shouldn't worry, you should just try your best and be happy.

M commented that the teacher looked to see how they worked and also whether they were behaving well. D gave examples of this as being "how you join in, like in sport, or if you put your hand up and say something." She was also aware that even if pupils were selected for the academic level, it was not definite that they would be able to stay there. She had been told it was better for some children to start in the middle ability level and move up later if they were doing well. I can confirm that teachers will want to make sure a child will not have a downward transition. They see it as better to start at a school with basic requirements and move up, than start at a school with higher requirements and have to move down.

R's mother Lesley found that the tension was tangible during the assessment process. "Children and parents feel under pressure," she said, "which was something I hadn't experienced before."

Doing extra homework

There is an element of impression management involved in getting an education in cantons that consider attitude and behaviour as part of the selection process. Working hard, keeping your books tidy, and joining in have all been mentioned. Doing additional homework can also be an indicator for selection. Martin H, a teacher and father describes how, as part of the plan for the week, his daughter M can choose how much homework to do in 3rd (H5) class. It is voluntary and the extra work has no impact on her marks. However, it shows the teacher something about M's capacity and willingness to work. My daughter described how a German teacher invited the pupils to say if they wanted to write extra essays in the 5th (H7) class. "We got into his good books if we did it," she comments.

Natalie M explains that in canton St Gallen, doing extra homework can be an indicator for teachers as they decide which pupils will go to which type of lower-secondary school. Pupils who want to take a higher level path and whose parents want them to take this route are often encouraged to do extra homework if the teacher offers it so that their level improves.

It is worth finding out what other parents are doing regarding homework. Andy in canton Solothurn says there is an unwritten rule among parents where he lives that if you want your child to do well at school, you should work with them for an hour a day from the 4th (H6) class and for two hours a day from the 5th (H7) class, until selection has taken place.

Teenage motivation

The first selection process tends to take place at the onset of puberty. At this time, motivation can be a big challenge for some teenagers and cause their parents much concern. I asked Beatrice Zeller, a psychologist and careers advisor for young people,[79] what parents can do if their child is not motivated at school and does not want to do homework. This was her reply:

> You can push your child, and try and force him to achieve. It is questionable whether it is good for the child's development. Each child has his own rhythm and his own path. You have to think carefully about how great your responsibility should be and what exactly your role should be. The task of parents is to observe the child, look at what the child does well, is good at, and at his abilities. These often do not correspond to school marks. Some children fail at school subjects although they are actually good at a lot of things. But there are so many bridges (*Übergänge*) and opportunities at different ages along the way that a child can catch up very quickly once he is motivated to learn. It is a porous system that can still get you into tertiary education.

If your child lacks motivation and has behavioural problems too, it might be helpful to get a professional learning therapist (*Lerntherapeut*).[80] A parent I spoke to could not praise his child's learning therapist highly enough. The therapist acts as a coach, offering psychological support for children who have difficulty at school with learning, marks, behaviour or motivation problems. The therapist finds out the source of the problems by talking to the child, the parents and possibly the teacher. He or she (gently) explores the child's approach to learning, psychological state, emotional development, and socialisation. Tests are carried out and the therapist finds out his level and gaps in school work, how gaps arose, his learning style, how he organises himself (for example in doing homework), and what strategies, if any, he uses to solve problems. Based on the data and impressions from this diagnostic phase, the learning therapist defines a development plan and discusses goals with the child. For example, an aim may be to reduce stress, or fear of tests. Progress is then assessed and goals are adjusted.

If you believe your child has tremendous academic potential but is just not making a good impression on the teachers at the age of 10 or 11, all is not lost. There will be more opportunities to change path along the way. The system design is based on the assumption that children mature at different rates. In particular, boys tend to mature on average later than girls, and provision is made for this. Longer-term, there are many pathways to tertiary education, as will be shown in later chapters. At the School of Business of the University of Applied Sciences and Arts where I work, the average age of students is around 24. Many obtained the Federal Vocational Maturity and then worked for a few years before having the desire to study.

Parental influence in career pathways

I have already described Pat's system of reward for good marks. Swiss parents may also reward their children financially for doing well at school. At the same time, they tend to accept it more readily than foreign parents if their children are not recommended for a path they think would reflect their potential.

My Swiss husband and I also thought it was up to our children to decide if they wanted to work hard at school, and that there were different options if they did not. It may be that you find this approach too laissez-faire, and if so, you will not be alone in this. I heard of many cases where foreign parents took a stand and actively argued for their child to be allowed to follow a more demanding path through the education system. They did this in spite of the recommendation of the teacher that their child should follow a more basic path. I am not saying that this will work in all cases. I would just like to show that 'going with the flow' is not the only way.

Alfredo in canton Geneva wished his child to remain on the academic path. He told me that his daughter chose law and economics in her first year of *collège* (gymnasium). She had good marks and was promoted to the second year. In the second year she chose the bilingual programme, English-French. She did not pass the year. At the time, *collège* pupils were allowed to repeat the year once. Alfredo was of the opinion that teachers did not encourage children enough to study and make an effort:

> The proposal of the teacher was to look immediately at other possibilities such as the *école de commerce* (commercial school) or the *école de culture générale* (specialised school). Our daugh-

133

ter didn't know what she would do afterwards but the *collège* (gymnasium) opens more opportunities. We went to tell the teacher our daughter would repeat the same grade but not leave the school to do other things as was suggested. We thought she could try to continue in *collège* . It was a good opportunity for her to realize the relevance of studying and making an effort. So she repeated her 2nd year but chose not to do the bilingual programme. She did work harder afterwards and passed her 2nd and 3rd year and is now preparing for her *maturité* exam.

Alfredo emphasised the importance of young people being disciplined and organizing themselves for studying, creating the appropriate environment, having a routine/ritual to study, to study every day and not only for special occasions such as the *épreuves cantonales* (the cantonal exams).

Section four

Upper-secondary school

Chapter 15   Gymnasium

The Gymnasial Maturity (or Baccalaureate) is a bit like a driving licence to drive a car. You do not get some licences that say you can only drive in country lanes and others that permit you to drive on the motorway. Similarly, you either have the Gymnasial Maturity or you don't. It provides pupils with an automatic entrance qualification to study most subjects at a traditional university. You don't apply to university; you just enrol. (Exceptions are human and veterinary medicine, dentistry, chiropractice and sport, for which there is an entrance exam). The standard (and cheapest) route to the Gymnasial Maturity is by obtaining a federally recognised cantonal Maturity from your local cantonal gymnasium.

Gymnasium education is considered to be of excellent quality and is free of charge although books and other materials may have to be paid for after the ninth year when compulsory schooling finishes. The exact contents of the Maturity exams on any subject vary from canton to canton and school to school, and depend on the content of the curriculum defined by the teachers of the particular school.

Structure

In the local languages, gymnasium is known as *Gymnasium, Kantonsschule* or *Kollegium* in German, *lycée, collège* or *gymnase* in French, and *liceo* in Italian. Pupils may enter gymnasium in the 9th (H11) and stay for four years. If they start in the 10th (H12) class but previously attended a 9th class (H11) of lower-secondary school that teaches at the academically advanced level required, they can complete gymnasium in three years. If not, it takes four years, giving them a total of 13 years of school. As explained earlier, in some German-speaking cantons there is also a longer six-year gymnasium (*Langzeitgymnasium*). In canton Basel-Stadt, gymnasium still lasts for five years in the old system being phased out. It starts in the 8th (H10) class for children born before 31 April 2002. See Chapter 28 for further details.

Admission criteria

As was stated in Chapters 12 to 14, selection takes place before entry to gymnasium. There are four main types of selection criteria used. These are (1) an entrance exam; (2) marks from continual assessment and class tests; (3) cantonal exams; and (4) the teacher's all-round assessment of the pupil. In some cantons there is an exam option if the pupil, parents and teachers are not in agreement whether the pupil should go to gymnasium. Selection also continues during gymnasium. Pupils have to keep passing each year. They may be allowed to repeat a year. If they pass, even if they just scrape through with a bare pass, they automatically qualify for university entrance.

Subjects

The range of compulsory Maturity subjects is extremely broad. According to national Maturity regulations, the Gymnasial Maturity does not primarily provide readiness for studies in a particular subject area in a particular faculty.[81] A major aim is to provide a broad education which results in personal and societal maturity. It is expected that the most influential positions in the country will be held by people who have obtained this broad education. They can, for example, make themselves understood in several languages, understand cause and effect in the economy and also have an understanding of basic scientific concepts and processes which help them to understand environmental issues.

The 11 compulsory subjects at gymnasium that are the same for everyone are as follows:

- first national language
- second national language
- third language (e.g. English)
- maths
- biology
- chemistry
- physics
- history
- geography
- art or music
- economics and law

The amount of time spent on the subject groupings is as follows:

- languages 30-40%
- maths and natural sciences 25-35%
- humanities and social sciences 10-20%
- art or music 5-10%

In addition, pupils choose a major subject, a minor subject and write a Maturity paper, all for a mark. Sport and IT are also compulsory, but the marks are not listed on the final certificate.

The elective major is generally taken for four years. Pupils may have the choice of:

- Latin and/or Greek
- a third national language
- English
- Spanish
- Russian
- physics and applied-maths
- biology and chemistry
- economics and law
- psychology, pedagogy and philosophy
- art or music

The elective minor is chosen for the last two years. The following subjects may be on offer:

- physics
- chemistry
- biology
- applied maths
- IT
- history
- geography

- philosophy
- religion
- economics and law
- pedagogy and psychology
- art
- music
- sport

There may only be three years of biology, chemistry and physics, no matter how many years the gymnasium programme lasts. Final marks for these are given in the second last year. Pupils who are interested in the natural sciences usually also take a science as their elective major. Some young people report that taking biology and chemistry as their elective major is good preparation for the *numerus clausus*, the stiff entrance exam for medicine and related courses.

The Maturity paper can be written on any topic a teacher is willing to supervise, from genetics to the theatre. A certain academic standard is required. I have known bicultural young people who have done field work and written about a topic related to their (or their parents') home country. One South African pupil went to South Africa to interview young people in prison. One of my daughters wrote about bilingualism, the other compared advertisements in different countries.

Marks

I am covering this topic in a fair bit of detail because many pupils start gymnasium and have to leave again. People who have not been through the Swiss system may be less familiar with this phenomenon. The drop-out rate varies, but can be 40% or more in some cantons. As Cathy in Geneva points out, it is fine to drop out of a particular school in Switzerland. "I only knew five dropouts in my whole school career in the US," she comments.

Pupils have to pass most of their subjects to be allowed to move up to the next year. They are allowed to fail a certain number (officially up to four, but sometimes less, depending on the canton) per year. However, they must double compensate each failed mark. If a pupil gets only a 3 in French and only a 3.5 in Italian, instead of the pass mark 4 in each, she is short of a total of 1.5 marks. She has to double compensate for these 1.5 marks by obtaining 3 marks elsewhere, for example by obtaining a 5 in three of her subjects, or a 4.5 in six of them, giving a surplus of 3 marks. She also has to get at least a 4 in all other subjects. So if she is particularly bad at one subject, she has to be particularly good at another one. Pupils spend a lot of their time making calculations to ensure they are good enough at everything and making sure they will be able to compensate when necessary. It can be quite nerve-wracking. In some cantons they can repeat a year if they fail, and may even be allowed to repeat a year once or twice.

Marks are given throughout the year for little tests, big tests, homework assignments, etc. Final marks from tests and continual assessment are given in the second to last year for the natural sciences, geography and history, so that these subjects are no longer taken in the last year. There are final written and oral exams in five subjects in the last year: the first school language; another national language; the elective major subject; maths; and one more subject as decided by the canton. Final oral exams are usually also conducted. In the language oral exams, pupils usually have to discuss and interpret a text on literature they have read in each of the two or three languages they are being examined in. One of my daughters had Spanish as her elective major subject and read a total of around 12 novels in preparation for her final oral exams in German, English, French and Spanish.

Value of marks

Teachers in gymnasium do not give marks away. There appears to be a continuing historical sense of the value of a mark and there is no 'social promotion' or inflation in this area. As EVAMAR, a study on all Maturity marks around the country in 2007 shows, the average *final* marks given were as follows:[82] The average mark was 4.41 in the final written examination in the first language of the school, and 4.63 when the marks for the oral and written examinations were combined. 19.6% of pupils did not pass the written exam and 4.7% did not pass the oral exam. In maths, the average was 4.03 for the written exam and 4.34 for the oral and written marks combined. 41.4% of pupils did not pass the written exam. 24.4% did not pass the oral and written exams combined. It has to be kept in mind that the examination marks are added to the mark for the year's work, which may raise the total average. In biology, the average mark for the year's work (as there were no final exams) was 4.68. 5.6% did not obtain a pass mark. The average mark for the year's work in the three natural sciences combined was 4.60. 5.6% did not obtain a pass mark.

Tips for success

Ex-gymnasium pupils suggest getting tuition in subjects where your marks are dangerously low. Kirsty suggests paying for an excellent tutor, preferably a teacher, who is recommended by other pupils. Isabelle recommends that pupils who are having difficulty do not just give up, but should get extra tuition from ex-pupils of the same school. "Find students who were pupils at your school, around four years ahead of you," she recommends. "They won't give you extra stuff you won't need to know. They know the teachers, the curriculum. It can give you confidence that you know you're doing a bit more." Isabelle also recommends proactively communicating with the teachers about low marks:

Loads of people are borderline. It's not a burden you have to bear by yourself. It is important to show that you are working. That counts a lot. You can ask for extra exercises. Write essays, hand them in. Show them you're trying. It's not like university where a machine works out your mark. By making yourself heard, being noticeable in positive ways, and laying your cards on the table, you'll also feel better.

Cantonal variations

According to the Swiss Federal Statistical Office, 19.8% of pupils obtained the Gymnasial Maturity nationwide in 2010.[83] The cantonal variation was between 12.3% in canton Glarus and 29.8% in canton Ticino. The statistics show that neighbouring cantons can vary, for example:

- Geneva (27.5%)
- Vaud (23.8%)
- Basel-Stadt (28.8%)
- Baselland (19.6%)
- Aargau (15.3%)
- Solothurn (14.6%)

There is also a gender gap. In 2010 the Gymnasial Maturity was obtained by 23.4% of the female population and 16.4% of the male population.

This variation is a cause for concern and is debated around the country. The numbers accepted for gymnasium are more influenced by cantonal education politics than ability. Local attitudes also play a role, as apprenticeships are more highly valued in some cantons than in others. It is not the case that cantons that accept more pupils into gymnasium then bring them all up to the same high level around the country. The EVAMAR II report tested the first language, maths and biology of 3800 final year gymnasium pupils and compared the results with the Gymnasial Maturity results.[84]

Pupils from cantons with fewer than 17.5% of pupils obtaining the Gymnasial Maturity did better overall than those in the cantons where over 19% of the pupils obtained the Gymnasial Maturity. The report also states that the performance level was higher at gymnasiums that take four years instead of three (giving a total of 13 years of schooling instead of 12). Pupils attending gymnasium for six years instead of four also do better. The work is more demanding.

According to the Education Report[85] (which refers to gymnasiums as *baccalaureate schools* and the Gymnasial Maturity as the *baccalaureate*), the fact that admission to baccalaureate schools is based less on actual aptitudes than on education policy considerations is all the more disturbing when it is considered that Switzerland is among the few industrialised countries that grant baccalaureate holders virtually unrestricted admission to universities and the different university programmes. For pupils and their parents this is worth understanding. It may be that a pupil who just scraped through gymnasium in a canton with a 14% pass rate may be academically more able than a pupil who scraped through in a canton with a 29.8% pass rate.

Making comparisons

There is officially no difference in the quality of the gymnasiums in a canton. They often share the same teachers, with teachers working for different schools. You can choose which gymnasium to go to in many cantons, but not all. In the Northwest of Switzerland (BS, BL, AG, SO) it will be possible to choose any gymnasium in the region from 2014. Some pupils are attracted to gymnasiums that specialise in a particular area, or offer particular subject combinations. Examples may be sciences and maths; modern languages; or Latin and Greek. There are often historical reasons for the school offering a particular combination.

In spite of the profiles, you will find pupils with particular interests or abilities do not necessarily head for the gymnasium that is known for the subject in question. The Swiss-wide *Simply Science* competition[86] was organised for gymnasium pupils at the Basel-based pharmaceutical company, Hoffmann-La Roche. The tasks included extracting the DNA of tomatoes.

A class from Kirschgarten Gymnasium was one of the ten classes to get into the final. This was not surprising as Kirschgarten Gymnasium specialises in maths and natural sciences. However, it was a class from Bäumlihof Gymnasium, a gymnasium that does not have a subject speciality, who won the first prize of a science week in California.

As well as playing down competition between gymnasiums, internal comparisons between pupils are also a bit taboo. Cathy in Geneva noticed with amusement how the lack of comparison of marks led her not to know how well her son was doing in *collège* (gymnasium):

> There is a 40% drop-out rate at *collège*. Any teacher you talk to will tell you that. Y had an average of 4.8 after his first year. You need 4.5 to continue. 'Having a gap' means that they have not managed the 4.5 required. Perhaps they got 4.1 or 4.2, but are allowed to continue into the second year with a warning to improve their performance the next year.
>
> Because there is no comparison of marks, you don't know how well your child has done. I overheard him talking to his friends. "In our group of 12 to 15 friends, only you, me and Amelia passed without a gap." He turned out to be one of the 20 – 25% who passed without any trouble.

In spite of the lack of competitive spirit, Cathy considers Y's gymnasium to be an elite school with a much more academic focus than in *cycle*, his lower-secondary school:

> Everyone is much more interested in studying. It is a great group of kids. There is peer pressure in a positive direction. He never had good friends to study with before. But it is not competitive and it is important to be like everyone else, and not stand out. You don't want to look like the smartest in the class. I had a conversation with him:
>
> Me: Did you get the best grade?
>
> Y: I don't know.
>
> Me: Did you ask anyone else what they got?
>
> Y: We're not supposed to.

Cathy describes a conversation she had with her nephew who was visiting from law school in the US:

> He said, 'We have this great study group. We are all in the top 25%. Our goal is to all be in the top 10%.' That is so different. In one way it is good that our children are not competitive. We are trying to teach them that the value of a person is not in their grades.

Immersion programmes and a bilingual Maturity

Immersion programmes leading to a bilingual Maturity were originally designed to take advantage of the multilingualism of Switzerland, offering the Maturity in two of the national languages. However, English has now taken the lead as the second language, in particular in the German-speaking part of the country. To qualify for the designation, at least two subjects other than languages have to be taught in the second language.

Bilingual classes tend to attract high ability pupils who are very motivated to work hard. They have to be willing to take course subjects like biology or chemistry in a foreign language. Over 70 of the 177 gymnasiums in 18 of the cantons had at least one class offering such 'immersion' classes in 2006[87] and numbers have continued growing since then. Over 10% of pupils now obtain a bilingual Maturity. In schools in some cantons, unfortunately, native speakers of the immersion language may not join the class. This is worth asking in your canton.

The International Baccalaureate at gymnasium

The International Baccalaureate (IB) programme may be of particular interest to bilingual pupils who have previously been educated in English. It was founded in Geneva in 1968 for internationally mobile pupils.[88] Participating schools worldwide use a standardised curriculum for the last two years of high school. Final exams must be passed at the end of the senior year in order to receive the IB diploma.

The IB is offered in many private international and bilingual schools in Switzerland. Interestingly, the IB is defined on the US National Association for Gifted Children website as an option for gifted children.[89] It is described as "A demanding pre-university program that students can complete to earn college credit. The IB emphasizes critical thinking and understanding of other cultures or points of view."

The two year curriculum of the IB diploma programme is offered in English at five German-speaking gymnasiums in addition to the Gymnasial Maturity. Other schools are looking into the matter and more IB programmes are likely to follow in the public sector over the next few years. The five schools are:

- Kantonsschule, Wettingen (AG)
- Neue Kantonsschule, Aarau (AG)
- Gymnasium am Münsterplatz, Basel (BS)
- Realgymnasium Rämibühl, Zurich (ZH)
- Literaturgymnasium Rämibühl, Zurich (ZH)

The IB is offered by Swiss gymnasiums in a format that meets the requirements of Swiss universities. They tend to offer the following subject combinations:

General subject areas

- Group 1: mother tongue
- Group 2: second language
- Group 3: mathematics
- Group 4: natural sciences: biology, chemistry, physics
- Group 5: social sciences: geography, history or economics
- Group 6: elective (one subject from Groups 2, 4 or 5 above)*
- In addition to the general subject areas, there is a theory of knowledge course (TOK) and pupils participate in 'Creativity, Action, Service' (CAS) activities.

All of the IB subjects except for TOK and CAS are also part of the Maturity programme, so there is little additional work for pupils.

The IB in Zurich

Markus Hugelshofer is a Zurich lawyer who is the president of the school board (*Schulkommission*) of the Literaturgymnasium Rämibühl in Zurich, where the IB is offered. He finds it positive that the IB allows teachers and pupils to work together on the same side towards a goal. Together they are given external feedback on their performance. He points out that the IB results are consistent with the in-house Maturity results at Rämibühl, confirming the high quality of the school's own programme. Markus

Hugelhofer's two children obtained the IB at Rämibühl. They both went on to Oxford University. A requirement for Oxford was that they had no mark below 5 in the Maturity.

The IB education was a help with the Oxford admissions process, which involved essay-writing and an interview process. They had learned to write essays with ease in English and summarise and present their findings succinctly and precisely. The IB also taught them a different way of thinking. He sees the combination of the relative curriculum freedom in the Maturity programme and the somewhat more rigid school programme of the IB as a good mix.

The IB in Basel

Here I provide more detailed information about the way the IB is offered at the Gymnasium am Münsterplatz[90] (or GM) in canton Basel-Stadt. From 2014 it will be available to pupils from four cantons (BS, BL, AG, SO). It costs around 1600 francs in fees paid to the IB organisation (or IBO). It combines the requirements of the Swiss Maturity qualification and the IB. In terms of content, there is not much extra work for pupils. Many of the subjects overlap and the only additional subject is Theory of Knowledge in addition to free time activities to fulfil the requirements of Creativity, Action, Service. Pupils may study some of their Swiss Maturity programme subjects (e.g. geography, biology, maths and history) in English, while others are in German. Their IB final exams are in May and the Swiss Maturity exams in June the same year.

Gymnasium lasts five years (from the 8th (H10) to the 12th (H14) class) in canton Basel-Stadt and the IB programme at Gymnasium am Münsterplatz starts in the 10th (H12) class. It has been designed in a way that caters for the linguistic needs of pupils from abroad or from an international school in Switzerland. They are accepted on the basis of their previous school report. It is preferable if they start in the 8th (H10) or 9th (H11) class. (It is increasingly difficult each year after that.) They take part in an intense language programme and are assessed after several months, in terms of their performance and their potential. If they are considered able, they are then accepted definitely. Two of the five classes each year are IB classes.

Pupils coming from other countries (or international schools in Switzerland) who are allowed to continue at the school after a trial semester have a good chance of obtaining the Swiss Gymnasial Maturity and the IB. The biggest challenge they face is learning two languages. They need to achieve a B2/C1[91] level in German as the school language, as well as B2/C1 in French by the 12th (H14) year in order to pass the final Maturity exam. Pupils who have previously been educated in English are dispensed from English classes and an intensive language programme is offered in both German and French.

There are language classes with a special German teacher, who gives them a mark for German as a foreign language, rather than the school language. There are also extra classes organised at a local language school, one-to-one or in a small group. Parents have to pay half of the additional costs for this. With regard to the others subjects taken in German, foreign language pupils have their marks compensated for a while until they have a good grasp of the language. The classes are generally much better at English. It is good for the English of German-speaking pupils that they are mixing with native speakers and others with a high level of English. They support each other, which is mutually beneficial.

Long-term prospects

The IB is internationally recognised and, with its standardisation and transparency of marks, is an attractive option for all young people living in Switzerland who wish to study at universities abroad. The Swiss Gymnasial Maturity is officially recognised by the Lisbon Convention. However, universities outside Switzerland with a high level of competition for places often stipulate breathtakingly high marks. As an example, 'no mark under 5' is required by some British universities, which requires absolute brilliance across the board. This is partly because admissions officers do not understand what the Swiss marks mean in the context of the candidate's class, school, canton and country. The IB is better understood. Taking the IB alongside the Swiss Gymnasial Maturity could also benefit academically-minded young people who have previously been educated in English in international schools in Switzerland.

They may wish to live and work in Switzerland after their studies abroad, especially if their parents have settled in Switzerland. Being fluent in the local language will be a great advantage if this is the case.

Independent learning

Both gymnasium pupils and their parents have commented on how mature a young person needs to be to manage gymnasium. As Cathy points out, "The teachers take the attitude that it is up to you to work. Their attitude is: this is not compulsory. If you're not into it, spare us the work and go away. You can go to other schools." Isabelle attended gymnasium and explains the types of skills needed:

> You have to concentrate and always listen, or you'll find yourself in a pickle, because they won't repeat things. Their philosophy is to leave pupils alone, to let them become independent, get knowledge themselves, learn how to make notes by themselves while someone's talking. That's quite difficult. It's as if they're saying, 'We're not going to teach them how to do it, because that would be taking the difficulty away. Then the ones who can do it, they're the ones we'll keep.'

Sophie is Scottish and Swiss and has experienced both Scottish and Swiss school systems. She thinks pupils are more spoon-fed in Britain. She describes what it was like in Swiss gymnasium at the age of 13:

> There is a lot of independent learning. Teachers will say, "Here's the sheet, learn it at home. If you have questions you can come to me." They will sometimes start talking about things and write something on the blackboard without explicitly saying, "You have to write this down. It's for the test." But because he's writing it on the board and it's quite extensive, we guess we should probably be taking a note of it. In Britain it would be unheard of. Everything has to be given in written form. In Britain teachers have to provide for example a model answer of set texts translated from Latin into English. Here, we do lots of translating in the language class, and then in a test we have a completely new text to translate.

Gymnasium is training young people for tough Swiss universities. In the EVAMAR II report,[92] students had to assess the importance of general study competencies and their personal competence level in each one. They assessed the following six competencies as most important:

- learning independently
- working independently
- taking responsibility for learning
- time management
- dealing with pressure
- solving problems

In all of these, they assessed their own ability as lower than required, with a definite dip with regard to time management.

Carl Honoré refers to studies from Britain and other countries that suggest that graduates from schools in the state system earn better degrees than those from elite private schools.[93] This is confirmed by a 5-year study conducted in the UK that tracked 8000 final year (A level) pupils in their university degree performance.[94] It was concluded that university students from non-selective state schools (known as comprehensive schools) are more likely to obtain higher classes of degrees than students with similar attainment from more selective private schools (referred to in the report as independent schools or grammar schools).

The researchers suggest that pupils from private schools are getting lots of support and are being pushed to their limits, while those in state (comprehensive) schools may not yet be fulfilling their full potential at school. It is also thought that state school pupils are more prepared for university because they have had less individual attention at school and are already used to the large amount of independent learning and self-discipline required at university. I see Swiss gymnasiums as similar to British private schools in terms of selectiveness but more like British state schools in the focus on independent learning. Pupils here are never pushed to their limits by their teachers; instead, they have to take on the task of pushing themselves if they are determined to succeed. It is worth knowing what the alternative paths are to ease the pressure if the gymnasium route turns out to be too difficult. Other paths at upper-secondary level are discussed in the next two chapters.

Chapter 16 Apprenticeships - Vocational Education and Training (VET)

What do Peter Voser, CEO of Shell (worldwide), Martin Senn, CEO of Zurich Financial Services and Sergio Ermotti, CEO of UBS have in common? One answer is that they are all Swiss and another is that they all did apprenticeships. Peter Voser did a commercial apprenticeship, as did Sergio Ermotti. Martin Senn went to a commercial school for his upper-secondary education, and followed this with a shortened commercial apprenticeship. None of these executives are considered to have a 'rags to riches' or *Tellerwäscher* (German for 'dishwasher') career. They were taking a safe, solid path to the top.

What people around you will describe as an 'apprenticeship' (*Lehre, apprentissage, apprendistato*) is now officially described in international English as Federal Vocational Education and Training or VET (*Berufsbildung, formation professionelle, formatione profession-ale*). Around 67% of young people in Switzerland complete a VET apprenticeship programme each year. VET programmes take place at upper-secondary level, from the 10th to 12th or 13th class (H12-14 or 15), starting around the age of 15. Their school starts to prepare them to find an apprenticeship from the 8th (H10) class onwards. In this chapter I discuss the nature of VET programmes, who does them, how they find them and what their future prospects are.

VET programmes consist of company-organised training and supervision in the workplace combined with related academic work in the classroom. National legislation defines the programmes. The government and industry work closely together to set high training standards and make VET programmes closely match the needs of the labour market. The result is that youth unemployment of 15 – 24 year olds is very low in Switzerland. At the end of 2011 it was 3.3%,[95] compared with an average of 22% across the EU-27[96] and 18.1% in July 2011 in the USA.[97]

The VET programme takes three to four years and students obtain a Federal VET Diploma (*Eidgenössisches Fähigkeitszeugnis (EFZ)/certificat fédéral de capacité (CFC)/attestato federale di capacità (AFC)*). Some students start with a two-year programme to obtain a Federal VET Certificate. If this goes well, they may then continue with a three or four-year programme. Pupils with good marks may go on take the Vocational Maturity, or Baccalaureate, (*Berufsmaturität, maturité professionnelle, maturità professionale*) in a subsequent year. There is also a faster route for particularly bright apprentices, who can do an 'M profile' apprenticeship, doing the Vocational Maturity during their three or four-year programme instead of spending an additional year on it afterwards. As stated elsewhere, this qualifies them to enrol for a bachelor's programme at a University of Applied Sciences and Arts. Pupils who have completed gymnasium and do not wish to go to university sometimes take a one-year shortened apprenticeship that is offered by some banks, insurance companies and law firms. With the Vocational Maturity people can take the *passerelle* (University Aptitude Test) to get into a Swiss cantonal university or Federal Institute of Technology (ETH or EPFL).

VET programmes can be part-time or full-time. Most are full-time, consisting of part-time studies combined with in-company experience. Students typically spend one or two days a week at a VET school to learn theoretical principles as well as academic subjects. They do their apprenticeship at a host company the other three to four days a week to gain practical skills. 30% of Swiss companies are hosts to apprentices. Full-time VET programmes with no apprenticeship are offered by trade schools or commercial schools. They then provide both the theoretical education and the practical training. Entirely school-based programmes are more popular among students in the French and Italian-speaking regions of Switzerland than in the German-speaking region.

The international perspective of Swiss apprenticeships

Many incomers underestimate the value of an apprenticeship qualification. Switzerland was given first place as the most competitive economy in the WEF global competitiveness report of 2011–2012.[98] It was praised for its strong collaboration between its academic and business sectors, combined with high company spending on research and development. It also ranks 7th worldwide for patenting. However, the report does not connect Switzerland's success with its VET programmes. It expresses concern that too few Swiss people go to university. It concludes that "maintaining its innovative capacity will require boosting the university enrolment rate, which continues to lag behind that of many other high-innovation countries." Indeed, Switzerland is in 51st place in the world in the report's category of tertiary education enrolment rate.

To gain quite a different outsider perspective of the VET system, I turn to a 2011 report by the Harvard Graduate School of Education, entitled 'Pathways to Prosperity'.[99] It describes how the USA needs to "build a more finely articulated pathways system – one that is richly diversified to align with the needs and interests of today's young people and better designed to meet the needs of a 21st century economy." The report describes the roadway from adolescence to adulthood in the USA as filled with potholes, one-way streets and dead ends. Although 'college for all' was promoted as the primary pathway to success in the last two decades, and the US job market now demands graduates, only 30% of young adults in the USA earn a bachelor's degree by their mid-20s. (In spite of this, in the WEF report, the USA comes 6th for its tertiary education enrolment rate).

In considering how to develop a more robust pathways system, the Harvard report turns to the empirical evidence of pathways networks as found in Europe. It homes in on VET type programmes in Austria, Denmark, Finland, the Netherlands, Norway, and in particular in Germany and Switzerland. These programmes lead to a qualification "with real currency in the labour market", as well as a pathway to tertiary education. The German and Swiss systems are described as exemplifying the three 'R's' of rigour, relevance and relationships. The report states that those who complete a VET programme are prepared for more advanced studies in institutions of higher education, such as polytechnics and universities of applied sciences.

The report also points out that while Swiss and German programmes make efforts to incorporate 'at-risk' students, employers otherwise expect their trainees to have a solid foundation of academic skills and a strong work ethic. They are "designed on the premise that many, perhaps most young people would prefer to learn from late adolescence on in an environment in which work and learning are integrated and in which there is a clear occupational goal in sight." This is seen as effective in meeting the developmental needs of young people, as apprenticeships "provide increasingly demanding responsibilities and challenges in an intergenerational work setting that lends a structure to each day. Adult relationships are built on support and accountability, mentoring and supervision."

The Swiss are aware that their apprenticeships are of a very high standard, both from their own experience and from what they read in the local press. The NZZ newspaper reported that some apprentices who had completed their education at the pharmaceutical company, Novartis, were sent for their year abroad to the company site in Boston, USA.[100] Managers in the USA commented that they had the same level of education as American university graduates with a bachelor's degree.

The World Skills competition[101] gives countries the opportunity to showcase their vocational qualifications. In England in 2011, Switzerland obtained 17 medals, 6 gold, 5 silver and 6 bronze.[102] They came in third place for the total number of medals, behind Korea and Japan. In his presentation for the 2011 competition, Michael Osbaldeston, the partnership director, used Switzerland as a role model for the high level of skills (namely, levels 5 and 6) that the UK needed to work towards. In Britain, intermediate level apprenticeships are at level 2, advanced level apprenticeships at level 3 and higher level apprenticeships at level 4.[103]

Reasons for doing an apprenticeship

Alongside school marks, factors influencing whether a young person does an apprenticeship in Switzerland are their gender, the canton they live in, and whether their parents did one too. In 2010, 36,769 boys and 30,594 girls completed one.[104] (This corresponds to some extent to the larger number of girls attending gymnasium). Apprenticeships are more popular in country areas than in the cities; and more in German-speaking Switzerland than the French-speaking and Italian-speaking parts. In canton Aargau, for example, half of the pupils who are recommended for gymnasium do not go there, but take the apprenticeship route instead. They are well-informed about them and their prospects. Natalie M explains the attitude as she experienced it in canton St Gallen:

> I went to the *Kantonsschule* (gymnasium), but I know others thought, "Why go there if you can have a really good apprenticeship and earn good money?" Many people think it is a good start, to have a bit of both, practice followed by further studies later on. My neighbours want their son to become an electrician, as it is a really useful course. The most prestigious apprenticeships take four years rather than three, such as a carpenter, an electrician or a draftsman. Some children who are offered a place at gymnasium do not take it. I am surprised by the intensive competition for places in gymnasium in Zurich.

Gymnasium or gardener

Many middle class incomers are concerned that their children have no future if they do not get into gymnasium and then university. As one mother was heard to say, "If the Swiss system is going to say that my son should become a gardener because his German isn't good enough to go to gymnasium, then I'm pulling him out of the local school." She possibly did not know that gardening is an apprenticeship with career prospects in Switzerland. Besides the clichés of liking to work outside, with your hands, the prerequisites for a gardening apprenticeship include being fascinated by plants, having aesthetic sense, being patient and persevering, and enjoying advising clients. The apprenticeship can be followed by more advanced tertiary qualifications such as an Advanced Federal PET Diploma (see Chapter 18) specialising in landscape planning, or a Bachelor of Science in environmental engineering from a University of Applied Sciences and Arts (UASA).

An apprenticeship lays a foundation, teaching you the nuts and bolts of a field of work. Dagmar Voigt is the Rector of the *Schule für Brückenangebote* (a school in canton Basel-Stadt offering 10th (H12) year bridge programmes). She studied and worked for many years in the USA and is aware of the difference in attitudes there and in Switzerland. "It is little understood in the USA," she explains, "but for technical and industrial fields, highly skilled people can go far, and the best way to get ahead is to start with an apprenticeship.

Engineers with a practical background are often more sought after by companies than those with an academic degree only." Dagmar went on to say that many people running their own companies in technical and industrial fields began with an apprenticeship in the field in question.

Apprentices may generally have lower school marks than those taking the academic route, but they are not necessarily less intelligent. 'Gifted apprentices' is now a subject of research in Switzerland.[105] There are many reasons for choosing this path. In some cases, they are 'one-sided', or good at a particular subject, for example, maths, IT, technical subjects or natural sciences, compared with gymnasium pupils, who have to work on a huge number of academic subjects over a period of several years, as was shown in the last chapter.

Some pupils do not make it into an academic-level class due to their teacher's assessment of their performance and potential around the age of 11. They decide not to attempt to transfer to an academic-level class later on. Another factor may be that peer groups can be very important around the age of 12 to 15 and some young people want to stay in the same school as their friends.

Some people choose apprenticeships because they are tired of being in the classroom all week and would prefer to be learning something useful that can be applied immediately. Some teenagers may (secretly or openly) not respect their school teachers but will have respect for the teaching practitioners from a particular field who will teach them about working in a real world setting. Others just look forward to earning their living and becoming independent. Their colleagues who are at university will probably only achieve this around the age of 25. Others do wish to study later on, usually at a University of Applied Sciences and Arts (UASA) with an applied focus, rather than a traditional research university. There is no age limit and many students are experienced practitioners.

In some cases, family circumstances make the apprenticeship route a necessity rather than a choice. An apprenticeship will provide young people with an income of around 800 francs per month from around the age of 15 or 16, and a reasonable salary from around the age of 19 or 20. This can be helpful to their parents if they have younger siblings to support.

Parents from other cultures may not be comfortable about their child taking the apprenticeship route because there is less focus on academic subjects. Maria is Spanish and is disappointed that her younger son R did not manage to get into gymnasium, although he is happy with his path:

He is doing an apprenticeship as a draftsman with an architect's office. I find it a pity that he is not getting so much language or any kind of cultural education any more. For me, 16 is too young to stop the pupils' general education. There is too strong a focus on marketable skills in Switzerland. He is happy about it but I think he was too young to enter the adult world. I wonder if I should have taken him out in first year of lower-secondary and sent him to a private school. He is going to do the *Berufsmatura* (Vocational Maturity) and then go to a *Fachhochschule* (UASA).

Denise is English and lives in canton Fribourg. Her son did an apprenticeship in IT at a vocational school, followed by a PET technical diploma. He now has a full-time job at Serono, a biotechnology company, and is doing a bachelor's degree at the School of Engineering, the *HES* (UASA) in Yverdon at the same time. Denise comments that it is a fairly recent development that young people with an apprenticeship continue their education at university level.

Where I live, the academic track used to be outside of people's experience. I suddenly realised my son was not even considering university. He did, however, want to go into IT and this was the path open to him. He was delighted to get the chance to go to the CPNV (*Centre professionnel du Nord vaudois*) for his IT apprenticeship. For me at least, this was an opportunity for him to be a student (also studying subjects like French and maths) rather than doing an apprenticeship within a company. Things are now evolving and a number of both my sons' friends in surrounding villages who originally did apprenticeships have gone on to take the *maturité professionnelle* (Vocational Maturity) and then to do a bachelor's degree too.

Finding an apprenticeship

There are around 230 VET occupations to choose from, from white and blue collar occupations, and from high tech to trades. The most popular ones in 2009 were in the commercial and retail sector, as well as health care and social care. These were followed by occupations as cooks, electricians, mechanical engineers and IT employees.[106] Commercial apprenticeships have the highest status of all (see the CEO examples above), and places tend to be reserved for pupils with very good marks. For a full list and description of occupations and courses of study, please see the excellent national jobs and careers advice website, www.berufsberatung.ch (in D, F and I).[107] Available apprenticeships, tips and blogs can also be found on the website www.yousty.ch (in D and F).

Lower-secondary schools help their pupils find out what kind of occupations are available. They attend vocational fairs with their class and have careers classes at school. Companies and trade associations may also give talks at the school. Chantal describes how she had such a class every week in her lower-secondary school in Valais, and that the pupils took turns to make a presentation on a particular job profile as well as career opportunities. She knew she was going to gymnasium, but as most pupils in her class were not, they all took part in these classes. Some pupils may miss out on this guidance if they change over from an academic level class or drop out of gymnasium. Then parents may need to be more active in helping them find an apprenticeship. Things are now changing so that pupils in all levels of lower-secondary schools are in future more likely to have careers classes too.

The national jobs and careers advice website mentioned above has reams of useful information, including documents in English and other languages to help explain the process of finding an apprenticeship.[108] It also offers an interactive platform in German and French (*myBerufswahl, myOrientation*) for pupils to create a log book and go through a set of seven steps in the job application process. Parents can create a separate account and receive information especially for parents. Pupils find out about themselves and about different schools and occupations, tailored to their canton.

Questionnaires help them to identify their skills, strengths and preferences, examining their interests, the school subjects they like and what they do in their spare time. (There are also books available to help German-speaking pupils as they do this.)[109] They compare their interests and strengths with the requirements of different occupations to find a good fit. The website also has videos of 40 occupations, where apprentices talk about their jobs and demonstrate what they do at work – for example, a day in the life of a pharmaceutical technology apprentice at Roche, the pharmaceutical company. An interesting cultural detail is that sample CVs show that the pupil should state their parents' jobs in their applications.

Another option is to visit the careers guidance office for your canton.[110] Andrea highly recommends going there for advice on a career path:

> I sent all my kids there and asked them to be tested for their skills, or abilities. It is good to do it during the 8th year of school, as they have to start applying for their apprenticeship at the beginning of the 9th year. The careers advisor was able to tell them if their school marks were high enough for the professions they were interested in, and make alternative suggestions if they did not have the marks required for what they wanted to do. She also wrote a letter of recommendation for my daughter to be accepted for the sports class at gymnasium and for my son to be accepted in a foundation course (*Grundkurs*) in chemistry at the local trade school (*Gewerbeschule*). When he applied for an apprenticeship in food technology, she wrote that he would be very suited to this, based on the tests and discussions he had with her.

The application process

Pupils are given job application skills as a school subject to help them look for an apprenticeship. Dagmar Voith emphasises the importance of talking to teachers and working with them on this, so that the young person knows that they are supported. "There is a lot of support around for kids who want to get into the process," she says. "Parents have to tap into it." She emphasises that it is very helpful to be able to speak the local language as some teachers are uncomfortable speaking English.

Beatrice Zeller is a careers advisor to young people.[111] She gives examples of how young people can find out what direction to take:

> They might have a special hobby or are passionate about something, for example excelling at sport, or in creating websites. Some young people are good at relating to others and bringing people together, selling an idea, organising, or craftsmanship.

They can choose an apprenticeship that will reflect something they are good at, and their other skills can be very useful later. They need to get some kind of paper qualification first and then their particular abilities will help them move in a specific direction. In the end, a career greatly depends on soft factors, like social competence and high energy levels, rather than marks at school. In contrast, having a university degree demonstrates intelligence but does not necessarily lead to a successful career. Great skill is needed to encourage the child but not overwhelm him, and to understand what motivates the child and what drives him crazy.

Once pupils have identified fields of work or particular occupations that might suit them, they may seek the opportunity to spend a few days in a company or organisation where this job is done. The trial days (known as *Schnupperwoche (D)* or *stage (F)*) may also give a potential employer the opportunity to gain an impression of the young person's personality, social skills, level of initiative, motivation and interest as well as their working style. Dagmar Voith strongly recommends that the young person is proactive and phones the company and asks if they can come for a few days' trial. "Many pupils will be applying to the same companies, so you have to stand out," she says. "This may compensate for not having the best grades." Pupils should not be worried about not being smooth or eloquent on the phone. They are very young, and companies appreciate this. It is impressive enough that they are taking the initiative to pick up the phone rather than just sending out written applications.

It is very common for parents in Switzerland to use their contacts among their friends and neighbours, as well as their colleagues at work, to find out if their son or daughter could do a trial week there. This can also be a way to find summer jobs or longer internships after they have finished school. Teachers may also have good connections. Dagmar Voith recommends that parents talk about their child to as many people as they can. "You as parents can give people a fuller picture of the young person than if others only see their child's report card," she comments. "This is when it is important to be aware of what your child does well." She also points out that opening a door like this gives a young person a start, but that they still have to prove themselves once they are there.

The careers guidance website www.berufsberatung.ch provides an extensive list of available apprenticeship places around the country. In September every year, a list of available apprenticeships for the coming year is released. Most, but not all companies advertise their vacancies there. Once they have established the field of work they would like, applicants start writing letters and filling in forms for companies advertising positions. They send documentation about their marks and abilities and attend interviews.

Companies are well aware of the career potential of pupils applying for apprenticeships. They look at their school marks and may also require them to take independent tests of their subject ability, such as *Basischeck* or *Stellwerk*, which tests pupils' maths, German, French, English and 'nature and technology' knowledge. Future employers are also interested in their marks in other tests, such as *Multicheck Junior*[112], a tool designed by Multicheck, a Swiss human resources company that conducts assessments of managers and executives, as well as 30,000 young people per year who seek an apprenticeship. *Multicheck Junior* tests pupils' spatial intelligence, ability to solve problems, think logically, memorise and concentrate. It assesses their potential in six fields of work and 70 professions. However, their school marks and other test results are not the only key factors. Some companies may base their decision on their impressions in a trial week and only use the marks to confirm their impressions.

It can be a tough time. Pupils are encouraged to be flexible and learn not to be discouraged by rejection. Many pupils change their plans if they cannot find a place in their chosen occupation. They can often still change direction later on.

Conditions

The Harvard report mentioned on page 152 referred to the "increasingly demanding responsibilities and challenges of apprenticeships in an intergenerational work setting." The reality of this can be a bit of a shock to young school-leavers. They have only five weeks holiday per year in addition to statutory days.[113] They have to start at the bottom and in some cases do the boring work. Apprentices often start work at 7 or 7.30 am and may work up to a maximum of nine hours per day or 45 hours per week in industry, office, technical and retail sectors. In all other sectors there is a maximum of 50 hours per week. A school day of six to nine hours counts as the equivalent of a full working day of nine hours.

The average pay of apprentices in Switzerland is less than 20% of skilled pay. This 'cheap labour' is acceptable to all concerned due to the fact that Swiss apprentices are being educated and receive a nationally recognised qualification, not just a company's internal certificate or seal of approval. In Switzerland, public subsidies cover the costs of part-time education in public colleges. The costs of training at the workplace fall to the employer (and the apprentice). It has been calculated that the company does not make a loss from training the apprentice, and that this makes it more attractive to employers to offer places.

The 10th school year (H12)

For students who do not find an apprenticeship position, there is also the opportunity to attend a bridge year course in a 10th (H12) school year first to gain practical training and pre-apprenticeship skills. For pupils who are new in Switzerland there may be special integration programmes too. The two main types of programmes are (a) purely school programmes and (b) programmes with work and school combined, usually two days of school and three days of work per week. Work can be done either in a school workshop or else in a company work placement. Either way, pupils are taught job application skills and given support in finding an apprenticeship. There are also helpful websites.[114]

As mentioned on page 158, Andrea's son did a one-year 'pre-apprenticeship' course in chemistry at the local trade school (*Gewerbeschule*). As she explained, "You have better chances of getting an apprenticeship afterwards." Other subject areas include health, wood, metal, physics, electronics and nutrition.

Dagmar Voith names three main reasons for young people doing a bridge-year course. "They can improve their grades; learn basic skills that are needed in the workplace, such as punctuality and perseverance; and they can find out what they want to do." It can be a matter of maturity whether they are ready to make that first decision regarding what to do with their lives.

Rudolf A sees it as potentially problematic for youngsters looking for an apprenticeship that they will in future have to start doing this at a younger age than before. As things stand now, pupils need to be thinking what type of apprenticeship they are interested in at the age of 14 and have their application ready by the age of 15. Some may have no idea what they want to do. The starting age for school is gradually being lowered in accordance with HarmoS, so that children who have just turned four by the end of July in a particular year will start kindergarten that August. This means that their 11 years of compulsory schooling (according to HarmoS) could finish before they have turned 15. I foresee that the bridge-year course will become even more necessary in future.

It is important to check who will pay for the bridge-year course if you live in a small community that does not offer this. It may be that your child can attend a bridge-year course in a larger town, but that your municipality will have to agree to pay the bill.

Apprenticeship qualifications without an apprenticeship

Yes, you did read that correctly. It is possible to obtain the Federal VET Diploma (*EFZ, CFC, AFC*) in some fields without having done an apprenticeship in that field. This is an excellent opportunity for young people who do not do an apprenticeship, or break it off. It is also a solution for pupils who do not yet speak the local language well. Once a pupil has completed their nine years of compulsory schooling, they can 'just work' for several years in one specific field, and then take the exams of the vocation. Additional courses are not always required.

As an example, they could take the exam if they have worked for at least six years selling furniture and doing the shop decor, or six years doing IT in an office, or seven years selling cars, or eight years as a hotel receptionist, or an unspecified time as a cable crane head of operations.[115] Once they have obtained the VET certificate, it is possible to take the Federal Vocational Maturity and gain entry to a UASA (University of Applied Sciences and Arts). See also www. validacquis.ch for further information on recognition of non-formal education and training.

Georgios is from Greece and originally started an apprenticeship as a painter and decorator. He broke it off after eight months. By chance he then found a temporary job for one month, working in a global pharmaceutical company's IT department doing odd jobs like unpacking laptops. It helped that there was little unemployment in the region. They kept extending the contract and he is still there today, after 11 years, working as a data acquisition specialist. His advice to young people is: "If you get a chance like I did, make the best of it. Prove you are good, and don't stop believing in yourself."

Vocational Maturity (or Baccalaureate)

The Vocational Maturity (or Baccalaureate) can be taken either during or after a VET programme, as either a school-based or a dual programme. It is intended to provide holders with direct access to Universities of Applied Sciences without having to take an entrance exam.[116] It is available in six different subject areas, determined by the apprenticeship occupation: technical or commercial studies, design, trade, natural sciences and health/social care.

Chapter 17 Specialised upper-secondary schools

Specialised upper-secondary schools (*Fachmittelschulen, écoles de culture générale, scuole medie specializzate*) are also sometimes known as specialised middle schools, or in English, just specialised schools. They are attended by around 3% of the population, with numbers increasing. In the past they prepared young people for educational and paramedical professions, where there was no suitable apprenticeship in the field. Specific occupational fields today consist of health/natural sciences; social work; education; design/art; communication/information; and music/dance/theatre. Only the first three of these six areas are offered by most cantons. A list of all schools and what they offer can be found in the www.edudoc.ch website.[117]

The basic certificate course runs from the 10th (H12) to the 12th (H14) year of school. It qualifies pupils to continue their education at tertiary level PET colleges (see Chapter 18) in the fields of health and social care (some types); and art. General subjects for all pupils are typically three languages; natural sciences; history and geography; economics and law; music and sport. After the first year, pupils choose an area of specialisation, based on their interests and more importantly, their marks. The highest marks are needed for the field of health, followed by education and then social work. Art is more specialised, and will depend more on natural ability than on marks.

If pupils wish to spend a further 13th (H15) year doing a Specialised Maturity or Baccalaureate (*Fachmaturität, maturité spécialisée, maturità specializzata*), they may also gain admission to a University of Applied Sciences and Arts to study the area of their specialism at bachelor's level: nursing, physiotherapy, midwifery, social work, primary teaching or journalism. Pupils need to have the Specialised Maturity in the subject they wish to study and there may be additional requirements. In French-speaking Switzerland most healthcare education continues only at Universities of Applied Sciences and Arts. It is worth checking carefully the entry requirements for your canton or region on a careers website.[118] The year spent on the Specialised Maturity involves writing a paper and may include doing an internship, as the next page shows.[119] The subjects in the last two rows are offered in fewer schools.

Specialised Maturity focus	Includes	UASA area of study/ occupation
Health	24 weeks internship in a health care institution.	Physiotherapy, occupational therapy, degree level nursing, health care management
Social work	40 weeks internship, at least 12 of which are in a social institution.	Social work, social pedagogy, socio-cultural activities
Education	Additional general education in two languages, maths, natural sciences, and human and social sciences. Internship option.	Primary school teaching
Design and art	Please ask the school for details.	Art and design (entrance exam and/or submission of portfolio)
Music, theatre, dance	Please ask the school for details.	Music, theatre, dance, choreography, acting, directing (and much more)
Communication, media	Varies according to specialism: internship in the media or stay abroad, foreign language exams, etc. (Please see the school for more details.)	Interpreting, tourism management, journalism (and much more)

Table 4   Specialised Maturity (or Baccalaureate) focus and future prospects

For some areas of study – for example, lower-secondary school teaching or speech therapy – a student with only the Specialised Maturity must take an additional entrance exam. It is to be hoped that there will one day be a *passerelle*, or shortened bridge course that will give them entrance to traditional universities, a route that is currently only available to young people with the Vocational Maturity.

Some pupils go to a specialised school if they cannot get into gymnasium. It is important that they consider what they want to specialise in afterwards. In some ways, an apprenticeship could offer more options (such as the *passerelle* to traditional university). The pupil follows a track, not a path, and it is difficult to change. A young person I know did the Specialised Maturity in order to study social work. There was a very long waiting list for social work at the UASA where he lived and he did not get in. He considered studying teacher education at the UASA, but would have needed to spend an additional year doing the Specialised Maturity again, this time with a focus on education. In the end he obtained a place studying social work at a different UASA.

Commercial school and IT school

In many cantons commercial school *(Wirtschaftsmittelschule, école de commerce, scuola media di commercio)* and IT school *(Informatikmittelschule, école d'informatique)* offer school-based programmes with a business focus, at the end of which pupils obtain a Federal VET Diploma, the same qualification as those doing apprenticeships. Pupils need good marks to get into commercial school and need to sit an entrance exam for IT school. Both courses are more general than an apprenticeship, but narrower than a Gymnasial Maturity programme. Both typically consist of two languages, maths, IT, accounting, history, political economics, micro-economics and law in addition to more intensive study of the programme's special focus.

The commercial school course takes three years. Students can continue for a further year to obtain the Vocational Maturity which qualifies them to study business administration at a University of Applied Sciences and Arts. For this they need to work for one year in an internship position in a company, followed by writing a paper and passing exams in all the course materials of the three-year course. In commercial schools in some cantons, the fourth year leading to the Vocational Maturity is now a compulsory part of the course. The IT school course takes four years, as it includes a one-year internship in a company, with a focus on programming.[120] The Vocational Maturity can be taken parallel to the course.

Commercial school is a good option for pupils who do not feel ready to enter the world of work by doing a commercial apprenticeship first.

Nan is from Scotland and her daughter C started kindergarten in canton Geneva in the year in which she became four in October. She was then still 14 when she finished *cycle* (lower-secondary school). She did not like school much and did not work very hard there. She did not want to go to *collège* (*gymnasium*) for the 10th (H12) class, as it was commonly known that only around half of the pupils passed the first year there. C was used to helping her administratively-minded mother organise family parties, using checklists and spreadsheets and enjoyed that. She then decided to go to the *école de commerce* where it turned out she enjoyed the business subjects like management, bookkeeping, and law. "She puts up with maths and French," commented Nan. "She has been getting much better marks than in the *cycle*. If she gets 4.6 as her average mark for her diploma, she will be accepted for a fourth year to obtain the Vocational Maturity certificate."

Section five

Tertiary education

Chapter 18   Three types of tertiary education

In this chapter I outline the main characteristics of tertiary institutions, and in Chapter 19 I provide a table showing the different routes that can be taken to gain entrance to each type.

The three types of institutions are:

- Traditional university (*Universität* or *ETH, université* or *EPFL, università*)

- University of Applied Sciences and Arts, or UASA (*Fachhochschule* or *FH; haute école spécialisée* or *HES; scuola universitaria professionale della Svizzera italiana* or *SUPSI*)

- Professional Training and Education or PET college (*Höhere Fachschule, école supérieure, scuola specializzata superiore*).

According to UNESCO statistics of 2011, 51% of the age-relevant population of Switzerland were enrolled in tertiary education in 2009 in three different types of tertiary institutions.[121] Nearly 36% of the population were in ISCED level 5A[122] programmes, which are offered at traditional universities and Universities of Applied Sciences and Arts. Level 5A programmes are largely theoretically based and are intended to provide sufficient qualifications for gaining entry into advanced research programmes. They have high skills requirements. Nearly 11% of the age-relevant population were in ISCED level 5B[123] programmes, which are PET programmes. These are more practically oriented and occupationally specific programmes. They do not prepare students for direct access to advanced research programmes. (The remaining 4% of those in tertiary education were in ISCED level 6 advanced research programmes.)

A binary system

Although UNESCO groups traditional universities and UASA together in ISCED level 5A, internally Switzerland still operates a binary system and embraces differentiation. Entry qualifications are different for the two types of institutions. Only the Gymnasial Maturity (or Baccalaureate) is designed to lead directly to a 5A traditional university programme. The Vocational Maturity (or Baccalaureate) is designed to lead to a 5A UASA programme (or a 5B PET programme). The Specialised Maturity (or Baccalaureate) is designed to lead to a 5A UASA (including a University of Teacher Education) programme. UASA partner universities abroad often do not really understand the special UASA status. When taking part in a lecturer exchange in Sweden, I had difficulty explaining to my partners at the Swedish university that, from the traditional Swiss perspective, I do not actually represent a 'university', and that the word 'university' is not used to describe UASA in German or French. More is said below about the two different types of institutions.

Traditional universities

There are 12 traditional Swiss universities which award bachelor's, master's, and doctoral degrees. The languages of instruction are as follows:

- Italian at the University of Lugano in Ticino
- German at the Universities of Basel, Bern, Lucerne, St Gallen, Zurich and the ETH (the Swiss Federal Institute of Technology, Zurich)
- French in the Universities of Geneva, Lausanne, Neuchâtel and the EPFL (the Swiss Federal Institute of Technology, Lausanne)
- French and German at the University of Fribourg.

Traditional universities used to offer mainly five-year degree programmes as well as doctoral programmes. Nowadays, with the option of bachelor and masters degrees, three to four-year programmes are also available. Students who leave after their bachelor's degree may be considered not to have completed their education.

Given the high rankings of Swiss universities, it is remarkable that their fees are not higher. Fees vary between 1000 and 2452 Swiss francs per year for residents.[124] Most universities charge students from abroad the same fees as local students.[125]

The three most influential and widely observed international university rankings are:

- the Academic Ranking of World Universities[126] (otherwise known as the Shanghai Ranking)
- the QS World Education Rankings[127]
- the Times Higher Education World Education Rankings[128]

Swiss results with each of these are shown in the table on the next page. It has been estimated that 70% of university students in Switzerland are studying at one of the world's top 200 universities, according to the Shanghai Ranking[129] while only 20% of students in the USA or Germany are doing the same. The Swiss university system has the advantage of focusing on around 20% of school leavers while in many other countries, universities have to educate over 50% of the population, including students with less academic ability.

Six or seven of Switzerland's universities are usually in the top 200 in the various rankings from year to year. With regard to the Shanghai Ranking, neighbouring country France had eight universities in the top 200 in 2011, Germany had 14, Italy had four and Austria had one. Further afield, the English speaking countries that did best in 2011 were the USA (with 89 universities in the top 200), and the UK (with 19). Universities in English-speaking countries have had a head start in that they have always been able to publish internationally in English as the language of their institutions and the mother tongue of many of their researchers. Academics in other countries used to working and publishing in *their* mother tongues have to first get their English to a high standard before they can compete in the international arena. Some Swiss universities may publish less in English, and this may also have an impact on their rankings.

Swiss university	Ranking agency		
	Times Higher Education Top Top 200	Shanghai (ARWU) Top 500 (2011)	QS Top 700 (2011-2012)
Swiss Federal Institute of Technology, Zurich (ETHZ)	15	23	18
Swiss Federal Institute of Technology, Lausanne (EPFL)	46	102-150	35
University of Zurich	61	56	106
University of Basel	111	89	151
University of Bern	112	151-200	143
University of Lausanne	116	(201-300)	136
University of Geneva	130	73	69

Table 5   Swiss universities in the top 200 in the world rankings of 2011-2012

Universities of Applied Sciences and Arts

There are seven public Universities of Applied Sciences and Arts (UASA) in Switzerland, in the regions of Western Switzerland (in French); Ticino (in Italian); and in Zurich, Bern, Lucerne, Northwestern Switzerland, and Eastern Switzerland (in German). There is also a private, but federally recognised UASA, namely Kalaidos.[130] In addition, there are 14 Universities of Teacher Education, which may also be referred to as UASA. The most popular UASA courses are three-year bachelor's degree programmes. The following remarks are of a very general nature, and there are many variations in the way UASA function. Some

UASA courses only accept students who are at least 20 years old, and many are older, preferring to gain expertise in a field before continuing their education. Some courses are part-time, so that students can continue to work while studying. UASA fees vary between 1000 and 1920 francs per year for residents of Switzerland.[131] Most UASA charge students from abroad the same fees as local students.

UASA subject areas offered are engineering and IT; architecture, building engineering and planning; chemistry and life sciences; agriculture and forestry; economics/business management and services; design, health and social work; music, theatre and other arts; applied psychology; applied linguistics; sports; and teacher education. The website www.kfh.ch provides links to all UASA courses offered in each of these subject areas under the heading 'bachelor degree programs' and 'masters degree programs'.

The UASA have small campuses, a low student-to-faculty ratio, small-group work, and a high level of interaction between students and faculty. They provide a practice-oriented education, accommodating the needs of both students and the job market.[132] Alongside an increasing focus on theory and academic standards, they have maintained their closeness to practice and serve industry and the community with their programmes.

Lecturers are often involved in research, professional practice or consulting. (It is for this reason that it no longer makes sense to call a traditional university a 'research university'.) A student writing a bachelor's or master's thesis combines theory and practice to make recommendations that are of practical application in the real world related to their field of study. The UASA also offer Certificates, Diplomas and Masters of Advanced Studies (CAS, DAS and MAS) as well as Executive MBA programmes which are tailored to the needs of the community or workplace.

Although the UASA offer both bachelor's and master's programmes that are internationally recognised, they are not permitted to offer doctoral degrees. They sometimes get round this by partnering with a university that can do so, either in Switzerland or abroad.

Professional Education and Training (PET)

Federal PET programmes are tertiary-level professional education and training programmes.[133] They are offered at local PET colleges (*Höhere Fachschulen, écoles superieures, scuole spezializzate superiore*). These are known as tertiary B level qualifications. PET programmes provide VET qualified students with very specific, more advanced qualifications and prepare them for managerial and specialised positions. There are around 400 PET programmes and two main levels of qualification:

- Federal PET Diplomas (*Eidgenössischer Fachausweis, brevet fédéral, attestato professionale federale*). Examples of subjects are human resources, management, marketing, social insurance, electrical safety, logistics and automotive diagnostics.[134]
- Advanced Federal PET Diplomas (*Eidgenössischer Diplom, diplôme fédéral, diploma federale*). Examples of subjects of study are: border control, construction, electrical engineering, food technology, and graphic design.[135]

PET examination candidates do not have to take courses in order to enter for the examinations. If they do, either they or their company generally pay high fees for their course. Programmes generally last two years full-time or three years part-time. They are narrowly focused and very much tailored to the needs of the labour market. The value of these federal PET qualifications should not be underestimated. In-company professional training is very well thought of in Switzerland.[136] If, for example, your 14 year-old daughter excels in maths and wishes to become an accounting expert, there is no need for her to first take the Gymnasial Maturity. In Britain you would even need an honours bachelor's degree in science or arts, as accountancy is taught as a post-graduate course.

In Switzerland, a typical path would be to do an apprenticeship and obtain the Federal VET Diploma in the field of commerce. This could be followed by preparation for a Federal PET Diploma exam in finance and accountancy. The final step is to take an Advanced Federal PET Diploma exam in order to obtain what is known in German as the *eidg. dipl. Experte in Rechnungslegung und Controlling* and in French as the *diplôme fédéral d'expert en finance et controlling.* This may sound to people from other countries as if they were doing some kind of diploma in invoicing and controlling (and foreign executives in Swiss banks do sometimes underestimate the qualifications of local specialists in this way). In fact they will finish up as a *Swiss Certified Expert for Accounting and Controlling*, a qualification that is equivalent to a master's level degree.

Many small and medium-sized companies in Switzerland are run by managers with PET qualifications. There are also top executives in multinationals, in particular banks, who have gone this route and have completed their education with a qualification such as an MBA abroad. An example of this is Sergio Ermotti, from Ticino, mentioned earlier. He became the CEO of UBS bank in 2011. He started with an apprenticeship at the Corner Bank in Lugano, followed by a PET diploma as an expert in banking. He then graduated from the Advanced Management Programme at Oxford University.

Chapter 19   University and UASA entrance requirements

In the previous chapters I described the main forms of upper-secondary education and the main types of tertiary education. In the next two chapters I address both parents and young people directly, as it is the young person who will ultimately make the decision as to what and where to study. Table 6 on the next two pages shows a simplified summary of the upper-secondary qualifications required for different types of tertiary education.[137] The real landscape, however, is somewhat more complicated and requirements may change from year to year. It is vital that you check the exact entrance requirements from year to year for a course or subject area of interest on the website of each individual university, UASA or University of Teacher Education. It might be advisable to phone them for additional information.

You may find your type of Maturity qualification does not give you entrance to the type of university or UASA course you are interested in. As the table shows, there are various ways to gain entrance to a different type of programme than the one you are qualified to enter. More is said about these below.

Bridges leading to traditional university

Pupils with the Vocational Maturity who wish to gain access to a traditional university need to take the *passerelle*, or University Aptitude Test, which is offered by the Swiss Maturity Commission. It does not stand alone, and is *only* valid for university entrance alongside the Vocational Maturity. Students need to have obtained an average mark of at least 4.8 in their exams. It is offered by cantonal Maturity schools and private schools around the country.[138] There are five examinations in five subject areas:

- mathematics
- first language
- second language
- science
- history or geography

175

The pass mark for each subject area is 4 (out of 6) but you may fail two exams providing your total average marks add up to at least 20. You can resit it (once) if you fail.[139] At present pupils with the Specialised Maturity do not have this *passerelle* option, although this may change. They need to spend longer on a Maturity programme for adults, as shown below. However, in some cantons pupils with good marks can change over from the specialised upper-secondary school to gymnasium, and this trend is on the increase.

Qualification obtained	Tertiary education goal	Route / additional requirements
Gymnasial Maturity (or Baccalaureate)	University ETH/EPFL[140]	Automatic admission for all courses except human and veterinary medicine, dentistry, chiropractice and sport (which have a *numerus clausus* or entrance exam)
	UASA	One year's work experience (possibly in related field). Occasionally additional admissions procedure, depending on the course
	University of Teacher Education	Automatic admission for kindergarten, primary and lower-secondary school teacher education. Additional requirements for speech therapy.
Federal VET Diploma (*EFZ, CFC, AFC*)	University ETH/EPFL	Obtain Gymnasial Maturity as a mature student. Takes up to 3.5 years. Entrance possible without Gymnasial Maturity at Fribourg, Geneva, Lausanne, Lucerne, Neuchâtel, Lugano. See university websites.
	UASA	Obtain Vocational Maturity or take entrance exam.
	University of Teacher Education	Several years work experience, admissions procedure (possibly foreign language requirement) and preparatory courses.

Vocational Maturity (or Baccalaureate)	University ETH/EPFL UASA	University aptitude test (*passerelle*) exam (2-3 semesters preparation). Entrance possible without *passerelle* at Fribourg, Geneva, Lausanne, Lucerne, Neuchâtel, Lugano. See university websites.
	UASA	Admission to courses related to type of Vocational Maturity taken (e.g. industrial, business, technical, etc.).
	University of Teacher Education	Admissions procedure and preparatory courses.
Specialised upper-secondary school certificate	University ETH/EPFL	Obtain the Gymnasial Maturity as a mature student. Takes up to 3.5 years.
	UASA	Entrance exam. One year's work experience required.
	University of Teacher Education	Several years work experience, admissions procedure and preparatory course.
Specialised Maturity (or Baccalaureate)	University, or ETH/EPFL	Obtain Gymnasial Maturity as a mature student. Takes up to 3.5 years.
	UASA	Admissions procedure for courses related to Specialised Maturity (e.g. social work).
	University of Teacher Education	For kindergarten and primary school teaching: Automatic admission with Specialised Maturity in Education. Additional requirements for lower-secondary teaching, speech therapy, etc. Admissions procedure and preparatory courses.
No qualifications	UASA	Submit portfolio (very difficult).

Table 6   Qualifications required for universities and UASA.

177

Federal Maturity and House Maturity

A more laborious route to university entrance for those without a Vocational Maturity involves entering a three or four-year Maturity programme for adults to prepare for the standardised Federal Maturity exams offered twice a year by the Swiss Maturity Commission and organised by the State Secretariat for Education and Research (SER).[141] Around 400 pupils per year obtain the Federal Maturity. For comparison, in 2010 around 20% of 19-year-olds, that is, 18,646 pupils (10,740 female and 7,906 male) obtained the cantonal Gymnasial Maturity. The intricacies of the Federal Maturity programme options are worth looking into, for example, by getting further advice from your local careers office.[142] Pupils may prepare for it in a publicly or privately run Maturity programme for adults that can be taken full-time, part-time or as distance learning with occasional teaching blocks.

The programme may last three to four years and fees vary greatly. An attractive alternative is to attend a public school that is authorised to award a 'House Maturity' qualification to adults, for example a local cantonal gymnasium that also offers evening classes. It is qualified to conduct continual assessment and set its own exams so that pupils may obtain their final mark for some subjects through class work and class exams. Some House Maturity certificates only qualify learners for access to the cantonal university of that canton. If the school does not offer a House Maturity, pupils have to take all exams externally as federal exams.

Bridges to Universities of Applied Sciences and Arts (UASA)

It is important to note that the Gymnasial Maturity does not necessarily provide automatic access to the UASA. This can be a surprise to pupils who were originally planning to go to a traditional university or who drop out of university. It is worth looking into this well in advance of enrolling so that you have time to meet additional requirements. You may be required to obtain a year's internship or work experience of 48 weeks in a field related to your future studies. This is, for example, the case for architecture, economics, and technical programmes at UASA. It takes a bit of organisation to fit this in during a gap year, so it is good to plan ahead if you do not want one gap year to turn into two. For demanding or popular UASA courses, such as midwifery, physiotherapy, social work or speech therapy, there may be a shorter internship requirement. Places may be limited for UASA courses as they tend to have smaller classes, and limited numbers. It might be necessary to apply for popular programmes one or two years in advance.

What suits you better?

If you are at gymnasium, it is possible that people will only talk to you about going to a traditional university. It is worth checking whether this is indeed the right path or whether a University of Applied Sciences and Arts might be more suitable for you. Questions you can ask yourself include:

- Did you have to work very hard just to pass your exams? Or did you not work very hard and just scraped through, but are planning to start working harder when you finally get to a traditional university? The system will let you enter university with a bare pass mark, but it is logical that people with higher marks are likely to find it easier. As an alternative, some students do a bachelor's degree at a UASA and then go on to a master's degree at a traditional university. They usually have to have high marks and obtain additional credit points to be accepted on the university programme. Not all programmes accept UASA graduates and each university master's programme stipulates its own requirements.
- Are you happy to attend lectures in the anonymity of large lecture theatres with 200 other people or would you prefer to be part of a smaller class of students who will do group work, make presentations and take part in discussions? In either case, check out the typical class size and forms of teaching of the course you are interested in. Universities tend to have larger classes than UASA.
- Do you like to increase your knowledge by going into a subject in great depth? Do you enjoy academic work for its own sake (university), or do you prefer to learn things that are useful and will have application to the work place (UASA)?

- Do you like to have plenty of freedom as to when and how much to study over the year or do you need a fairly tight structure and regular deadlines? UASA courses tend to provide a tighter structure, although some university courses do too.

- Do you prefer to know in advance where your studies will take you? Would you like to be provided with a road map that specifies the destination? If this is the case, a UASA might offer clearer pathways.[143] If you prefer to leave everything open as long as possible, some traditional university courses leave you with plenty of choice right up until you have obtained your master's degree.

Some young people do not realise university is not for them until they have tried it out. Robyn started studying biology at the University of Basel. She compares herself with her father who is a scientist and works in the pharmaceutical industry. "There are people like my dad, who love to gain knowledge and learn for the sake of learning," she explained. "They can excel at university. They soak it all up. For myself and others it's more blurred. Knowledge alone didn't do it for me when I was studying biology." Robyn did not mind that her course was very theoretical, but she was unhappy about the five or more years ahead until she got her master's degree, because she could not see where all the hard work was leading. She could not visualise her future career. She left university after one semester and passed the tough entrance exam and interview process for midwifery at a University of Applied Sciences and Arts. It turned out to be exactly what she wanted. It was important to her to find something where she could both study and know what specific profession it led to. Along with the course, she was being given the road map of the destination.

Anna, a colleague of Robyn's, experienced studying biology quite differently: "I just love university, and people giving me knowledge," she said. "I want to do a master's and then go on to do a PhD. I would like to work in research afterwards. I was always a kid with an academic focus."

Chapter 20   Applying to universities abroad

A certain number of students with a Gymnasial Maturity from Switzerland wish to study for a first degree abroad. Establishing the value of the 'currency' of Swiss marks is a challenge for them. Katie is British and was in her final year of Swiss gymnasium when she briefly considered applying to university in the UK. She discovered that she would need an average of a 5 to get in to the university of her choice. She was at that time heading for a 4.8. She was used to the idea that the Gymnasial Maturity would give her automatic access to all traditional Swiss universities to study almost anything she liked. She chose to study psychology at a Swiss university instead. Her older sister Sophie would not have been able to study law, her chosen subject, in the UK either. She had only obtained a 4.8 average across the board in her Maturity, although she had a 5.5 in Latin, history and economics and law. She obtained her bachelor's degree in law at a Swiss university with an average mark of 5.1 for all her subjects. Her average went up once she could focus on the subjects she was good at.

Pieter is English and a lecturer at a University of Applied Sciences and Arts. His daughter is studying in England. He comments that in the UK you only have to take three to four A-levels while in Switzerland you have over ten subjects to get high marks in. But people think Swiss universities are so good that there is no need to go elsewhere.

> The Swiss don't explain their grading system abroad, which is not necessarily consistent with increasing trends in educational mobility. Students very rarely get a 6, the top mark, for example. Even a 5.5 is higher than an A. Nationally we still have a lot to do in Switzerland regarding the benchmarking of grades. Consequently, Swiss marks are underrated and misunderstood by the Anglo-Saxons.

Until recently it was common that people's qualifications from one canton were not valid in another. It is quite another challenge to make them translate well further afield, and young people and their parents in Switzerland may struggle with this. Tim is the head of the Modern Languages department at an English sixth form college. He says that the UK entrance boards are deeply suspicious of anything they cannot understand. It has been helpful in recent years that a few gymnasiums now offer the International Baccalaureate, a better-known alternative currency, as described in Chapter 15.

Pieter's daughter Eva obtained the Gymnasial Maturity in canton Bern. She was top of her year among the pupils with a linguistic speciality, with an all-over mark of 5.3. However, 5.3 was the average mark required for her course at Bath University in the UK. Bath also required that she had no marks below 5.0, including music, which she achieved too. "My UCAS application pack contained an additional transcript explaining the complexity of Swiss grades and their relation to my studies," she told me. "The greatest challenges have probably been since then. When requesting admission to more maths-based economics modules, I find it extremely hard to put my level of maths into context, despite having a 6 in my written and 5.5 in my oral maths Matura exam."

Marilyn Stelzner lives in canton Vaud and specialises in advising young people applying to universities in the US.[144] "Compared with the UK, the US secondary system is a bit more like the Swiss system in that more subjects are studied all the way through," she explains. "In addition, students applying to the US take standardized SAT or ACT tests, covering reading, writing and maths. There are also subject tests that can be taken. These are benchmarked across a wide set of applicants, which gives the US universities more of a basis for evaluating Swiss applicants." Marilyn suggests taking both types of tests and using the better results for an application. She also points out that universities in the USA wish to know about the distribution of grades in the school the student attended, and where the student falls in relation to these. Another option she suggests is to start studying in Switzerland, and then transfer to the USA. "Any US university will give advanced standing, that is, credit for a semester to a year of university courses based on a Swiss Maturity."

No currency converter

There is a small amount of data available on Swiss gymnasium marks, but it is not of the type to act as a marks 'currency converter' for foreign admissions offices. As mentioned in Chapter 15, Swiss teachers do not give marks away. The average Gymnasial Maturity mark given nationwide in the first language of the school was 4.63. For maths the average was 4.34 and for biology it was 4.60. There is also data available from the ETH Zurich, a top university that ranked number 23 in the world in the Shanghai rankings of 2011.[145] It is a tough university with a strong natural sciences focus. Out of 5,216 students, only around 260 (which amounts to around 5% of the ETH student population) had achieved an average mark of 5.5 or more in their Gymnasial Maturity between 2004 and 2007. The average Gymnasial Maturity mark of the whole cohort was 4.86. In the *Basisprüfung*, ETH's own first year exams with this cohort, the average mark was 4.2.

Corinne F is an English teacher in a gymnasium in canton Neuchâtel. She comments that she and her colleagues are not supposed to have an average mark for a class below 3.8 or above 5.2. This is problematic for her if she has eight native speakers of English in the class. She then has to argue the case to the headmaster and he may allow a higher average as an exception.

Nicola is English and lives in canton Vaud. She thinks you need to be a good all rounder with a spark of genius to get into a British university with a Swiss qualification. She describes an interesting approach she took to helping her daughter L get into a British university. L wanted to study a combination of maths and philosophy. Nicola was concerned that her daughter had an average of 4.8. She did have a 6 in her maths final oral exam, but other subjects pulled her marks down. For example, she only had a 3.5 in art. (All pupils have to take either art or music.) In the end they were helped by a Swiss university professor of maths:

> He tried to find out at which British universities candidates were accepted to study maths as a result of a departmental decision, and at which ones it was a faculty decision. At faculty level, someone in an office adds up the figures with no real understanding of the individual candidate's profile. So we focused on the universities where it was a departmental decision. I contacted individual maths and philosophy departments and asked, "What do you need to know?" One answer we got was, "Where does she come in the pecking order? How did she compare with others in her school?" Now that is completely

secret information in Switzerland. There was no data available. So I contacted the school headmaster and said, "You've got to give us the percentage of pupils who got a 6 in maths, French and English over the last few years. English universities need to know where she ranks." As it turned out. only 0.5% of pupils had obtained a 6 in French, their mother tongue, in the previous years. So we included a letter from the headmaster with the percentages in her application to that university and they took her.

On request, gymnasiums often provide a letter or other document for pupils to send to universities abroad to put their marks in context. They cannot provide a lot of data but they may be able to provide information as to how many pupils obtained a particular average, etc. As an example, Nan in canton Geneva told me that in her daughter's *collège* (gymnasium), there had been 360 pupils at the beginning of the 10th (H12) class. By the end of the 13th (H15) class there were only 140 left. Around 10 pupils out of the 140 were given a prize for having an average of 5.0 or more in their maturity exams over the two years. "The 7% who obtained a mark above 5 tended to be extremely studious," reflected Nan.

The higher demands made by foreign universities does not automatically mean their courses will be more challenging. Dan is English and grew up in Switzerland. For reasons that will be explained at the end of this chapter, he studied history and archaeology at Sheffield University in England for one year before changing to Zurich University. Sheffield required him to have a 5 average in his Gymnasial Maturity, while Zurich only required him to have a pass mark. He then experienced both the universities and found the course in Zurich to be intellectually more demanding:

A 5 was a fairly respectable grade. In comparison, however, I found that the studies in Switzerland were tougher for me. Failing grades are much easier to 'achieve' in Swiss universities compared with British ones. I also found that students in Switzerland, in the humanities and elsewhere, are required to do fairly long research papers on a regular basis. Seminars far outweigh lectures. In Sheffield, in contrast, lectures, exams and short essays formed the bulk of my study time. It is much more fact-based rather than method-based, and felt largely like an extension of the lessons in school. I personally found the Sheffield studies easier both to do and to get into, but I can see how the

'Zurich method' helps prepare students better for actual work, be it in history or elsewhere. Of course, a good background knowledge of historical facts is also important for work, and I found this aspect somewhat lacking in Zurich.

Students from abroad who wish to apply for Swiss universities may need high marks, but they do not need as many subjects as students from Switzerland. According to CRUS, the Rectors' Conference of the Swiss Universities, the "Swiss Maturity Certificate requirements for three languages and three natural sciences would be too much to be required of school leaving certificates from other countries."[146] In addition, the 'arts' (art or music) is not a requirement. While each university can make its own entrance criteria, many follow the CRUS agreement. Access to most Swiss universities is possible with an upper-secondary foreign school-leaving certificate that qualifies as general education. The last three years of schooling must include at least six general education subjects, independent of one another, in accordance with the following list:

- first language (native language)
- second language
- mathematics
- natural sciences (biology, chemistry or physics)
- humanities and social sciences (geography, history or economics/law)
- elective (one subject from category 2, 4 or 5)

School certificates with five core subjects only partly fulfil the requirements for Swiss universities, and those with fewer than five subjects are not equivalent and are not recognised. A British student with three or four A levels would therefore officially not meet the entry requirements.

Roots and wings

When you are planning where to go to university, it is worth considering whether you really want to live your life in another country. Switzerland has what I call a 'roots' culture, where you maintain many of your relationships from your schooldays throughout your life. Your strongest network as an adult may be based on these. A 'wings' culture is one where people see it as part of growing up that you find your wings and 'fly off' at some point to experience the world and possibly settle somewhere quite different than where you grew up. Many Swiss would call this 'uprooting yourself'. It is good to be aware of this distinction and what appeals to you more as you assess your options. Dan, who was mentioned above, went to Sheffield University in England although all his classmates went to Basel or Zurich University. However, after a year, he transferred to Zurich University. He explains why he went to Sheffield:

> My parents sort of pointed me in that direction and helped me with the applications. I think I agreed to the idea because I myself fancied a change of scenery after leaving school. I saw it as a chance to start afresh and meet new people. However, having grown up in Basel, I never really got used to life in Sheffield: Possibly a combination of culture shock and homesickness, I didn't feel comfortable or happy in the long term. Maybe I would have gotten more to grips with that if I'd stayed on, but I felt at the time that I would rather be back in my old environment. I also possibly thought that I wasn't maximising my academic potential.

His mother, Val, comments, "When he was back half an hour, his phone started bleeping. In Switzerland people live at home or within striking distance. Students come home at weekends and socialise with people they already know. They only slowly get to know new people. All his classmates that went to Zurich commuted every day at first. It is an evolution rather than a revolution."

Dan does not wish to scare anyone off, based on what was a very personal experience. At the same time his advice to others is to think very hard about both the university and the location, and make sure it is right for them. As he puts it, "While differences between countries may seem small, especially for the children of international families, the contrasts can become starker than you expect."

I can imagine that the experience of visiting grandparents and other relatives in their 'home' country can give young people a false impression of the degree to which they will actually feel at home in a new place in the country they have previously only visited.

Section six

Working together
with the school

Chapter 21   The role of parents and teachers

The role of teachers and parents of children in Swiss schools could be described as one of unequal partners. As mentioned in Chapter 3, parents are not consumers with a say in the policy and practice of schools. Isabelle Chassot, president of the EDK, made a speech in which she outlined the responsibilities of teachers and parents as follows: Teachers are responsible for marks, didactics, teaching concepts, choice of teaching materials and the teaching process. The school has the right to be supported by parents in pedagogical measures taken. Parents, in turn, have the right to be heard by school officials and actively participate in decisions being made about their child, for example before a decision is made regarding which school they should attend next.[147]

Regarding communication, Isabelle Chassot stated that the school has a duty to inform parents openly and transparently. The minimum requirement is that there must be at least one parents' evening per year for the whole class. There must also be a one-to-one evaluation meeting per year with the parents or guardians, and an open day at least every two to three years. The school leadership has to inform parents at the beginning of the year about important projects and events in the coming year.

Isabelle Chassot's speech also addressed the need to have a fixed arrangement (*verbindliche Vereinbarung*) for parents to be involved in school matters at the content level rather than just 'helping out'. In the podium discussion following her speech, it was agreed by representatives from parents' organisations that parental involvement requires a formal framework such as a parents' council. The needs of children and the general quality of the school should be central topics. I was surprised to read this, as the quality of the school is usually the domain of the teachers and the head teacher, and parents' councils tend to discuss other matters, as will be shown below.

Taking responsibility as parents

What teachers want parents to do is be good, responsible parents rather than unpaid teaching assistants. A head teacher in canton Basel-Stadt commented in a letter to the *Basler Zeitung* newspaper that parents should not primarily work in the school, but rather, for the school.[148] The school is satisfied if parents:

- make sure that their child turns up on time in the morning;
- do not excuse their child for needless absences
- do not extend their holidays without permission
- if they notice when there are problems with alcohol, nicotine or drugs
- do not install a TV in their child's bedroom
- take a look at their child's school work during term time
- talk to their child during a meal at least once a day

in short, if they take parental responsibility.

Then their work in the school can consist of parents' evenings and conversations with the teachers.

Most of the items on the head teacher's list are not enforceable, but a few of them are. The school will note absences,

Permitted absences from schools

Parents may need to obtain permission (often by filling in a form) if they wish to take their child out of kindergarten or school during term time, for example, to go on holiday or to visit relatives abroad. Some cantons offer 'joker' days, a specific number of extra days off school per year. Otherwise, parents can be fined if their child has days off without permission. Schools tend to be sympathetic to parents requesting extra time for visits to family 'back home', for example at Christmas, or special occasions like a wedding. It is important to ask in advance, rather than explain afterwards.

counting those with and without an excuse. It may be that a pupil arriving late will have it noted as a half day absence. This may appear on the pupil's report card.

Parents' organisations

There are various ways for parents to be involved in school matters. Alfredo in canton Geneva recommended joining the parents' association (*Conseil d'établissement*). It helped him a lot to understand school dynamics and Swiss ways of doing things. He explains its role at school:

The *Conseil d'établissement* is a group composed of a representative of the *Mairie* (the city council), the director of the school(s) and four to six parents elected by vote by all the parents of the school or schools concerned. Issues discussed include: relations between children and teachers; curriculum; optional activities such as sports; visits to museums; trips to other parts of Switzerland; language classes such as Italian, Portuguese, etc; specific problems (violence at school, drugs, etc.). Parents at the *Conseil* are approached by other parents to share some concerns and the *Conseil* tries to respond to these.

Parents' associations exist in many schools around the country. They tend to consist of the head teacher, one or more other teachers and one or two parent representatives from each class. As Alfredo describes, they can discuss a wide range of issues related to school, although the degree of influence of parents can vary greatly. In some communities their main role is to organise events, such as school bazaars or other events that are open to the public. They may have different names, but are often known as the *Elternrat* in German.

Ute is German and describes how parent involvement went further at her son Jan's primary school in canton Basel-Stadt:

> His teacher created a parents' consultation group (*Elterngruppe*) of around five parent volunteers who met four to six times a year. Each year a different set of five parents took part. She said that she valued our input as her own children were much older and she wanted to know how children tick and what matters to them nowadays. It was a really good platform for both sides: for us to find out what was going on in the classroom, and for her to know what children were telling us at home, or what fights were going on that she didn't know about. For example, we discussed how to organize the amount of homework more effectively. In another class the *Elterngruppe* explored what could be done to break down barriers between the boys and the girls, so that they would be friendlier to each other. This was a much more effective way for parents to be actively involved at school than to join an official parents' organisation (the *Elternrat*).

Jan's teacher, Verena S, explained to me how she developed her approach to working with parents during a post-graduate course she took on the subject. She set up her first parents' group in 1979 and ran them until she retired in 2011. Over the years the *Elterngruppe* idea was also adopted by the head teacher and the other teachers at her primary school. Verena S's approach was to see parents as partners rather than just as an *Instanz* (a legal term referring to people with a certain authority who have to be consulted if there is an issue to discuss):

> There is a lot I don't see going on outside the classroom. The parents can tell me what's happening on the way to school. For example, one year parents reported that the children were swearing a lot. I didn't know that. They didn't do it in the

classroom as it was not allowed. In another case, there was one boy who had problems at home that affected his behaviour at school. Sometimes the parents came with ideas, like they wanted to roast chestnuts for the whole class, or we organised a parents' evening about a specific topic. Running a group like this requires confidence on the part of the teacher, as parents could make demands on you. You need to be able to set limits. It was clear that I was still in charge of teaching content.

Helping with school activities

It is common for parents to be asked to help out with outings, partly to help with 'crowd control'. Although it is not automatic that parents are involved in the classroom, I know several ways this has been done where I live. Some of these may be activities you can suggest via the parents' organisation of your local kindergarten and school.

Crumbs in the kindergarten

When I went to sing in English with my daughter's kindergarten class, I took a tin of biscuits along as a visual aid. As we were singing, "Biscuits in the tin, shake them up, shake them up," I demonstratively shook my tin of biscuits. Suddenly, the lid came off and the biscuits flew through the air and landed all over the room. I am sure I was the talk of the town and that the kindergarten children will always remember that song.

While my daughter was in kindergarten the teacher invited me to go along one morning and teach the children songs in English. I have also heard of cases where parents can sign up to go and read a story to the kindergarten class.

In the 4th (H6) and 8th (H10) classes of my daughters' schools, parents were invited to go to the school to talk about their jobs. Verena S also took a systematic approach to involving mothers as 'reading mothers' (*Lesemütter*) from the 2nd (H4) class. A mother had told her about the idea and she googled it to find out more. She then adapted the concept for her situation. Five or six mothers came to the class for one lesson once a week for six weeks. This happened two or three times a year. Each mother worked with a group of pupils who were at a similar level and who read aloud from the same book at their own pace. If a child lost the place, they had to either stand up for a moment, or give back one of the pebbles they had been given at the beginning of the reading session. In this way the children had intensive reading practice (as well as practice in concentrating), and could ask if they did not understand something. Parents had the opportunity to support the school with a clearly-defined task. I do not wish to give the impression that this is typical in Switzerland, but it seems to be on the increase.

Chapter 22   Communicating about your child

Few chats in the classroom

Kirstin Barton lives in France and coaches many parents in the Basel area of Switzerland.[149] She sees the fact that in the Swiss system it is not usual to come to the school gate and into the classroom as a challenge for incoming parents who are keen to communicate and integrate. "For me, in the French system, that's where I got all my friends, all my children's after-school play dates, all my contacts, chats with the teachers, popping into the classroom asking questions."

In this chapter I address how to go about communicating with teachers about everyday matters and difficult issues.

Whether it is a custom for parents to enter the classroom without an appointment can vary somewhat around the country, although it appears more common in Romandie, the French-speaking part. Sarah M, from the *bureau d'accueil pour l'école primaire* explains that, in canton Geneva, each school has its own rules in this regard. She gives one *école enfantine* (kindergarten) as an example:

> While parents can accompany their children to the *école enfantine* for the first few months, from round about mid-October, a sign is placed on the door at the entrance to the building showing a child saying, "We are big enough to come in on our own now."

The approach at kindergarten level in Geneva is similar to the approach at playgroup for younger children in German-speaking Switzerland. It is expected that the parent may come right into the classroom with the child in the beginning, but it is hoped that this will not drag on. It is assumed that the child will settle better if the mother leaves fairly confidently and quickly.

Cathy in Geneva liked it that at her children's kindergarten and in the first primary year there was flexibility in arrival times in the morning and that parents were even welcome to look at the children's work during that time. In German-speaking Switzerland it is more unusual for parents to enter the school building without an appointment. Karen felt she did the wrong thing at first:

> I took my children right into the classroom. In the UK parents
> are free to wander round the classroom in the morning in
> primary school. They can chat to the teacher without having
> to make an appointment. Here I have to make an appointment
> if I have issues to discuss.

Mary missed early warnings from her ten-year-old son's teacher that something was wrong. "We didn't find out about a behaviour issue between him and some others boys until we were called to a meeting with other parents," she explains. "In the UK, it would be handled early by chatting informally to the parent at the school gate with a 'Can I have a word?' from the teacher." After the meeting, Mary had to rely on her son to report if his behaviour had improved. In the UK she would pop into the classroom first thing in the morning from time to time to ask.

As with everything else in this book, there are always exceptions. Valerie found it worked well on one occasion to pop into the classroom one morning just before school started, to ask the teacher something regarding her son. They had a brief chat and she got her answer.

Main channels of communication

Different approaches parents can take to communicating with teachers include phoning or emailing them, writing notes, and making an appointment to see them. Newcomer parents may be reluctant to disturb teachers at home, so it is a good idea to ask teachers what channel of communication they prefer. If they prefer you to phone them, ask when is a good time to reach them. Some teachers will say they are happy to talk to parents in the lunch hour, while others may prefer late afternoon or evening.

Cathy mentioned the system of a weekly *carnet* (notebook) in her canton, with the homework assignments recorded, as well as dates of tests, etc. This was also the vehicle for her to get messages to the teacher with regard to absences or their family situation. She also found teachers very flexible regarding setting up meetings:

> Although timing was not always easy for me, a working mother,
> the teachers were always willing to find a time to discuss the
> children's work and school life. I never felt that they were

unapproachable or that I would be putting them out to take some of their time to talk about my children.

My children had an *Elternheft* (a notebook for parents) that I had to sign when I had received a letter from the teacher. My daughter told me that if pupils were not doing their homework regularly, parents also had to sign it to confirm that their child had done it.

After their child started Swiss school, many parents described the intensive communication they had with their child's teacher regarding settling in and language learning. You can emphasise to your child's teacher that you would like to support them and that they should contact you whenever anything is not working well. Teachers expect you to approach them if you are concerned about something. You can also take the initiative to contact them from time to time when things seem to be fine, just to check if everything is going well. My husband and I used to arrange an additional appointment with our daughter's primary school teacher every year around November, just to find out how she was getting on. The official meeting with the teacher was usually in January.

Talking about homework

It can be helpful for the teacher to hear from you if school matters are impacting on your child's home life. A classic example of useful parent feedback is when homework is too difficult or is taking too long. Each canton has stipulations as to how many minutes per day or week should be spent on homework. Lise in Ticino gives an example of how she talked to the teacher about her son's homework, as she was unable to help him:

> My son's homework was too difficult for him to do alone, but my Italian wasn't that good. I told the teacher that I didn't see the point in him repeating my mistakes in Italian, so she made it easier.

Not surprisingly, schools generally recommend that parents do not do their children's homework for them. The task should be set in a way that children can complete it on their own. Parents should resist doing the maths or writing the presentation themselves, and instead try to encourage their children and provide them with a quiet work environment. If they have difficulty over several days, parents should speak to the teacher and to other parents. Natalie M gives the following advice:

> Whether you decide to help your child with the homework or not, don't let them go to school with homework which has been done correctly by you, but that they couldn't have done on their own. The teacher will assume that the child can do this. Either make sure your child can really do it (so if you've helped them with two thirds, let them do the last third all alone to make sure they can do it!) or don't let them finish it and send a note with them, telling the teacher that your child has not understood this.

In practice, many parents do help their children, in particular, when they have tests ahead, even if teachers do not encourage this. It is important to talk to other parents and find out when they are giving their children extra help to compensate for any difficulties they are having.

Kate in canton Zurich describes how her younger son C was not handing in any homework in his first four weeks of 4th (H6) class. The teacher contacted Kate and said, "We need to talk." It turned out that C's teacher had a split blackboard, with a side for homework, and kept adding to it. Some homework was given on Tuesday for Friday, or on Wednesday for the following Wednesday. C was writing his homework down, but understood the deadline given to hand it in was the date he had to sit down and do it. Kate had assumed that after two years of Swiss school, she could leave him to get on with his homework in his bedroom.

After the talk with the teacher, Kate had C doing his homework at the kitchen table. Later he was back in his bedroom but he showed her afterwards that he had done everything. She just looked through it, but did not correct it, which is what teachers prefer. She explains that there was also an organisational challenge involved:

> It was a male teacher who was extremely good, but the level went up several gears at once in 4th grade. C didn't know how to organise himself. My older son J had been given a plastic concertina file by his teacher, who had explained how to use it. C just got millions of pieces of paper which he was expected to organise himself. I then found C a plastic concertina file too and he keeps his papers in there with a section for homework to hand in.

Discussing marks with teachers

In primary school the class teacher has a clear overview of your child's ability in all subjects. At lower-secondary this may no longer be the case. Communicating with teachers regarding how your child is doing across the board can be helpful at times, as the following story shows.

Angus is from the UK and lives in canton Baselland. He describes how it looked as if his 15-year-old son Iain might have to repeat the final year of lower-secondary school instead of moving up to upper-secondary. To obtain a 'satisfactory' report, he was not allowed more than three fail marks out of a total of ten subjects. Angus explained what he did in the situation:

Iain is quite bright, but he was not very motivated. He was having trouble especially with subjects that required steady application, even his favourite ones. Therefore he certainly could not afford to lose marks on the more practical subjects like home economics and sport, in which his marks were now borderline. I decided to take action. I knew that the teachers all gave marks separately and might not communicate with each other or know what others were giving. We had agreed with some teachers at a parents' evening to keep in touch so I telephoned a couple of them to let them know that Iain was borderline.

Once the sports and the home economics teachers were informed that it was a critical stage, and he might have to repeat the year, things changed. They were grateful for the information. The sports teacher noted that Iain's asthma should be taken into account especially for swimming, which was not his best sport anyway. The home economics teacher said Iain hadn't yet done all of the marked tasks, including the clearing up activity, and that most pupils were able to get a 6 for that exercise. So I was able to say to him, "The marks are there to be had; if you get on with it and show you are willing." I believe the home economics teacher also had some words of encouragement for him.

Although Iain was embarrassed that I had talked to the teachers, the news that he was still in with a real chance seemed to have a positive effect on him generally. Of particular importance, we also found (independently) an excellent learning therapist[150] for him whom he trusted so that he started working harder on his favourite subjects – history, English and maths. Within a couple of months he had also worked himself up from a 3.5 to a 5.0 average in home economics. In the end he did not have to repeat the year. We all felt a corner had been turned.

Providing the parents' perspective

Karen recommends treating teachers as the experts. "You have to remember you're foreign, in their country. It's their school system," she reminds other incoming parents. "I go along and ask for advice. I'm not going to go in and demand things. If you want something, it is important that you show respect."

In a magazine interview, Maya Mulle, a parent coach, explained that as a mother her aim was to give the school a perspective from the outside.[151] "What do I hear my daughter saying? What am I seeing? I am concerned about her development. Going to the school with questions and observations like this is the right way to do it."

Ursula is a Swiss mother of three children who described to me how, over the years, she learned to communicate with teachers in a way that they kept listening. In the early days she tended to tell the teachers what they were doing wrong. Teachers would then defend themselves. In later years, following the Thomas Gordon model, she learned to use 'I messages', which were non-blaming and non-judgmental. She explains that rather than saying, "My daughter is unhappy in your class", she would now say, "I experience my daughter as being different at the weekend than on school days," and then go on to describe the differences she observes in her daughter's behaviour.

Alice is South African and lives in a village in canton Aargau. She put this into practice after she sat in on her daughter's kindergarten class six weeks after she had started kindergarten. She noticed that her daughter was very withdrawn, spoke little, and played alone. "When I discussed it with the teacher, she was surprised to know that my daughter is usually outgoing and very lively," Alice told me. "She resolved to draw her out more, and this was very helpful."

The importance of asking questions

Many experts recommend taking an inquiring approach, or asking questions when talking to teachers, head teachers and school authorities (as opposed to telling them what to do). It shows you are considering the teacher as the professional in charge, whose job it is to find a solution to a problem on their patch. One of the advocates of asking questions is Christian Waser, the head of *Schulsupport*, a consultancy company in Zurich for school authorities when crises seem likely to escalate. In a magazine interview he describes the situation as 'Mars meets Venus', where two planets (the teachers and the parents) encounter each other and are unable to imagine each other's worlds or systems.[152] He refers in particular to fathers showing muscle in the same way as they would do in the business world. He believes parents often identify with their children so much that they feel personally injured if their child is not successful or has problems. He recommends that parents ask questions to understand how the school and the teachers are thinking. They will probably then notice that the school also wants the best for their child.

Discussing thorny issues

Discussing the child's performance with teachers can be a cause of concern, but the really thorny issues parents need to speak to teachers about include the quality of teaching, the pupil's behaviour, the teacher's behaviour and the behaviour of other children towards their child. The correct procedure is first to speak to the teacher about any problem you have. If the problem is not resolved, you can then approach the head teacher, and if you are still in disagreement (or if there is no head teacher), you can take the issue to the school authorities. It may be that you do not find a satisfactory solution to a school problem, and wish to make a formal request that your child changes class or school. Please see Chapter 26 for further information on this.

Where parents told me about a problem with teaching quality, it tended to be either a case of a newly qualified teacher, or else a teacher working with young people in early puberty. It is my impression from my many interviews that the toughest age group to teach is 11 to 14 year olds.

I heard about the most behavioural problems with this age group too. As a teacher/lecturer of young adults, I have great admiration for teachers of children and young people. They are in a people profession that is particularly vulnerable to burnout. They are dealing with multiple pedagogical challenges, group dynamics issues and behaviour problems at the same time. They have to be on the alert all the time, and cannot just stare out the window or retreat behind their laptops if they need some down time. However, while it is very understandable that teachers may have phases in their working lives where they lose their drive and motivation to teach, it is also important that children do not leave school with gaps in their knowledge, or are unable to pass a key subject due to poor quality teaching.

If teaching quality is a problem, or learning is not taking place because the teacher is not managing to control the class, the first step should be to talk to the teacher about it. It may be that several of the parents are concerned about teaching quality, and individual meetings with the teacher do not help. David F, a lower-secondary school teacher, suggest that parents work as a group to have something done:

> Call each other and ask, "Do you have the same experiences? What does your child tell you?" Then send one or two representatives from among you to discuss it with the teacher. Decide carefully which parent would be suitable to communicate this in the correct tone. They need to be able to get to the point quickly but not just confront the teacher with an accusation. Ask the teacher to suggest measures to take to improve things. Ask what you can do to support him or her. Allow time for things to change. If nothing changes, have your reps approach the head teacher and ask for the teacher to be supported in solving the problems (supervision, coaching, etc. are all possible). It may be that you are on your own in this, as the other parents may wish to sit out the problem.

Problem solving styles

It may be the case that when parents complain about teaching quality, the head teacher takes measures to help the situation to improve, but will not discuss these with parents. In the magazine interview mentioned above, Christian Waser describes it as a problem that some schools communicate badly.[153] They may not be able to say exactly what they are doing about a problem for reasons of confidentiality, but they need to show that they are taking criticism seriously. In the same article, Angelina Forte, the president of a parents' organisation, comments that when action is being taken, it would be helpful if schools would send a letter to concerned parents to say that they are looking for solutions.

Martin H is a teacher at lower-secondary level. "Some head teachers will take up a parents' complaint while others will feel attacked," he comments. "They may be inexperienced as a head teacher as it is a new type of role in many schools." Until recently, each teacher in a school was fairly autonomous. One person would be made responsible for some administrative tasks only, like timetabling. Head teachers may be reluctant to take disciplinary action against their colleagues or make tough decisions related to their livelihood. Having said that, many schools do have very proactive school management and some have an official way for parents to approach the school if a particular problem affects many of them. Barbara in canton Schwyz describes the arrangement at her daughter's school of having a *Pate* (godparent) for the class, who informs the teacher if the parents have an issue:

> The approach in the school is very democratic. If there is an issue with the teacher, parents team up and inform the head teacher, or write a letter together, sign it by everyone, then send it officially, also to the head teacher. As an example, a complaint about the teacher's communication behaviour, where the teacher seemed to prefer some kids and was upset with one kid, or seemed to be leaving out a kid who was always answering, and the pupils jumped to conclusions about what that meant. So the teacher took the opportunity to sit down with the class to discuss it with them, then things got better.

Chapter 23 Dealing with bullying

In this chapter I provide examples of how bullying is dealt with in Switzerland and how you can address this issue if your child is affected. A few parents from other countries commented to me about how they had been reluctant to send their child to Swiss schools because they had heard that bullying was rife and that children had to deal with this on their own. It used to be the standard view that children should deal with low levels of aggressive behaviour by themselves. If one child hit another, the child being hit should just hit back, and that would be the end of it.

This is no longer the position taken by teachers in most communities. Most will address aggressive behaviour and bullying if they are made aware of it. They may do it discretely, and depending on how much your child tells you, you may or may not be informed that they took action at all. You are also unlikely to hear if your child is doing some of the bullying, as that is something they do not report at home. Karen describes how teachers dealt with her son T being bullied:

> T is quite gentle. He is surrounded by sisters. In the 1ˢᵗ class he was set upon in the playground in the break by older boys in the 3ʳᵈ class. His older sister waded in and threw them off. Then she went and got the teachers. She told me about it when she got home. She said the teachers came straight away and the boys were given detention. I saw that the teachers had dealt with it and that I did not need to contact the school. I wouldn't have known about it if he didn't have siblings in the school. T was satisfied that the teachers had dealt with it fairly. UK parents would have gone to the school anyway. I stand back a little bit. I have six children. I ask, "What did you do to them? Did you antagonise them in some way?"

In this case, the school took action immediately. For some parents it may sometimes seem as if the school is doing nothing. Lorna reported that her son C was being bullied when he was 10, just after he had started a new school:

> It was escalating. Three other boys regularly waited for him after school and pushed him around and took his bag. They punched

him, and they congregated outside our gate and shouted at him. They phoned our house at midnight. C's older sister dealt with that by taking the phone and telling the boys in Swiss-German that they would be phoning the police if they rang once more. Eventually I rang the class teacher, who said "What do you think I should do about it?" I said, "I don't know. You're the teacher. I'm not the teacher." After that I heard nothing. I was reading websites and books about bullying, saying he should laugh, walk away, tell a teacher, tell us, and so on. Also to conform, wear the same style of t-shirts and shoes as the others in his class. So we were trying to deal with it on our own. We were considering it as our problem.

Lorna was then really surprised when suddenly, out of the blue, she got 'contracts' in the post from the bullies, sent by the school *Heilpädagogin* (the special needs teacher). C then said, "Oh yes, I forgot to tell you about that." The special needs teacher had taken him and each of the bullies out of the room and asked for their stories. Then each of the boys had to write in a contract what they had done, and had to sign that they would not do it any more. It was very specific. The contracts were countersigned by the parents of all the boys except one. Lorna was very relieved. "That was basically the end of it. It happened sporadically after that and C seemed to be able to cope with it much, much better."

Research and courses on bullying

Attitudes to bullying have changed in recent years in Switzerland. I see the research of Françoise Alsaker, an expert in developmental psychology at the University of Bern, as playing a role in this. She and her team have researched the subject of bullying at kindergarten. One study was conducted with 70 kindergartens in canton Bern.[154] They define bullying (referred to as *Mobbing*) as a situation where one child is bothered again and again over a period of time by another child or group of children. It does not need to be physical. A child may be left out, others may take away her things, or push and shove her. At kindergarten it is often verbal, consisting of humiliating a child, saying he is stupid, he stinks, or comparing him with animals.

The study divides children into bullies, passive victims, aggressive victims, and uninvolved children. Passive victims are most likely to be sad, depressed and fearful. The Alsaker team conclude that teachers have to watch carefully because the children they notice first are the aggressive victims, who respond to provocation by being impulsive and uncontrolled. Bullies are often clever children who know they are doing something wrong and cover it up. This invisibility can make bullying difficult for adults to spot. In addition, the bully is often a popular child.

The Alsaker team offers courses for both teachers and parents.[155] The Bern *Be-Prox* programme, for example, helps kindergarten and school teachers to develop strategies to deal with bullying.[156] The approach is no-blame, but everyone has responsibility for the problem. Respect and clear communication are encouraged. The topic of bullying is discussed in class and children are encouraged to say 'stop' and get help if they are bullied. Children on the edge are encouraged to get involved to put a stop to bullying.

As well as the *Be-Prox* programme, there are many different approaches taken to deal with bullying around Switzerland. Natalie M in canton St Gallen describes mediation courses for older pupils at lower-secondary school to help younger ones. The children all attend conflict management classes, and then they choose their mediators.[157] Other approaches I heard about ranged from enforcing 'time out' (having to sit beside the teacher) for kids who get physical at kindergarten to getting the Swiss Red Cross (*SRK*) in to the school to give the children some *Chili Training*,[158] to learn to address conflicts openly and improve their social competence. Parents and teachers are all involved in this.

Steps you can take

If your child is being bullied by other children, the first step should be to talk to the teacher. If the teacher thinks the child needs to deal with the problem alone, you should make an appointment to see the head teacher, if there is one, and the school authorities, if there is not. Teachers may sometimes be slow to do something about bullying, trying not to intervene too early, but they usually take action in the end. They may also not agree with you about what type of action to take, and it is important to let them deal with it their way. In rare cases, they do not see that action needs to be taken at all. A next step might be to see the school psychologist, who will know the school and may support your child and help the teacher to deal with it too. All cantons have school psychological services.[159] If there is a school social worker available, this can also be helpful (see box on page 206).

If the bullying is taking the form of threats, physical violence or theft, it can even be considered as a legal matter. As well as speaking to the school, you can contact a victim support group in your canton (*Opferberatung, Centre LAVI, UIR*[160]). If your child is suffering to the extent that he or she has physical symptoms or mental health issues as a result of the situation, you should see your paediatrician. It may be that they recommend that your child changes class or school, and will give you a medical certificate prescribing this.

The external expert's opinion will be respected by the school. One mother who got a doctor's certificate when her child was being bullied by a teacher put it like this: "You are getting the opinion of a local expert instead of a 'hysterical' foreign mother. The doctor had 100% credibility and I had zero credibility." I know of several cases where a doctor's certificate was issued. In each case this led to the school taking measures to improve things, usually either involving the school addressing the bullying, or the child being allowed to change class or school.

Martin H thinks that changing class can sometimes be the solution for a child being bullied if there is a particular constellation of pupils. The composition of the whole class can play a role.

In other cases, the problem continues. The child is bullied in their next school and may have to move again. Teachers tend to see moving a child as a last resort rather than something to try out to see if things improve. Others say that this should not be necessary if the school addresses it properly. Please see Chapter 26 for further information on requesting to have your child's class or school changed.

School social workers

School social workers can also provide support in a case of bullying. They are usually attached to lower secondary schools. Nationwide, there is around one social worker for 1000-1500 pupils.[161] It is the goal of *Avenir Social* (an association of Swiss social work professionals) to have one social worker per 400 pupils. Pupils, parents and teachers may all go and consult the school social worker. Typical topics include: a fight with a friend, comments on Facebook, family problems, motivation at school, absenteeism and homework. Social workers also address questions related to sexual orientation and drugs. They will talk to the pupil and often recommend a psychologist.

In a magazine interview, school social workers Michael Krisztmann and Lukas Mühlemann point out that they are not there to 'wipe away' (*wegwischen*) every little problem.[162] However, Lukas Mühlemann comments that in a case of bullying, "If someone no longer has the courage to walk home from school alone, the school has to intervene." They then look at the class as a system and address the responsibility of the whole group to improve the situation: "We pick some of them out – the main actors (*Täter*), the followers (*Mitläufer*) and neutral young people who have a strong social role in the class. Then they have to find a solution. They all know perfectly well what role they have. The person who is bullying the most also knows it."

Working with other parents

With this chapter I wish to show that it is no longer the standard Swiss approach to leave children to sort out bullying by themselves. It has been clearly defined by the Alsaker team and shown to be unacceptable. There is now a wide range of culturally appropriate best practices from around the country to deal with it. It may be that you will have to be the first to act. Try to involve other parents too if their children are affected. In researching this chapter, I spoke to Sally, a mother in a village in canton Aargau where low-level bullying had been going on at the kindergarten and the school for a long time, but the teachers said it was not their problem. Six months later she gave me an update on her experience, which I condense here:

> I think it is very useful to give people the advice that they should take action, and use all the options that they have, and that they should persist, because even low-level mobbing (bullying) can be very damaging to a child. In our village, more parents are coming out into the open with their concerns, so I am not alone in this. I was the first to do something about it but it was only when the Swiss mums took it up that the school really took notice.
>
> I managed to get most of the other mums of the kids in my daughter's class together, and we agreed the level of conflict between the kids in the school is too high, and that the way the school deals with it (or not) is inadequate. Our request for a round table discussion was met with surprise, but the school leadership finally gave in. The discussion was very useful in highlighting our concerns, although the teachers refused to acknowledge that these incidents had been occurring, and put the onus on us to inform them every time something happens at the school. We asked them to reinforce the 'stop' rule (where a 'victim' says 'stop' when they have had enough, and the perpetrator must respect this). They have now put this in a newsletter, and asked parents for support in making the children aware of its importance and complying with it. There is also going to be a session in the school on *Mut tut gut* (Courage does you good), including conflict resolution.

Chapter 24   Special needs

In this chapter, I describe the broad range of special needs provision that may be on offer, referring to recent developments in the legal framework. I also make suggestions as to how to work with the school and experts to obtain a diagnosis and support for your child. At the end of this chapter I provide a list of websites of charity organisations that can advise you further. In Chapter 25 I address provision for gifted children and in Chapter 26, I outline how to appeal a school decision you cannot accept.

Myriam K is a trainee primary school teacher and describes how her 2nd (H4) class's learning needs are met in the course of the week in a city school in canton Basel-Stadt. 13 of the 20 pupils leave the classroom at least once a week for a special lesson: six have integrative schooling (ISF) in the form of extra support for school subjects; four have coaching for gifted children; two have speech therapy; and one has speech therapy and therapy for dyscalculia. The need is defined by the teacher or teaching team and the school psychological services may be consulted too.

Meeting special needs within the regular classroom programme is a fairly new phenomenon and it is very challenging for the teaching team, as will be shown later in this chapter. It is a recent development in some municipalities that so much provision is made in the regular classroom for children with special needs. This approach is by no means universal in Switzerland. As with everything else, it varies greatly from canton to canton, and in some cases from school to school and teacher to teacher.

The legal framework

Recent changes in Swiss law have given people with disabilities more rights. With regard to schooling, there is now an emphasis on mainstreaming, or integration of children with special needs into regular classes, with additional support. These changes are mainly due to the Disability Discrimination Act of 2004[163] that was adopted by Swiss people by popular vote in 2002. The following is my translation of two important points from Article 20 of the act:

1. The cantons are to ensure that children and young people with disabilities receive an education that is adapted to their special needs.
2. The cantons are to promote the integration (or mainstreaming) of children and young people in regular schools as much as possible for their own good.

Following the adoption of this legislation, an intercantonal agreement (or *concordat*) was passed regarding cooperation in special education.[164] The aim of the agreement is to provide a comparable offer in all cantons to integrate children and young people (aged 0 to 20) with a disability. 12 cantons had joined by 2010 (AR, BL, BS, FR, GE, LU, OW, SH, TI, UR, VD, VS) and it came into effect for them on 1 January 2011. Others are likely to follow. The 12 cantons agree to a specific use of terminology, quality standards and evaluation procedures (known as *SAV* in German and *PES* in French).[165]

All other cantons are now required by law to develop their own cantonal concept for special education in accordance with the Disability Discrimination Act. In addition, there is now an intercantonal agreement (*IVSE* in German, *CIIS* in French and Italian[166]) that has been accepted by all cantons whereby schooling or residential care to meet special needs will be provided in institutions outside the person's canton where there is no suitable offer within the canton.

Another change in the law is that, since 2008, national Invalidity Insurance (*IV* in German, *AI* in French and Italian) has withdrawn from responsibility for special education from primary school onwards and the cantons are now financially and legally responsible for this. The IV/AI still pays for assistance and special education for serious conditions up to and including kindergarten level.

Levels of provision in the 12 cantons

In accordance with the intercantonal agreement on special education, there are several levels of provision to be implemented by the 12 cantons involved. If you move to one of these cantons, you can expect it to adhere to these. I base the following outline on the way the concept is applied in Basel-Stadt and Baselland.[167] The standard approach is that teaching teams in schools teach in a way that differentiates between pupils within a class. They challenge the brightest pupils while supporting the weakest. (See, for example, the 'plan for the week' on pages 97 – 98.) If this is not sufficient, additional provision (*Förderangebot* in German, *offre de base* in French) is offered, such as extra lessons in one of the school subjects, language lessons in the school language, support for learning difficulties, coaching for gifted children, speech therapy and development of psychomotor skills. All of this is paid for by the school's budget and several children from the same class or school can benefit.

If more intensive provision, or measures (*Verstärkte Mass-nahmen* in German, *mesures renforcées* in French) are required for a particular child, the teaching team and the head teacher contact the school psychological services and the parents. The school psychologist talks to the parents and the child and conducts an evaluation using the *SAV/PES* process mentioned earlier. Additional measures are then recommended. In most cases the canton will pay for these. The canton also pays for special schools. Some cantons may also offer special classes as part of the more intensive measures – for example, a first class that takes two years instead of one.

Using this approach as a starting point may help you ask the right questions in order to find out about levels of provision in your canton if it has not joined the intercantonal agreement. It is impossible to outline all the cantonal concepts that vary from this approach. For more information on each canton, please see www.integrationundschule.ch, available in German, French and Italian.

Levels of provision around the country

Christian Liesen is an expert in special needs education. In a paper written in English he describes how special needs funding is provided by every canton but that they split the costs with the municipalities.[168] High-level provision (similar to the intensive measures described above) involves a higher share of cantonal funding, for example, to fund special schools for pupils with severe disabilities. Low-level provision (similar to the additional provision described above) usually means a higher share of municipal funding, for example, to support a child with mild problems in language acquisition within the regular school.

There are a range of measures in between with different funding mechanisms. There is often mixed financing with insurances, charitable trusts and private parties. Some cantons are ahead of others and have a level of provision that is capable of handling a wide range of issues. Christian Liesen gave me an example of a maximum amount of low-level provision as having a second teacher in the classroom for 16 hours a week. A maximum amount of high-level provision may involve special schooling. This is the most intensive measure.

Special schooling

Special schooling may consist of special classes (*Sonderklassen* or *Kleinklassen* in German, *classes spécialisées* in French) within regular school for children with behavioural or learning difficulties. Children may spend several years in a special class. Introductory classes can also be used as a temporary measure to help children to build a solid educational foundation. Natalie M explains:

> Children who are a bit different or who need longer can do the first school year over two years. They get more time to do the same work. It is a great opportunity. "You're a year older, but you haven't lost anything. The first class is so important learning to read and write, getting a feeling for numbers. Then you're all set up for second grade. My friend was recommended to put her child in the introductory class and she refused. The child then had problems reading in the first class. In the introductory class he would have had time to play and read and would have had a good foundation for the rest of his school years.

There are also special day schools and boarding schools (*Sonderschulen* in German, *écoles spéciales* in French) for children who need more intensive treatment. They specialise in a particular form of disability or learning or behavioural difficulty.

An evaluation is made and cantonal approval must be given for a child to attend a special school. Just as with regular school matters, parents have no right to choose the place of provision of special schooling. They may, however, *request* a transfer to a different school. Municipalities are expected to consider their request, but may decide against meeting it. Parents can also send their child to a private special school. Some of the cost may or may not be paid for. It can become a legal matter and parents may contest a decision they do not agree with. In some cases they can claim that their child is being discriminated against. (See Chapter 26 on making an appeal against a school decision).

Special schooling may be followed by practical training for work. INSOS is an umbrella organisation of 750 institutions for people with disabilities. Their website outlines the details of a two year practical-training course, akin to an apprenticeship, for people with learning difficulties.[169] If it goes well, this may be followed by a regular two year basic apprenticeship, which in turn may be followed by the standard federal three or four-year VET programme (*EFZ, CFC, AFC*).

Before and after the school years

Special schooling can be preceded by financial support for pre-school children with a disability. Parents should register their child's condition to obtain invalidity insurance (IV / AI). These insurances will pay for children who need help to manage everyday tasks (due to their disability, not their age), an intensive care supplement and transport costs.

Integrative schooling

High-level provision may also be provided within the regular school, for example, highly individualised support for a child, with the assistant taking part in school life. Magda told me how her son was given a diagnosis of autism from the Department of Child and Adolescent Psychiatry (KJPD) at the University of Zurich.[170] The diagnosis was sent to the boy's kindergarten with the recommendation that he have a special needs teacher in the classroom for several hours per week to help him with his disruptive behaviour, which the school duly organised. The table below shows how a mainstreaming approach to provision can be portrayed as a continuum with the aim of integrating the child as far as possible in regular school. This can range from attending a regular school part-time to receiving support with one subject only in a regular school.

Degree of Integration	Type of School	Lesson Plan Design	Additional resources
Less integration		Individual learning goals in all subjects	Individual
	Special school and regular school	Individual learning goals in 3-5 subjects	Collective (for all pupils)
		Individual learning goals in 1-2 subjects	
More Integration	Regular school only	Standard lesson plan with standard learning goals	None

Table 7   Integration as a continuum[171]

Low level provision

Low level provision can be very low key, as was shown in Myriam K's example at the beginning of this chapter. The recent change in policy to integrate children with special needs has meant that teachers have become pedagogical choreographers in some cantons. They work closely with special needs teachers, holding meetings to plan learning content as well as the logistical aspects of the programme to make everything fit together. In addition, they may have to run the class in a certain way to meet special needs. For example, a kindergarten teacher told me that she now has an Asperger's child in her class. It is important for him to have the same routine every day, so she can no longer vary her programme from day to day as she used to.

In rural areas, a school may be too small to have its own additional support staff for special needs. Martin H in canton Lucerne describes how he and his colleagues provided the additional support (*integrative Förderung*) offered to pupils with a weakness in a particular subject. At first this had to be done when the teacher offering the support had a free period. The teachers found it problematic, as pupils were taken out of their class and therefore missed their regular class in one subject in order to be given support in another. (This is similar to the challenge of incoming children being taken out of regular classes for their extra classes in the school language). Martin H and his colleagues then managed to change the programme so that extra German support happened at the same time as the rest of the class had German.

Dancing in step

There has been a huge increase in special needs provision in Switzerland in recent years. A study in canton Zurich showed that 46 out of 100 children were given support for special needs in 2008/9.[172] International parents I spoke to tended to be appreciative if the school picked up on their child's speech, motor skills or learning difficulties and offered them extra support. Caz reports from canton Zurich:

> My son had a few problems with pronouncing certain letters at the age of 4. Fish were *pish* and spoon was always *poon* amongst others and this was picked up very quickly by the *Logopädin* (speech therapist) who does a visit to the kindergarten twice a year. This has resulted in my son having one-on-one sessions in German to improve this and I have to say the change is great. It is great fun and he cannot wait to go to the sessions.

Some Swiss parents and teachers (as well as some paediatricians) are concerned that children are now being labelled unnecessarily and that they should be given more time and space to develop at their own pace. The German-Swiss parents' magazine, *Wir Eltern*, ran an article discussing the issue, and I summarise some key points from Swiss experts quoted there.[173] Special needs expert Andrea Lanfranchi pointed out that children who don't 'dance in step' (literally: *aus der Reihe tanzen*) in German-speaking Switzerland very quickly end up with corrective measures. In canton Ticino, for example, there is less money and teachers cannot be perfectionistic or seek therapeutic measures or a special class for every noticeable difference. A Ticinese teacher will try to find local solutions, in their own class, with the child's parents, or with peers in the class. Andrea Lanfranchi and educational expert Urs Moser both recommend that teachers and parents first work together, as many problems will then be solved without expert help.[174] In some cases it can be sufficient to consult the school's own special needs teacher. Once the school psychological services are involved, the therapy machinery starts to move and is difficult to stop.

How to obtain support

It may be that you are concerned that your child has special needs and is not being given adequate support. It is good to go and talk to the teacher as the first step, and ask what he or she recommends. Barbara Graham-Siegenthaler[175] is a Swiss lawyer and mother based in canton Basel-Stadt. She suggests the following:

> If you don't speak the language well, and you feel you don't understand what is going on and don't have a means of communicating with whoever is in charge, I would advise taking along a friend who is sympathetic to the cause, who will understand the issues and will be able to explain them to you in your language. Ask as many questions as possible. Make sure you understand the procedures and decision to be taken as well as the time aspect involved.

Peter Lienhard, professor of special needs education, used to be a school psychologist. He gives the following advice:

It is not helpful to approach the teacher with a ready-made diagnosis provided by a parents' support group. It is better to go to the teacher and say, "I am very concerned. I would like to find a solution." Give the school the chance to look into the matter. In some cases, the teacher will not think there is a problem needing special attention and parents may then consult the school psychologist.[176]

There is no standard around the country as to what a school psychologist will recommend. It is very much a matter of personal judgment and negotiation with the parents. It can be that one psychologist decides to recommend eight hours of support per week for a child where another would recommend only two hours.

Christian Liesen describes variations in the route parents take to reach a diagnosis:

The school might not agree with parents about what difficulties the child is experiencing, or they may think it is not a serious issue. There will usually also be financial considerations. If your child is emotionally and behaviourally challenged, they could be more likely to do something about it because it affects them in the classroom. If the school doesn't listen, some parents involve the school psychologist. Others may take a short cut, which may be problematic from the school's point of view. Instead of the school or school psychological services, they go straight to a clinic and get a medical report.

Barbara Graham-Siegenthaler points out that it can take time for the school to work out a provision plan, and that this can lead to misunderstandings. It may be that the school does not keep the parents informed along the way. She recommends that parents be proactive in communicating with the school:

If you hear nothing, contact the teacher, or the head teacher, or the school authorities, and ask for news. If, for example, your child has been assessed at kindergarten for special provision at school, you may hear nothing in the holidays. Take the initiative and phone and ask. Also, once a decision has been communicated, if you are not happy with it, ask what the decision is based on so that you really understand and do not assume anything or jump to conclusions.

Variations in provision

A parent of a child with special needs pointed out that there may be constraints in time, manpower or finances that need to be taken into account. Provision can be a bit patchy in some places. It is worth linking up with parents of children with similar challenges in different cantons or municipalities to find out what is being offered. Stephanie, an Australian mother, describes how much provision can vary:

> It is a challenge that special needs are not always catered for in some towns and villages. A lot depends on the resources of both the canton and the particular municipality. A family I know moved from one canton in order to have their child's special needs catered for.

In some cases, you can 'borrow' an idea from one canton to suggest in another. A mother told me that her daughter had been allocated a few hours per week of specialist help in the classroom for her learning needs. She argued for having an assistant for 35 francs per hour rather than a specialist for 126 francs per hour. She was well networked and knew that it was happening in other places, but it was a new idea to the school. There was some resistance at first, but in the end the school agreed and her daughter received many more hours of assistance than had originally been planned.

Specialist advice

In some cases, it will be clear that your child has special needs or a disability well before they start kindergarten. A mother of a child with a serious condition gives the following advice to parents:

> Parents need to take responsibility for their child's condition, rather than being in denial and saying, 'It's just a phase' or 'It is the responsibility of the school or doctor to sort it out'. In our case, it was like a wild, long, 'terrible twos'. For complex disability issues, it is worth getting a good diagnosis from a well-respected specialist in the field of your child's disability (and paying for if it necessary) rather than solely relying on your family doctor or school psychologist who may not have sufficient experience and

misdiagnose or incompletely diagnose the condition. Having a specialist report is like having the right currency for Switzerland.

The authorities are unlikely to listen to a worried parent, however well informed, but will respect an official professional report. For some recognised disabilities, a diagnosis will lead to registration with the *IV* (or *AI*) which can unlock funding for specific measures to assist the child. Assistance may also be provided for children without an *IV* diagnosis on a discretionary basis.

If your child has a serious condition, it is also well worth contacting a charity organisation such as *Procap* or *Proinfirmis* (see box below) to get advice on how to go about getting a diagnosis.

Advice and support groups for parents

You will need advice that is specific to your canton. National websites offering support to parents usually provide lists of cantonal advice centres and group meetings around the country. To get you started, the following organisations can give you general advice as well as legal advice regarding financial support:

- www.allspecialkids.org (English, with many useful links)
- www.procap.ch (D, F, I)
- www.proinfirmis.ch (D, F, I)
- www.egalite-handicap.ch (D, F, I)

The following websites may also be helpful:

- *Attention deficit (hyperactivity) disorder*: www.elpos.ch (D), www.aspedah.ch (F) and www.aida-ti.ch (I)
- *Autism*: www.autism.ch (D, F, I), also: http://aba-parents. ch/ (D, English, as it was started by Ray Pierce, an American)
- *Dyslexia and dyscalculia*: www.verband-dyslexie.ch (D), www.adsr.ch (F) and www.dislessia-ticino.ch (I)
- *Mental disability*: www.insieme.ch (D, F)
- *Visual impairment*: www.visoparents.ch (D) and www.szb. ch (D, F, I)
- *Hearing impairment*: www.svehk.ch (D, F)
- *Behavioural problems*: www.triplep.ch (D, F)

Chapter 25   Gifted children

H is a child with outstanding talent. She was able to read the local newspaper before she even started kindergarten. Her younger sister K read Harry Potter while she was in kindergarten. Both children started local school in canton Zurich at the age of five. They both skipped the 5th (H7) class and went on to pass the stiff six-year gymnasium entrance exam at the end of the 6th (H8) class. Their mother is a Zurich lawyer and told the German-Swiss *Wir Eltern* magazine that other parents had accused her and her husband of stealing their children's childhood from them.[177] The article comments that starting school early is on the increase in canton Zurich, having increased sixfold in the space of four years.

> **Terminology**
>
> In this chapter I talk mainly about gifted children, using the word in English that is closest to the German *begabt* and the French *doué*. I also use the terms *talent* and *outstanding talent*. A child with outstanding talent is *hochbegabt* in German and *surdoué* in French. There is a tendency in some circles to refer to children with an IQ of over 130 as being gifted,[178] but in others there is a reluctance to quantify this.

This chapter is to some extent a continuation of the previous chapter on special needs, and many of the points discussed there also apply to the needs of gifted children. As the example above suggests, attitudes of the school authorities towards giftedness may be changing dramatically in some parts of Switzerland. It is relatively new that provision is made within the regular classroom curriculum or with extra lessons, and it is not available everywhere. It may depend on cantonal policy, provision at municipal level and the individual teacher. The chemistry between pupil and teacher as well as teacher and parents may also play a role. There are private schools specialising in the education of gifted children, and other private schools with small classes that can focus on individual needs which may include the needs of gifted children. A few cantonal or municipal authorities may pay part or all of the cost of special schooling for children with outstanding talent, although they will not advertise the fact.

Internal differentiation

Internal differentiation is the first step in provision for gifted children. This means that the teacher aims to provide a classroom programme that meets a wide range of needs. Examples of this have been mentioned in previous chapters, for example, providing greater challenges in lessons, by means of activities with varying levels of difficulty as part of the plan for the week (see Chapter 9). German-Swiss experts in the field, Brunner, Gyseler and Lienhard, point out that there is a difference between developing talent (*Begabung*) and developing the talented (*die Begabte*).[179] The first should be a general teaching principle and the second involves specific measures for individuals. The more talent development is practised in the classroom in general, the less there will be a need for special development of the talented. The specialists emphasise that characteristics of talent development should be more learning and less teaching. The teacher should not be central, but rather, the pupils should engage in active learning, for example, developing knowledge, strategies and processes to solve problems. In some cantons, for example in canton Zug, children may even spend a few lessons per week working on their own research project.

Additional coaching

In addition to internal differentiation within the classroom, the child may be taken out of the class for one-to-one or group coaching or mentoring, or may join another older class for part of the week for more challenging lessons. B, a mother in canton Bern comments that teachers may suggest a child take 'pull out' courses if they are gifted. Parents have to agree that the child be tested. If they achieve an IQ above 130 they can take a morning off their regular class and go to a special class. Here they can learn not to give up when the task gets difficult, which is something they do not experience in their regular class.

Identification of children who would benefit from a greater challenge can be very low-key. Wendi in canton Thurgau described how the children in her daughter's primary school class were assessed by the special needs teacher during class work. Her daughter and one other pupil were to be sent to another class for extra lessons for two hours per week to challenge them more.

When he worked as a school psychologist, Peter Lienhard arranged additional coaching for gifted children in one of their areas of strength, for example, in science. At the same time he gave them the task of exploring the difference between the two worlds they were in, their own personal world as a gifted child and the world of their classroom. In their class they could either try to fit in or stand out and be special. Fitting in required understanding how the rules of the classroom world worked and what they would have to do there if they did not want to stand out. If they always stood out, and always attracted attention as special, they might get on the nerves of other children, who might then not want anything to do with them. This was more important before puberty. By the age of around 11, they started to want to fit in and be part of the group.

Swiss gymnasium is often considered enough of a challenge for gifted children, and it varies as to whether there is an additional offer to challenged gifted children. Pieter, a British father in canton Bern has a gifted daughter who is now studying politics and economics in England. When she started gymnasium, the family was pleasantly surprised to discover that school advisors recommended a fairly low-key additional programme for a few of the children who were under-challenged with the class work. She took additional music classes and the French teacher encouraged her to take an external French exam, the C1 DELF. She found it hard, and it stretched her a bit, but she managed to pass. In general, they gave her extra tasks and encouraged her. If she felt she needed a bit more maths, they gave her additional work.

Identifying giftedness

Lichtblick für helle Köpfe is a book in German for teachers of gifted children.[180] It is accompanied by a free questionnaire, also available in English that can be downloaded by parents, to help find out if their child is gifted.[181] The questionnaire includes ways to identify under-challenged children who should undergo psychological testing.

ASEP, the Swiss association for gifted children in French-speaking Switzerland and Ticino has a booklet in English about intellectually gifted children.[182] It provides tips for spotting a gifted child at school. Measures it mentions include acceleration, or jumping a year of school, for example going straight to the 2nd (H4) class after kindergarten. It points out that for children with an IQ of over 145, skipping one year will not be enough. However, if they skip two years, they will be more behind in motor and other skills.

Skipping a class

The example of the two gifted children at the beginning of this chapter may be misleading, as having a child start school early or be moved up a class is a fairly unusual measure. It is not automatically considered the best way to advance the child's education. H and K, mentioned earlier, had exceptionally high IQs. Parents often disagree with the school regarding whether their child is gifted, and whether special measures are required. Swiss specialists say that success at school depends on personality traits and behaviour as well as academic ability.[183] (As previous chapters have shown, being organised and disciplined become crucial behavioural aspects in Switzerland). I imagine that H and K were also reasonably mature for their age.

The teacher looks at the all-round picture of the child's development. If the gifted child is immature or does not have good social skills, teachers will probably not recommend skipping a class. They are also taking a long-term perspective.

A gifted child is not necessarily more mature when puberty hits, and it can then become a disadvantage to be a year younger in the class.

Corinne H agrees that some children are genuinely ready for school at an earlier age than others. She sees great differences in their cognitive and emotional development, irrespective of their ages:

> As an example, a boy of a newly arrived family isn't ready for school. His parents are highly educated and are keen for him to start as soon as possible. There is also pressure from their circle of friends, relatives and work colleagues. He has speech problems, and the school psychologist does not recommend sending him to school, but we will let him go because his parents are keen and he is keen. Children can be trained by their parents, but this is not the same thing as being self-directed. Another five year old is very advanced for his age and we have recommended that he starts school. Our aim is to help such children to obtain a certain level of all-round maturity so that they can then start to read and write, and are ready for academic challenges.

Parents sometimes regret having moved their children up a class. A couple told me how they think it was possibly a mistake that their son M started Swiss school a year early. He had attended an international school until he was five, and learned to read and write there. He then changed over to Swiss kindergarten. He was tested by the school psychological services and was recommended to start school a year early instead of doing the second year of kindergarten. A few years down the road he was a bright child but was having difficulty with the schoolwork. At the end of the sixth year of primary school, again in consultation with the school psychologist, they decided to have him repeat the year.

Going back a class

It can be worrying for parents when they first arrive in a new community if their gifted child is recommended to go back a year in order to have time to learn the language thoroughly. Kimberly's older daughter M is a gifted pupil. When she was in 2nd grade in the USA, John Hopkins University took her into a special programme for talented youth. When they came to Switzerland, Kimberly and her husband were told that she would have to repeat 5th (H7) class because of her birth date. To Kimberly's surprise, this turned out very well:

> It caused us a little worry as she is so advanced anyway, but it was the BEST thing. She is now one of the oldest in the class and it makes tons of difference socially. She is exceptionally bright in math. Last year her teacher let her work with the older kids in the class (it was a 4th/5th/6th grade combo class) or gave her additional work to do. This year the teacher is new and extra work is built into the work syllabus for the kids who finished correctly and quickly. After only 18 months in Swiss school, and only 12 months in the regular classroom, M managed the stiff entrance exam for *Langgymnasium* (six-year gymnasium).

The class teacher of Kimberly's younger daughter B gave her additional German in her first year in Swiss school and additional maths in her second year. He also emphatically requested that B come to homework help. M was invited too. During that time he worked with her on organization and executive skills as well as extra German.

The article discussing H and K also reports on studies in Germany that show how older pupils in a class do better. Now twice as many parents in Germany are holding their children back a year (known as 'redshirting' in the USA)[184] so that when they start kindergarten they are among the oldest in the class. This is thought to give them a head start that can be long-lasting. Some US studies suggest that the youngest children in each year group lag behind in test scores until 8th grade and that older kids maintain a slight advantage throughout elementary and middle school. Others, however, report that the oldest kids in a particular year group can lose their head start within three years.

Private schools

If children are not challenged enough by the measures mentioned above, and if skipping a year or two will not help enough, some municipalities will consider paying for them to go to a private school that caters for gifted children. They usually do not want to publicise this, so it is difficult to find out which ones might do so. It is very much a judgment call in a grey area for them, because a private school that caters for gifted children is not a 'special school' and local authorities tend to try to avoid subsidising private schools with public money. There is always a fear that a precedent will be set and more and more parents will want public funding for their chosen private school.

Benedicta is now looking for a private school for her five-year-old son. She describes how his behaviour at his kindergarten in Baselland was attracting attention:

> When the teacher explained something, he understood it immediately. He then got frustrated when the other children took longer to understand things or did not follow instructions immediately. He tended to get aggressive. The school had him tested (a five hour test) and it turned out that he is *hochbegabt*, meaning he has outstanding talent. He has the same level as a 12-year-old in some types of intelligence. It is a dilemma, as his brain is very advanced, but he loves playing. He could start school a year earlier, but then there would be less opportunity to play. Our municipality in Baselland may pay for a private school for him. The school psychological services need to recommend it, and it then has to be approved by the authorities. I know a family who moved from another canton to this municipality because of the provision made for gifted children.

There are several private schools in Switzerland that have special programmes for gifted children. They can be found by contacting the parent support groups listed on page 229. Talenta in Zurich is a small fee-paying private school for gifted children, for the six years of primary school only and the two years of kindergarten before that.[185] The Talenta management consider the canton of Zurich gymnasium programme (which roughly 18% of pupils complete) as tough enough to keep gifted children occupied and interested to some extent.

Susanne Heer is responsible for admissions at Talenta and explains that children need to qualify to be given a place, to ascertain whether they will be able to manage the work. They can be tested by a children's hospital, their school psychological services, a private psychologist or a private organisation. They are considered gifted if they have an IQ above 130, although she warns that the numbers game has its limitations. Her school takes a much broader perspective than this. The child's motivation also plays an important role:

> A child can have an outstanding test result at the age of 5, and then the fire just goes out of her a bit later on. Another child might score 160, but is just not motivated to learn. He does not want to use his intelligence. It is often due to personality, but other factors may play a role. A third child may have a result a little under 130, but, when she comes to visit the school, we see she is extremely keen to learn and would benefit from the programme.

Susanne Heer encourages parents who are in Switzerland short term to think carefully before sending their child to Talenta, or any other Swiss school for that matter. Their education will be in the local language and it may be difficult for them to move to another type of school system in another country later on.

Natalie M teaches at KiTs,[186] a bilingual private school with a programme for gifted children in canton St Gallen. She compares this with the regular kindergarten her daughter attends:

> Our daughter can read and write but they do nothing with those skills. She is very happy playing in her kindergarten, so it's ok for us, but we think it's just a shame that she is not encouraged. Our private school has a *Basisstufe*, which combines kindergarten and school, so our pupils can start reading, writing and doing sums as soon as they feel ready. I think, a lot of Swiss people feel strongly that kindergarten should be 'fun' and playing and not about (formal) learning. What they don't see is that (formal) learning could be fun. It is difficult for parents who think or know they have a gifted child, because some teachers will think that they are just trying to 'push' their child.

Gifted children in distress

Given that many public schools aim to cater to the needs of gifted children, I asked Susanne Heer how parents can know if their gifted child needs a special school. She sees it as a question of how settled and happy the child is at school. In her experience there is often a difference in how girls and boys express any unhappiness:

> Gifted girls who are frustrated at school might show symptoms at home, for example, they get depressed, or they get a stomach ache, or headaches. At school they hide their unhappiness and try

to fit in. They may get test results below their (outstanding) ability in order not to stand out. They are easy to teach, are no trouble, and are often appreciated by the teacher. But it could also be that a girl has these symptoms because of a fight with her friend, or the teacher, not because she is gifted and frustrated. It has to be investigated carefully. Gifted boys who are frustrated at school are more likely to be disruptive, or even aggressive at school, playing the fool and disturbing the others. They may also be aggressive at home. The teacher is more likely to get in touch with the parents to discuss having the child assessed because of his behaviour. Then it comes out that he is gifted. This does not mean that every child who is disruptive is gifted. In the case of both girls and boys, parents sometimes look for a solution because the whole family is suffering at home.

Behavioural problems

Some parents end up in conflict with teachers because of their child's behaviour, for example if the child is frustrated or disruptive in class. This can be a result of special needs such as your child being gifted, and may require a classroom assistant, an enriched programme, or a move to a school for gifted children. A mother in canton Schwyz moved her son to a private school so that he could have more attention in smaller classes, and be pushed to do more math and reading where he excelled. The teachers also addressee behavioural issues:

> His two teachers in the private school (both English and German-speaking) know him very well, and more on a personal level. They know his strengths and weaknesses. His strength is that he is academically advanced: he speaks three languages, is strong in maths and is very gifted in art. His weakness is his behaviour. They said he can be very sweet at times, but is temperamental and can be aggressive when upset, and not listen. When this is the case, they give him a task (i.e. writing sentences, no break time, cleaning up, etc), and then he improves. If he doesn't behave, we take away privileges at home (i.e. the television, dessert, or he goes to bed extra early, etc.) This works as well. When he eventually matures, we will consider sending him back to public school; perhaps in a few years.

With regard to behavioural issues, a programme mentioned to me by several people for behavioural problems is *Triple P*, a *Positive Parenting Programme* (www.triplep.ch) for parents of children and teenagers. It aims to help you strengthen your relationship to your child, encourage good behaviour and deal constructively with bad behaviour. The website is in German but lists courses, reading materials and trainers for almost all cantons. Trainers may be teachers, doctors or psychotherapists. Teachers may also take action to help the child with a behavioural problem, and will want to report to the parents how things are going. Alli describes how her daughter F was acting up and distracting other children around the age of five until she was seven:

> Her teacher instituted a 'traffic light' system, with a picture of a traffic light on the wall. The first time F acted up she would move the marker from green to yellow, and the second time from yellow to red. Then every week she would send home a report of how F had been behaving each day, on a six-point scale from frowny-face to smiley-face with a crown. I don't think there was any punishment as such, the idea was more to make her aware of her actions and how they affected the class.

In some cases, teachers with big classes are already at their limits and cannot cope with an additional disruptive child. On several occasions I heard of a teacher who refused to have the child in their class. As mentioned already, some cantons will even pay part or all of the costs of a private school for children who cannot be catered for in the local public school. It is worth finding out if this is possible before you arrange to go private and pay for it yourself.

Organisational problems

It is possible that some gifted children will not get an adequate education if it depends on them developing age-appropriate organisational skills as required by their local school. The following account is my translation of a conversation in French in the online forum www.asep-suisse.org. A mother commented that nothing had been offered in lower-secondary school for her high potential, hyper-active child, who had real difficulties with organisation and precision in his school work. His attention deficit did not help matters. As a result, he was the weakest in his class and relatively demotivated.[187]

Another parent explained how she dealt with this. She colour coded her son's school books and notebooks by covering them with different colours of paper: red for German, blue for maths, yellow for French. She used plastified paper so that he could not be distracted by drawing on the cover. It then became automatic for him to take the right books to school. In the 8th (H10) class she started gathering together all his bits of paper from the whole week and filing them with him. Every day she looked at his diary and planned his tasks for the week for him. She wrote in *her* diary what he needed to do each day. She stayed at his side as he did his homework, especially when preparing for tests. Her son was reassured and his school results were better. She commented, "I have the impression that I am taking care of a child under 10, but it is good like this, and peaceful. He will certainly fly with his own wings some time. For the moment he needs his parents ... a bit wearing (*usant*), but it is like that." It can be helpful to make contact with organisations like ASEP to get tips from other parents and find out how they manage special challenges at school.

Advice and support groups for parents

www.begabungsfoerderung.ch (D) has a list of contact people at the schools departments of all German-speaking cantons.
www.hochbegabt.ch (D) has a list of mentors and psychologists.
www.ehk.ch (D) has a list of regional parents groups and contact people in German-speaking Switzerland.
www.asep-suisse.org (F, I) has a list of ASEP members who can be contacted in all French-speaking cantons and in Ticino. It also has an online forum and information about activities and courses for parents and their children.
www.mensa.ch (D, F, I, English)

Schools with special sports classes

It has been commented that although outstanding intellectual talent has only been addressed quite recently, Switzerland has been very proactive in organising special programmes within the regular school system for talented sports people. From lower-secondary level onwards there are programmes for them in different types of schools around the country. There are five special sport schools nationwide and a further 40 or more regular schools with special sports classes. These are organised to make it easier for talented pupils to attend school and practise their sport too. See the Swiss Olympic website for details.[188] (Some talented young musicians are allowed to join sports classes, because the structure frees them up to practice their music.)

An example of someone who benefited from special sports classes is Marco in canton Basel-Stadt. As I write, he is 23 years old and just about to start a bachelor's degree in Business Information Technology at the UASA where I work. At the age of 13 he had the number of points required to get into five-year gymnasium in canton Basel-Stadt. However, his teachers did not recommend it, saying he was not mature enough for it. He was also playing football and did not think the academic route would be compatible with professional sport. His parents encouraged him to do what he thought was right. He was a bit of a minimalist at his lower-secondary school, just making sure he got the required marks average to get into commercial school (WMS) for his upper-secondary education.

He attended a new sports class in his commercial school at the *Bildungszentrum kvBL* in Baselland, where it took four years to complete the three year course. Pupils had two full days of school per week plus three days a week with two hours of sport twice a day, between lessons. They were also given coaching by the school to manage the different aspects of their lives. He then went on to do the Vocational Maturity (or Baccalaureate). He did his internship working for the cantonal government, where he developed his IT skills working with controllers. He did this over two years instead of one year so that he could continue with his football. He went to work twice a day and did sports training twice a day too. He now works in the pharmaceutical industry, where he applies his IT knowledge combined with his communication skills to facilitate the communication among programming specialists during the migration of several programmes from different regions of the world into a central database. He will continue to work there part-time for the duration of his studies.

It is admirable how Switzerland has taken the initiative to make provision for children who are gifted in the realm of sports by providing special school programmes around the country. Something akin to this is now starting to be provided for children who are intellectually gifted, so that they can also take part in special programmes within the state sector instead of having to be sent to a school in the private sector.

Chapter 26 Appealing school decisions

The previous few chapters have flagged up some difficult issues parents may have to deal with. It is a real dilemma for all
parents to know when they and their children should try and
cope with a situation that is detrimental to their child's education or well-being, and when to take things further. It is particularly difficult to have to go through this process in a foreign
country and in a foreign language. This chapter explains what
is involved in formally appealing a school's decision, and suggests how you can get advice and support from experts regarding your canton. My aim is not to encourage you to go the legal
route, but rather to help you to have local knowledge so that you
know what your options are.

In researching this book, I spoke to several parents who had
experienced serious problems with a decision made by the school
and did not know that they had a right of appeal. They ended
up just taking their child out of local school and paying the fees
for a private school (local or international) instead. Interestingly,
the parents from other countries who had children with special
needs were much more aware of the appeals process. They were
well networked with Swiss parents' support groups and knew
someone who had gone through an appeals process in order to
get the level of provision for their child that they had a right to
from their municipality, as stipulated by cantonal law.

First steps

It is worth weighing up whether a school issue is a temporary
problem that can be borne for a while, or whether it may have
long-term implications for your child's education or well-being.
To summarise the discussion from the previous chapters, it is
important to talk to teachers, then the head teacher and the school
authorities about problem areas and to listen to their perspective.
In particular, if you wish your child to change class, or even leave
the school, you may need to work your way up through different
levels of authority. Head teachers usually make the decision about

whether the child may change class, while the school authorities may decide whether he or she may change school.[189] Barbara Graham-Siegenthaler warns that it is unusual for the authorities to allow a child to change school. You have to have really good reasons. The best argument is the well-being of your child. It may be that none of these steps help you find even a partial solution, and the school refuses to meet your request. Barbara recommends getting the school to tell *you* about the next step to take:

> Let the school know you are thinking about taking things further if you don't find a solution just by talking. For example, your child may have to repeat a year, or you as parents want your child to skip a class, or your child does not get enough special needs provision or language support, or you think your child needs to be transferred to another class. You can inquire at the next level, one higher than the teacher and ask, "What legal possibilities of appeal do I have?" Not in an adversarial tone, more that you are just trying to understand how things work, and find out what options you have.

The formal appeal process

It may be that the school tells you about your rights of appeal, but they may not. In the following outline of how to take things further, I follow the advice of *Hilfe in Schulalltag*, a Swiss book by Walter Noser, a social worker and expert on school matters.[190] Comments by Barbara are included too. Examples of issues addressed in the book include complaining about the way a teacher treats a child and insisting that school transport needs to be provided for children who would otherwise have to walk along a dangerous road.

As the topic is rather complicated, I have only written the legal terms (in bold) in English in the text below. There is a glossary in the table on page 235 showing the equivalent terms in German and French.

- Write a formal letter to the school authorities stating your request and the steps you have already taken. Request a formal reply.

- In return the school authorities should send you a **decree** or **instruction**, which, depending on the canton, may contain the following elements: a **decision** (for example a refusal of your request); an **explanation** for the decision made; **the legal basis** for it; and notification of your **right of appeal**. Barbara finds it helpful that the authorities provide reasons, which give a factual basis for the discussion.

- If the authorities write a normal letter back, without the above details, you can insist on a formal **decree or instruction that you can appeal**. It should contain information as to whom you should address your **appeal** and within what time period, if you are not satisfied with the decision. Barbara says they may not write on it "This is a decree". However, if it is a decision by the authorities as to what will happen to your child, it is one. These letters often do not include your right of appeal, or it is written in small print. She suggests asking them, "Is this a decree that I can appeal?"

If you decide on further action, the next step is to make the appeal. You should write a letter to the higher authority named in the formal instruction. Barbara comments that the appeal normally has to be made in the local official language. However, some places accept appeals in other national languages or English. Explain what decision you are contesting, and state what you want, giving all reasons. It might be helpful to explain why the matter is urgent, so that it is dealt with quickly. It does not cost anything to make an appeal, unless you have a lawyer.

It is important to know that not many people have a decree reversed. Barbara is also a member of a school appeals board and explains why:

> Generally speaking, we have to respect the decisions made by those who have been authorised to make them. The **appeals board** are further away from the scene of action, and we should not reverse a **judgment call** made by those who are closer, unless we have very good reasons. Good reasons might be procedural mistakes, for example in a psychological assessment, that have to be put right. I would guess that around one in ten decrees are reversed. With regard to appeals to have a child change class or school, if the school has already refused, the authorities seldom agree to this.

English	German	French
A decree	Eine Verfügung	Une décision
An instruction	Eine Anordnung	Une injunction (une instruction)
The explanation	Die Begründung	La motivation (la justification)
The legal basis	Die rechtliche Grundlage	La base légale
The right of appeal	Die Rechtsmittelbelehrung	L'indication (f) des voies de droit
A decree that you can appeal	Eine Beschwerdefähige Verfügung	Une décision susceptible de recours
An appeal	Ein Rekurs (Beschwerde, Einsprache)	Un recours
The appeals board	Die Rekurskommission	La commission de recours
A judgment call (decision based on the person's judgment)	Eine Ermessensentscheid	Une décision par appréciation

Table 8   Legal terms in French and German

Getting advice with legal matters

It can be difficult to understand who is actually in charge of matters like this in your municipality, and therefore difficult to know exactly who to write to next if the school refuses your request for action. You may also be concerned about how to word the letter. One option is to obtain advice from a lawyer in your canton, who may charge you at an hourly rate of around 180 to 300 francs. Barbara

235

comments that the court in your canton may offer legal aid, possibly free of charge. You may have taken out a legal insurance policy. These are helpful for issues related to property rental or conflict with neighbours. However, I have been told that they do not usually cover school issues, so it is important to check this out.

You can also obtain legal advice and legal aid for all cantons of Switzerland at a reasonable price from a publishing company. The *Beobachter* is a German language Swiss magazine that offers its subscribers a self-service database (in German only), as well as free email and telephone tips and advice (which could be given in English) on legal matters.[191] Subscriptions cost 89 francs per year. You may be unable to read the bimonthly magazine in German, but it could be worth subscribing just to have access to the advice.

Areas of expertise offered are work, home, consumer issues, family matters, social insurance, the authorities, money matters and, lastly, child rearing and social matters. This last category is called *Erziehung und Soziales* in German. Advice is given regarding school matters for schooling all over the country. The website contains sample formal letters in German to show

subscribers how to formulate a letter to the school authorities. A *Beobachter* advisor can tell you to whom you should write an official letter in your canton, and how to take things further if necessary. They are used to advising German speakers living all over Switzerland, so can help you with issues related to all cantons. I spoke to Toni Wirz, the head of the *Beobachter* advice centre and he confirmed that it is likely that their advisors will be able to conduct a conversation with callers in English. They do not, however, officially offer their services in English.

Subscribers may also have a first consultation with a local lawyer recommended by the *Beobachter*, at a reduced price. The *Beobachter* also offers a subscription that includes personal legal protection insurance, *Beobachter Assistance*, in cooperation with *Coop Rechtsschutz*, for 133 francs. This needs to be taken out at least three months before it is first used. It provides legal assistance in the form of a first telephone consultation with the *Beobachter*, followed by the services of a recommended mediator, lawyer or expert up to the value of 500 francs. If the problem is still not resolved, the *Coop* insurance company assesses further needs. Assistance up to the value of 5000 francs may then be paid for. This offer is subject to change, and details should be checked on the *Beobachter* website.

I spoke to Veronika Imthurn,[192] a lawyer in canton Zurich who is recommended by the *Beobachter*. She specialises in legal issues related to children and young people. I wanted to know at what point she recommends involving a lawyer in a school case. She recommends that parents should first try to arrange a meeting with the authorities to discuss their problem before writing a formal letter. If they find a solution, the matter is resolved. If not, a lawyer could then be consulted. Veronika Imthurn finds it important that the lawyer first talks informally to the authorities to try to solve the problem.

If you end up meeting the authorities with your lawyer, they may also have a lawyer present, so be prepared for this. In the experience of Veronika Imthurn, the problem is often resolved at this stage. If you do not reach agreement, it is time to decide whether to write the formal letter. If you have a lawyer, he or she can help make sure the most important points are mentioned in it.

Veronika Imthurn also reminds parents of the cost issue:

> The cost of all services should be discussed with both your legal insurance provider and your lawyer before entering into the client relationship, and before each further step. It should be kept in mind that if the matter goes to court, and you lose the case, you will have to pay your share of the costs, even if you have legal insurance.

I sincerely hope you will not find yourself in the situation where you have to appeal a school decision. However, as I said at the beginning of the chapter, it is important that you know what your options are. Appeals are a last resort if all else fails. A successful appeal could mean that your child can continue his or her education in the local school system rather than having to change over to a private school.

Section seven

Cantonal variations

Chapter 27   Cantonal tables

The following cantonal tables provide you with some general information about the public school system in your canton. However, the school system is undergoing fast-paced change in many cantons and there may also be differences from one municipality to another. It is important that you check the details with your local municipality or school.[193]

Three cantons (BS, GE, NE) have started using the HarmoS numbering system (see pages 14 and 15 for explanation about HarmoS), and I use this numbering system too for these three cantons in the tables below and give the old numbering system in brackets. For the other cantons, I only refer to the old numbering system. (Please see page 253 for a conversion table of the old and new numbering systems).

Table 9   Kindergarten and primary school by canton

Canton[194] (old and new structure)[195]	Name for kindergarten	Is kindergarten compulsory? (attendance and offer)[196]	Name for primary school 1st – 6th class (H3 –H8)
AG old	Kindergarten	a.c. no o.c. 1 yr	Primarschule only 1st to 5th class
AG new	Kindergarten	a.c. 2 yrs o.c. 2 yrs (from 2013)	Primarschule 1st to 6th class (from 2014)
AI	Kindergarten	a.c. 1 yr o.c. 2 yrs	Primarschule 1st to 6th class
AR	Kindergarten	a.c. 1 yr o.c. 2 yrs	Primarschule 1st to 6th class
BE (F)	Ecole enfantine	a.c. no o.c. 1 yr	Cycle / classes primaire 1st to 6th class
BE (D)	Kindergarten	a.c. no o.c. 1 yr	Primarschule 1st to 6th class
BL old	Kindergarten	-	Primarschule only 1st to 5th class
BL new	Kindergarten	a.c. 2 yrs o.c. 2 yrs	Primarschule 1st to 6th class
BS old	Kindergarten	-	See chapter 28
BS new	Primarstufe: (Kindergarten)	a.c. 2 yrs o.c. 2 yrs	Primarstufe: (Primarschule) 3rd to 8th year (*Pre-HarmoS: 1st to 6th class*)
FR (F)	Ecole enfantine	a.c. no o.c. 1 yr	Ecole primaire 1st to 6th class
FR (D)	Kindergarten	from 2013: a.c. 2 yrs o.c. 2 yrs	Primarschule 1st to 6th class
GE	Ecole primaire : Cycle élémentaire 1P & 2P	a.c. 2 yrs o.c. 2 yrs	Ecole primaire: Cycle moyen 3P to 8P (*Pre-HarmoS 1st to 6th class*)
GL	Kindergarten	a.c. 2 yrs o.c. 2 yrs	Primarschule 1st to 6th class

GR	Kindergarten	a.c. no o.c. 1 yr	Primarschule 1st to 6th class
JU	Ecole enfantine 1E & 2E	a.c. no o.c. 2 yrs	Ecole primaire 1st to 6th class
LU	Kindergarten	a.c. 1 yr o.c. 1 yr From 2016: o.c. 2 yrs	Primarschule 1st to 6th class
NE	(Ecole enfantine) Cycle 1: degrés 1-2H	a.c. 2 yrs o.c. 2 yrs	Ecole primaire : Cycle 1: degrés 3-4H Cycle 2: degrés 5-7H Orientation: 8H (in planning)[197] (Pre-HarmoS 1st to 6th class)
NW	Kindergarten	a.c. 1 yr o.c. 2 yrs	Primarschule 1st to 6th class
OW	Kindergarten	a.c. 1 yr o.c. 1 yr	Primarschule 1st to 6th class
SG	Kindergarten	a.c. 2 yrs o.c. 2 yrs	Primarschule 1st to 6th class
SH	Kindergarten	a.c. 2 yrs o.c. 2 yrs	Primarschule 1st to 6th class
SO	Kindergarten	a.c. no o.c. 2 yrs	Primarschule[198] 1st to 6th class
SZ	Kindergarten	a.c. 1 yr o.c. 1 yr	Primarschule 1st to 6th class
TG	Kindergarten	a.c. 2 yrs o.c. 2 yrs	Primarschule 1st to 6th class
TI	Scuola dell'infanzia 1-3 years	a.c. no o.c. 3 yrs	Scuola elementare only 1st to 5th class
UR	Kindergarten	a.c. no o.c. 1 yr	Primarschule 1st to 6th class
VD	Cycle initial CIN1 & CIN2 (Ecole enfantine)	a.c. no, o.c. 2 yrs from 2013 a.c. & o.c. 2 yrs	Cycle primaire: CYP1 (1st-2nd) CYP2 (3rd-4th) CYT (5th-6th)
VS (F)	Ecole enfantine	a.c. no o.c. no	Ecole primaire 1st to 6th class
VS (D)	Kindergarten		Primarschule 1st to 6th class
ZG	Kindergarten	a.c. 1 yr o.c. 1 yr	Primarschule 1st to 6th class
ZH	Kindergarten	a.c. 2 yrs o.c. 2 yrs	Primarschule 1st to 6th class

Table 10   Date school year begins by canton

Canton	In 2012	In 2013	In 2014
AG	13 August	12 August	11 August
AI	13 August	19 August	11 August
AR	13 August	12 August	11 August
BE (D)	13 August	12 August	11 August
BE (F)	20 August	20 August	18 August
BL	13 August	12 August	18 August
BS	13 August	12 August	18 August
FR compulsory school	20/23 August	19/22 August	25/28 August
FR upper-sec. school	3 September	2 September	1 September
GE	27 August	26 August	25 August
GL	13 August	12 August	11 August
GR	20 August	19 August	18 August
JU	20 August	19 August	18 August
LU	20 August	19 August	18 August
NE	20 August	19 August	18 August
NW upper-sec. school	27 August	26 August	25 August
NW compulsory school	27 August	19 August	18 August
OW Engelberg	20 August	12 August	11 August
OW others	20 August	19 August	18 August
SG	13 August	12 August	11 August
SH	13 August	12 August	11 August
SO	13 August	12 August	11 August
SZ	13 August	12 August	11 August
TG	13 August	12 August	11 August
TI	3 September	2 September	1 September
UR	20 August	19 August	18 August
VD	27 August	28 August	25 August
VS (F)	20 August	19 August	18 August
VS (D)	16 August	19 August	18 August
ZG	20 August	19 August	18 August
ZH	20 August	19 August	18 August

Table 11   Minimum age to start kindergarten in a particular year by canton

Most cantons allow a degree of flexibility, and children born a few months before or after the official date can start kindergarten at a time that suits their stage of development. In some cantons, kindergarten is not compulsory, and in others it is compulsory for one year only (see Table 9, page 240).

Canton	Starts KG in 2012 Birthdate by	Starts KG in 2013 Birthdate by	Starts KG in 2014 Birthdate by
AG	30 April 2008	Municipalities will shift date from 30 April to 31 July by 2018	
AI	1 April 2008	1 April 2009	1 April 2010
AR	30 April 2008	30 April 2009	30 April 2010
BE	30 April 2008	31 May 2009	30 June 2010
BL	15 May 2008	31 May 2009	15 June 2010
BS	31 May 2008	15 June 2009	30 June 2010
FR 1 yr KG	30 April 2007	-	-
FR 2 yrs KG	31 July 2008	31 July 2009	31 July 2010
GE	30 Sept 2008	30 Sept 2009	30 Sept 2010
GL	31 July 2008	31 July 2009	31 July 2010
GR	31 Dec 2007	31 Dec 2008	31 Dec 2009
JU	1 June 2008	1 June 2009	1 June 2010
LU	31 Oct 2007[199]	31 Oct 2008	31 Oct 2009
NE	31 Aug 2008	31 Aug 2009	31 Aug 2010
NW	30 June 2008	30 June 2009	30 June 2010
OW	30 June 2008	30 June 2009	30 June 2010
SG	31 July 2008	31 July 2009	31 July 2010
SH	30 April 2008	31 May 2009	30 June 2010
SO	31 May 2008	30 June 2009	31 July 2010
SZ	31 July 2008	31 July 2009	31 July 2010
TG	31 July 2008	31 July 2009	31 July 2010
TI	31 Dec 2009	31 Dec 2010	31 Dec 2011
UR	31 July 2008	31 July 2009	31 July 2010
VD	30 June 2008	31 July 2009	31 July 2010
VS	30 Sept 2008	30 Sept 2009	30 Sept 2010
ZG	31 May 2007	31 May 2008	31 May 2009
ZH	30 April 2008	30 April 2009	15 May 2010

Table 12   Minimum age to start school in a particular year by canton

Most cantons allow a degree of flexibility and children may start school one year earlier or later if it suits their stage of development. This may be decided in consultation with the kindergarten teacher and the school psychological services. In several German-speaking cantons there is also a *Basisstufe* or *Grundstufe* as an alternative to kindergarten and the first one or two years of primary school. There is then no formal changeover from kindergarten to school.

Canton	Starts school in 2012 Birthdate by	Starts school in 2013 Birthdate by	Starts school in 2014 Birthdate by
AG	30 April 2006	30 April 2007	30 April 2008
AI	1 April 2006	1 April 2007	1 April 2008
AR	30 April 2006	30 April 2007	30 April 2008
BE	30 April 2006	30 April 2007	30 April 2008
BL	30 April 2006	30 April 2007	15 May 2008
BS	30 April 2006	15 May 2007	31 May 2008
FR 1 yr KG	30 April 2006	30 April 2007	30 April 2008
FR 2 yrs KG	31 July 2006	30 July 2007	31 July 2008
GE	30 Sept 2006	30 Sept 2007	30 Sept 2008
GL	31 July 2006	31 July 2007	31 July 2008
GR	31 Dec 2005	31 Dec 2006	31 Dec 2007
JU	1 June 2006	1 June 2007	1 June 2008
LU	31 Oct 2006	31 Oct 2007	31 Oct 2008
NE	31 Aug 2006	31 Aug 2007	31 Aug 2008
NW	30 June 2006	30 June 2007	30 June 2008
OW	30 June 2006	30 June 2007	30 June 2008
SG	31 July 2006	31 July 2007	31 July 2008
SH	30 April 2006	30 April 2007	30 April 2008
SO	30 April 2006	30 April 2007	31 May 2008
SZ	31 July 2006	31 July 2007	31 July 2008
TG	31 July 2006	31 July 2007	31 July 2008
TI	31 Dec 2006	31 Dec 2007	31 Dec 2008
UR	31 July 2006	31 July 2007	31 July 2008
VD	30 June 2006	30 June 2007	30 June 2008
VS	30 Sept 2006	30 Sept 2007	30 Sept 2008
ZG	31 May 2006[200]	31 May 2007	31 May 2007
ZH	30 April 2006	30 April 2007	30 April 2008

Table 13   Cantons changing the minimum age to start kindergarten

Can-ton	Starts in 2012 Birthdate by	Starts KG in 2013 Birthdate by	Starts KG in 2014 Birthdate by	Starts KG in 2015 Birthdate by	Change complete
AG	30 April 2008	Municipalities will shift date from 30 April to 31 July by 2018			
BE	30 April 2008	31 May 2009	30 June 2010	31 July 2011	By 2015: 31 July
BL	15 May 2008	31 May 2009	15 June 2010	30 June 2011	By 2017: 31 July
BS	31 May 2008	15 June 2009	30 June 2010	15 July 2011	By 2016: 31 July
SH	30 April 2008	31 May 2009	30 June 2010	31 July 2011	By 2015: 31 July
SO	31 May 2008	30 June 2009	31 July 2010	31 July 2011	By 2014: 31 July
ZH	30 April 2008	30 April 2009	15 May 2010	31 May 2011	By 2019: 31 July

Table 14   Cantons changing the minimum age to start school

Can-ton	Starts in 2012 Birthdate by	Starts in 2013 Birthdate by	Starts in 2014 Birthdate by	Starts in 2015 Birthdate by	Starts in 2016 Birthdate by
AG	30 April 2006	30 April 2007	30 April 2008	Municipalities will shift date from 30 April to 31 July	
BE	30 April 2006	30 April 2007	30 April 2008	31 May 2009	30 June 2010
BL	30 April 2006	30 April 2007	15 May 2008	31 May 2009	15 June 2010
BS	30 April 2006	15 May 2007	31 May 2008	15 June 2009	30 June 2010
SH	30 April 2006	30 April 2007	30 April 2008	31 May 2009	30 June 2010
SO	30 April 2006	30 April 2007	31 May 2008	30 June 2009	31 July 2010
ZH	30 April 2006	30 April 2007	30 April 2008	30 April 2009	15 May 2010

Table 15 Lower-secondary school names and types by canton[201]

Canton	Name for lower-secondary school 7th - 9th class (H9-H11)	Lower-secondary types of schools, classes or levels (from most to least demanding)
AG	Sekundarstufe I[202] 6th to 9th class	Bezirksschule Sekundarschule Realschule
AG new	Sekundarstufe I 7th to 9th class from 2015	Bezirksschule Sekundarschule Realschule
AI	Sekundarstufe I 7th to 9th class	(Gymnasium from 9th class) Sekundarschule Realschule or Niveau h (hoch) Niveau m (mittel) Niveau e (einfach)
AR	Sekundarstufe I 7th to 9th class	(Gymnasium from 9th class) Home rooms of mixed levels and ages or Stammklasse E (erhöhte Anforderungen) Stammklasse G (grundlegende Anforderungen) (with Niveaus e, m and g)
BE (D)	Sekundarstufe I 7th to 9th class	(Gymnasium from 9th class) Sekundarschule Real- und Sekundarschule Realschule (with Niveaus e and g)
BE (F)	Cycle secondaire I 7th to 9th class	Section préparant aux écoles de maturité (p) Section moderne (m) Section générale (g)
BL old	Sekundarschule 6th to 9th class	Niveau P: progymnasial Niveau E: erweitert Niveau A: allgemein
BL new	Sekundarschule 7th to 9th class	P Zug (progymnasial) E Zug (erweitert) A Zug (allgemein)
BS old	Please see chapter 28.	
BS new	Sekundarschule 9th to 11th year (*Pre-HarmoS 7th to 9th class*)	P Zug (progymnasial) E Zug (erweitert) A Zug (allgemein)

Canton	Name for lower-secondary school 7th - 9th class (H9 - H11)	Lower-secondary types of schools, classes or levels (from most to least demanding)
FR (F)	Cycle d'orientation 7th to 9th class	Classes pré-gymnasiales (PG) Classes générales (G) Classes à exigences de base (EB)
FR (D)	Orientierungsschule 7th to 9th class	A: Pro-gymnasiale Abteilung B: Sekundarabteilung C: Realabteilung
GE	Cycle d'orientation 9CO – 11CO (Pre-HarmoS 7th to 9th class)	R 3 (exigences élevées) R 2 (exigences moyennes) R 1 (exigences de base)
GL	Sekundarstufe I 7th to 9th class	(Gymnasium from 7th class) Sekundarschule Realschule Oberschule or Mixed level home rooms
GR	Sekundarstufe I 7th to 9th class	(Gymnasium from 7th class) Sekundarschule Realschule
JU	Ecole secondaire 7th to 9th class	Mixed level home rooms: - Cours communs - Cours à option - Cours à niveaux
LU	Sekundarstufe I 7th to 9th class	(Gymnasium from 7th class) Niveau A & B: Sekundarschule Niveau C: Realschule Niveau D: Werkschule
NE	(Ecole secondaire) Orientation: 8H[203] Cycle 3: degrés 9-11H (Pre-HarmoS 6th to 9th class)	Section de maturités Section moderne Section pré-professionnelle
NW	Sekundarstufe I 7th to 9th class	(Gymnasium from 7th class) Niveau A Niveau B Werkschule
OW	Sekundarstufe I 7th to 9th class	(Gymnasium from 7th class) Niveau A Niveau B
SG	Sekundarstufe I 7th to 9th class	(Gymnasium from 7th class) Kooperative Sekundarschule/ Realschule (with Niveaus e, m, g)

Canton	Name for lower-secondary school (H9 - H11)	Lower-secondary types of schools, classes or levels (from most to least demanding)
SH	Sekundarstufe I 7th to 9th class	(Gymnasium from 9th class) Sekundarschule Realschule
SO	Sekundarstufe I 7th to 9th class	(Gymnasium from 6th / 7th class) Sek P (Progymnasial) Sek E (Erweiterte Anforderungen) Sek B (Basisanforderungen) Sek K (Kleinklasse)
SZ	Sekundarstufe I 7th to 9th class	(Gymnasium from 9th class) Sekundarschule or Stammklasse A Realschule or Stammklasse B Werkschule or Stammklasse C
TG	Sekundarstufe I 7th to 9th class	(Gymnasium from 9th class) Stammklasse E (erweiterte Anforderungen) Stammklasse G (grundlegende Anforderungen) (with Niveaus e, m, g)
TI	Scuola media 6th to 9th class	Mixed level home rooms 6th-7th Ciclo di osservazione 8th-9th Ciclo di orientamento: level groups for maths and German.
UR	Sekundarstufe I 7th to 9th class	(Gymnasium from 7th class) Sekundarschule Realschule Werkschule
VD	Degré secondaire I Degrés 7 à 9	VSB (baccalauréat) VSG (générale) VSO (options)
VD (from 2013)	Degré secondaire I Degrés 7 à 9	2 levels: Voie prégymnasiale Voie générale
VS (F)	Cycle d'orientation 7th to 9th class	(Gymnasium from 9th class) Niveau I Niveau II
VS (D)	Orientierungsklasse 7th to 9th class	(Gymnasium from 9th class) Niveau I Niveau II
ZG	Sekundarstufe I 7th to 9th class	(Gymnasium from 7th class) Sekundarschule Realschule Werkschule
ZH	Sekundarstufe I 7th to 9th class	(Gymnasium from 7th class) Abteilung A Abteilung B (Abteilung C)

Table 16   Basis of selection for lower-secondary school path by canton[204]

Can-ton	Teacher's qualitative judgment[205]	Classwork/ marks/ canton-wide tests)[206]	Parents' or pupil's opinion	External exam (option)[207]
AG	Yes	(Yes)[208]	No	Yes
AI	Yes	(Yes)	No	No
AR	Yes	Yes	No	No
BE (D)	Yes	Yes	Yes	Yes from 2013[209]
BE (F)	Yes	Yes	Yes	No
BL old	Yes	Yes	No	Yes
BL new	Not yet known[210]			
BS old	Yes	Yes	No	Yes
BS new	Not yet known[211]			
FR	Yes	Yes	Yes	No
GE	No	Yes	No	No
GL	Yes	(Yes)	No	Yes
GR	Yes	Yes	No	Yes
JU	No	Yes	Yes	No
LU	Yes	Yes	Yes	No
NE	Yes	Yes	No	No
NW	Yes	Yes	No	No
OW	Yes	Yes	No	No
SG	Yes	Yes	No	No
SH	Yes	Yes	No	No
SO	No	Yes	Yes	No
SZ	Yes	Yes	No	No
TG	Yes	Yes	No	No
TI	No selection at this stage			
UR	Yes	Yes	Yes	No
VD	Yes	Yes	No	No
VS	Yes	Yes	Yes	No
ZG	Yes	Yes	Yes	Yes
ZH	Yes	Yes	Yes	Yes

Table 17 Names and years of gymnasium by canton

Where gymnasium starts in the 10th year, its duration depends on the level of teaching in the 9th year. If this was in a stream with a gymnasium-level standard, gymnasium may only take three years. Otherwise it will take four years. Pupils who change to gymnasium from another path may have to repeat a year.

Canton	Names used for gymnasium	Years of gymnasium
AG	Gymnasium / Kantonsschule (Kanti)	$10^{th} - 13^{th}$
AI	Untergymnasium / Gymnasium	7th, 8th or 9th - 12th
AR	Gymnasium / Kantonsschule (Kanti)	$9^{th} - 12^{th}$, $10^{th} - 13^{th}$
BE (D)	Gymnasium	$9^{th} - 12^{th}$, $10^{th} - 13^{th}$
BE (F)	Gymnase	$10^{th} - 13^{th}$
BL old	Gymnasium	$10^{th} - 13^{th 212}$
BL new	Gymnasium	$10^{th} - 13^{th}$
BS old	Gymnasium	$10^{th} - 14^{th} / 15^{th}$ year (*pre-HarmoS:* $8^{th} - 12^{th} / 13^{th}$ *class*)
BS new	Gymnasium	$12^{th} - 15^{th}$, $13^{th} - 16^{th}$ year (*pre-HarmoS:* $10^{th} - 13^{th}$, $11^{th} - 14^{th}$ *class*)
FR (F)	Collège	$10^{th} - 13^{th}$
FR (D)	Gymnasium / Kollegium / Collège	
GE	Collège	$12^{th} - 15^{th}$ (*pre-HarmoS:* $10^{th} - 13^{th}$)
GL	Gymnasium / Kantonsschule (Kanti)	7th or $9^{th} - 12^{th}$
GR	Untergymnasium / Gymnasium	7th or $9^{th} - 12^{th}$, $10^{th} - 13^{th}$
JU	Lycée / Ecole de maturité	$10^{th} - 12^{th}$

Canton	Names used for gymnasium	Years of gymnasium
LU	Gymnasium / Kantonsschule (Kanti)	7th or 9th – 12th, 10th – 13th
NE	Gymnase / Lycée	12th – 14th (pre-HarmoS:10th – 12th)
NW	Untergymnasium / Gymnasium / Kollegium	7th – 12th, 10th – 13th
OW	Untergymnasium / Gymnasium / Kantonsschule (Kanti)	7th or 9th – 12th, 10th - 13th
SG	Untergymnasium / Gymnasium / Kantonsschule (Kanti)	7th or 9th – 12th, 10th – 13th
SH	Gymnasium / Kantonsschule (Kanti)	9th – 12th, 10th – 13th
SO	Untergymnasium / Gymnasium / Kantonsschule (Kanti)	6th, 7th or 9th – 12th, 10th – 13th
SZ	Gymnasium / Kantonsschule (Kanti)	9th – 12th, 10th – 13th
TG	Gymnasium / Kantonsschule (Kanti)	9th – 12th, 10th – 13th
TI	Liceo	10th – 13th
UR	Untergymnasium / Gymnasium / Kollegium (Kollegi)	7th or 9th – 12th, 10th – 13th
VD	Gymnase	10th – 12th
VS (F)	Lycée / collège	9th – 13th, 10th – 14th
VS (D)	Kollegium (Kollegi)	9th – 13th, 10th – 14th
ZG	Untergymnasium / Gymnasium / Kantonsschule (Kanti)	7th or 9th – 12th, 10th – 13th
ZH	Langzeitgymnasium / Gymnasium / Kantonsschule (Kanti)	7th or 9th – 12th, 10th – 13th

Table 18 Entry requirements for gymnasium by canton[213]

Note: Conditions of entry to specialised upper-secondary schools, commercial schools and IT schools may be similar to those given for gymnasium. Please check the details with your local school.

Canton	Based on teacher's judgment	Class-work /marks	Based on entrance exam	Entrance exam option[214]
AG	No	Yes and final exam	No	Yes
AI 7th yr	Yes	(Yes)[215]	No	No
AI 9th yr	No	No	Yes	-
AR	Yes	(Yes)	Yes	-
BE (D)	Yes	(Yes)	No	Yes
BE (F)	Yes	(Yes)	No	Yes
BL old	No	Yes	No	No
BL new	Not yet known[216]			
BS old	Yes	(Yes)	No	Yes
BS new	Not yet known[217]			
FR (D)	Yes	(Yes)	No	Yes
FR (F)	Yes	(Yes)		
GE	No	Yes	No	No
GL	No	Yes	Yes	-
GR	No	Yes	Yes	Yes
JU	No	Yes	No	No
LU	Yes	(Yes)	No	No
NE	No	Yes	No	No
NW	Yes	(Yes)	No	No
OW	Yes	(Yes)	No	No
SG	No	No	Yes	-
SH	No	No	Yes	-
SO	Yes	(Yes)	Yes	-
SO	Yes	(Yes)	No	Yes
SZ	Yes	(Yes)	Yes	-
TG	Yes	(Yes)	Yes	-
TI	No	Yes	No	Yes
UR	Yes	(Yes)	No	No
VD		Yes (Certif. d'études)	No	Yes
VS (D)	No	Yes	No	Yes
VS (F)	No	Yes	No	Yes
ZG	Yes	(Yes)	No	No
ZG	No	Yes	No	Yes
ZH	No	Yes	Yes	-

Chapter 28   Structural changes in various cantons

A. Change in numbering of school years

An important change in the school system in the cantons of Basel-Stadt, Geneva and Neuchâtel is the new HarmoS way of numbering the years of schooling. Kindergarten is now counted as the first and second classes of primary school instead of just being 'pre-school'. I have included this new numbering in brackets throughout this book (e.g. *H3* to describe the old *1ˢᵗ class*), as an orientation guide to parents in these cantons. The new numbering will be introduced in canton Vaud from 2013.

The new numbering is easy enough to explain, but more difficult to use, as it is rather like a country changing its currency from 'old money' to 'new money'. The conversion table below shows how this works.

What parents are still likely to say (*using Pre-HarmoS numbering*)	Official HarmoS numbering now used in BS, GE and NE
1ˢᵗ and 2ⁿᵈ kindergarten	1ˢᵗ and 2ⁿᵈ year
1ˢᵗ to 6ᵗʰ class	3ʳᵈ to 8ᵗʰ year
7ᵗʰ to 9ᵗʰ class	9ᵗʰ to 11ᵗʰ year
10ᵗʰ to 13ᵗʰ class	12ᵗʰ to 15ᵗʰ year

Table 19   Pre-HarmoS and the official HarmoS numbering of school years

B. Change in number of years of primary and lower-secondary school

In accordance with HarmoS, the cantons of Baselland, Basel-Stadt and Aargau are changing over to six years of primary school and three years of lower-secondary school. As a result, Ticino will be the only remaining canton to continue to have five years of primary school and four years of lower-secondary school.

1. Canton Basel-Stadt

In accordance with HarmoS, Basel-Stadt is undergoing the most radical change of all cantons. It is phasing out one of its school stages, namely the three-year-long *Orientierungsschule* (OS), in order to have the same structure as most cantons in Switzerland. Primary school will last six years instead of four and lower-secondary school will last three years instead of two. OS teachers will change over to one of the other two school stages as part of the restructuring. The two structures are explained below. Diagrams of the old and new structures can be found on the Basel-Stadt schools website.[218]

Old structure

The old structure applies to pupils born up to 30 April 2002. They were in kindergarten for 2 years (H1-2) and primary school for 4 years in the 1st to 4th class (H3-6). The *Orientierungsschule* lasts for 3 years, from the 5th to 7th class, which is now officially known as the 7th to 9th year. Pupils are then streamed into either gymnasium for the 8th to 12th or 13th class (now officially the 10th to 14th or 15th year)[219] or the Weiterbildungsschule (WBS) for the 8th to 9th class (officially the 10th to 11th year). The WBS is followed by post-compulsory education such as an apprenticeship or a specialised upper-secondary school.

Organisation of levels within the old structure:

Orientierungsschule (OS): Pupils are in mixed level classes. From the second half of the 6th class (officially the 8th year), pupils are divided into levels for German, maths and French only.

Weiterbildungsschule (WBS): There are two class types, the higher E Zug and the basic A Zug. Pupils in the A Zug who perform well will possibly be able to move up to the E Zug after the 1st semester.[220] Pupils in the E Zug who perform well can possibly move up to gymnasium after one year,[221] or after two years by doing an additional bridge year, the *ÜK* or *Übergangsklasse*.

New structure

In the new structure, pupils born after 30 April 2002 are in kindergarten for two years and primary school for six years. These eight years are now officially known as the 1st to 8th year, rather than the 1st and 2nd kindergarten and the 1st to 6th class. There is a 7th year (5th class) of primary school for the first time in 2013 and an 8th year (6th class) for the first time in 2014. These pupils will change over to *Sekundarschule* in 2015, where they will stay for three years, from the 9th to 11th year (7th to 9th class). This is followed by post-compulsory education from the 12th year (10th class). This may be gymnasium, an apprenticeship or a specialised upper-secondary school.

2. Canton Baselland

In canton Baselland there will be six years of primary school instead of five. (Baselland does not use the new HarmoS numbering system.)

Old structure

In the old structure, pupils born before 30 April 2003 were in kindergarten for two years (H1-2) and are in primary school for five years in the 1st to 5th classes (H3-7). They are in *Sekundarschule* for four years, for the 6th to 9th classes (H8-11). This is followed by post-compulsory education from the 10th class (H12). This may be gymnasium, an apprenticeship or a specialised upper-secondary school.

New structure

In the new structure, pupils born after 30 April 2003 will be in kindergarten for 2 years (H1-2) and primary school for six years in the 1st to 6th class (H3-8). There will be a 6th class of primary school for the first time in 2015. These pupils will change over to *Sekundarschule* in 2016, where they will stay for three years, from the 7th to 9th class (H9-11). This is followed by post-compulsory education from the 10th class (H12). This may be gymnasium, an apprenticeship or a specialised upper-secondary school.

3. Canton Aargau (use if the vote is accepted)

Canton Aargau is planning a similar change to canton Baselland, as there will be six years of primary school instead of five. Canton Aargau does not use the new HarmoS terminology.

Old structure

Pupils born before 30 April 2002 were in kindergarten for two years (H1-2) and are in primary school for five years in the 1st to 5th classes (H3-7). They will be in the *Sekundarstufe* for four years, for the 6th to 9th classes (H8-11). This is followed by post-compulsory education from the 10th class (H12). This may be gymnasium, an apprenticeship or a specialised upper-secondary school.

New structure

Pupils born after 30 April 2002 will be in kindergarten for 2 years (H1-2) and should be in primary school for six years in the 1st to 6th class (H3-8). The first 6th class of primary school will start in 2014. These pupils will change over to the *Sekundarstufe* in 2015, where they will stay for three years, from the 7th to 9th class (H9-11). This is followed by post-compulsory education from the 10th class (H12). This may be gymnasium, an apprenticeship or a specialised upper-secondary school.

Section eight

Appendices

Appendix 1   Contact details of the 26 Cantonal Departments of Education.

The information in table 20 below is derived from a list on the website of the Conference of Cantonal Directors of Education (referred to in English as the EDK, www.edk.ch). It provides the official initials used for each canton, followed by the name of the canton as it is known in the cantonal language(s). The official name of the Cantonal Department of Education is given in the local language(s), followed by the telephone number. You can phone this number to ask for the telephone number of the local school or the school authorities where you live or plan to live. The country code for Switzerland is + 41. The EDK also provides links to the web sites of these 26 member cantons. You can find it by googling 'list of EDK members'.

Table 20   Departments of education by canton

Full name of canton	Cantonal Department of Education	Telephone number
AG	Aargau (D)	Departement Bildung, Kultur und Sport des Kantons Aargau	(0)62 835 20 01
AI	Appenzell Innerrhoden (D)	Erziehungsdepartement des Kantons Appenzell Innerrhoden	(0)71 788 93 61
AR	Appenzell Ausserrhoden (D)	Departement Bildung des Kantons Appenzell Ausserrhoden	(0)71 353 68 20
BL	Basel-Landschaft (D)	Bildungs-, Kultur- und Sportdirektion des Kantons Basel-Landschaft	(0)61 552 51 11
BS	Basel-Stadt (D)	Erziehungsdepartement des Kantons Basel-Stadt	(0)61 267 84 40
BE	Bern (D), Berne (F)	Erziehungsdirektion des Kantons Bern (D), Direction de l'instruction publique du canton de Berne (F)	(0)31 633 85 11
FR	Fribourg (F) Freiburg (D)	Direction de l'instruction publique de la culture et du sport du canton de Fribourg (F), Direktion für Erziehung, Kultur und Sport des Kantons Freiburg (D)	(0)26 305 12 06
GE	Genève (F)	Département de l'instruction publique de la culture et du sport du canton de Genève	(0)22 546 69 00
GL	Glarus (D)	Departement Bildung und Kultur des Kantons Glarus	(0)55 646 62 00
GR	Graubünden (D) Grigioni (I), Grischun (Romansh)	Erziehungs-, Kultur- und Umweltschutzdepartement des Kantons Graubünden (D), Dipartimento dell'educazione, cultura e protezione dell'ambiente del Cantone dei Grigioni (I), Departament d'educaziun, cultura e protecziun da l'ambient dal chantun Grischun (Romansh)	(0)81 257 27 02

JU	Jura (F)	Département de la formation, de la culture et des sports du canton de Jura	(0)32 420 54 03
LU	Luzern (D)	Bildungs- und Kulturdepartement des Kantons Luzern	(0)41 228 52 03
NE	Neuchâtel (F)	Département de l'éducation, de la culture et des sports du canton de Neuchâtel	(0)32 889 69 00
NW	Nidwalden (D)	Bildungsdirektion des Kantons Nidwalden	(0)41 618 74 01
OW	Obwalden (D)	Bildungs- und Kulturdepartement des Kantons Obwalden	(0)41 666 62 43
SH	Schaffhausen (D)	Erziehungsdepartement des Kantons Schaffhausen	(0)52 632 71 95
SZ	Schwyz (D)	Bildungsdepartement des Kantons Schwyz	(0)41 819 19 15
SO	Solothurn (D)	Departement für Bildung und Kultur des Kantons Solothurn	(0)32 627 29 05
SG	St Gallen (D)	Bildungsdepartement des Kantons St. Gallen	(0)58 229 32 29
TG	Thurgau (D)	Departement für Erziehung und Kultur des Kantons Thurgau	(0)52 724 22 67
TI	Ticino (I)	Dipartimento dell'educazione della cultura e dello sport del Cantone Ticino	(0)91 814 44 50
UR	Uri (D)	Bildungs- und Kulturdirektion des Kantons Uri	(0)41 875 22 44
VS	Valais (F), Wallis (D)	Département de l'éducation, de la culture et du sport du canton du Valais (F), Departement für Erziehung, Kultur und Sport des Kantons Wallis (D)	(0)27 606 40 00
VD	Vaud (F)	Département de la formation, de la jeunesse et de la culture du canton de Vaud	(0)21 316 30 30
ZG	Zug (D)	Direktion für Bildung und Kultur des Kantons Zug	(0)41 728 31 83
ZH	Zürich (D)	Bildungsdirektion des Kantons Zürich	(0)43 259 23 09

Appendix 2 Standard school terminology in four languages

The following tables provide the German, French and Italian equivalents of certain terms used in English in this book.

Table 21 Official bodies

English	German	French	Italian
EDK: Swiss Conference of Cantonal Ministers of Education	EDK: Schweizerische Konferenz der kantonalen Erziehungsdirektoren	CDIP: Conférence suisse des directeurs cantonaux de l'instruction publique	CDPE: Conferenza svizzera dei direttori cantonali della pubblica educazione
OPET: Federal Office for Professional Education and Technology	BBT: Bundesamt für Berufsbildung und Technologie	OFFT: Office fédéral de la formation professionnelle et de la technologie	UFFT : Ufficio federale della formazione professionale e della tecnologia

Table 22 Compulsory education

English	German	French	Italian
Compulsory education	Obligatorische Schulzeit	Ecole obligatoire	Scuola dell'obbligo
Kindergarten	Kindergarten	Ecole enfantine	Scuola dell'infanzia, or asilo
Primary school	Primarschule	Ecole primaire	Scuola elementare
Lower-secondary school	Sekundarstufe I	Secondaire I	Secondario I (Scuola media)
Bridge year courses	Brückenangebote	Offres transitoires	Formazioni transitorie

Table 23   Upper-secondary school-based education

English	German	French	Italian
Upper-secondary school	Sekundarstufe II	Secondaire II	Secondario II
Gymnasium (or baccalaureate school)	Gymnasium, Kantonsschule, Kollegium	Gymnase, lycée, collège	Liceo
Six-year gymnasium	Langzeitgymnasium, Langgymnasium, Untergymnasium	-	-
Gymnasial Maturity (or Baccalaureate)	Gymnasiale Maturität (or Matura)	Maturité gymnasiale	Maturità liceale
Specialised upper-secondary school	Fachmittelschule (FMS)	Ecole de culture générale (ECG)	Scuola media specializzata (SMS)
Specialised Maturity (or Baccalaureate)	Fachmaturität	Maturité spécialisée	Maturità specializzata
Commercial school	Wirtschaftsmittelschule	Ecole de commerce	Scuola media di commercio
IT school	Informatikmittelschule	Ecole d'informatique	-

Table 24 Vocational education

English	German	French	Italian
VET school	Berufsschule	Ecole professionnelle	Scuola professionale
Vocational Education and Training (VET) Programme	Berufliche Grundbildung	Formation professionnelle initiale	Formazione professionale di base
Apprenticeship (informal term)	Berufslehre	Apprentissage	Apprendistato
Federal VET Certificate	Eidgenössischer Berufsattest	Attestation fédérale	Certificato federale di formazione pratica
Federal VET Diploma	Eidgenössisches Fähigkeitszeugnis (EFZ)	Certificat fédéral de capacité (CFC)	Attestato federale di capacità (AFC)
Vocational Maturity (or Baccalaureate)	Berufsmaturität	Maturité professionnelle	Maturità professionale

Table 25 Tertiary education

English	German	French	Italian
University	Universität	Université	Università
Swiss Federal Institute of Technology	ETH: Eidgenössische Technische Hochschule (Zürich)	EPF: Ecole Polytechnique Fédérale (de Lausanne)	politecnico federale
University of Applied Sciences and Arts (UASA)	Fachhochschule (FH)	Haute école spécialisée (HES)	Scuola universitaria professionale della Svizzera italiana (SUPSI)
University of Teacher Education	Pädagogische Hochschule (PH)	Haute école pédagogique (HEP)	Alta scuola pedagogica (ASP)
PET (Professional Education and Training) college	Höhere Fachschule (HF)	Ecole supérieure (ES)	Scuola specializzata superiore (SSS)
Federal PET Diploma	Eidgenössischer Fachausweis	Brevet fédéral	Attestato professionale federale
Advanced Federal PET Diploma	Eidgenössisches Diplom, Diplom HF	Diplôme fédéral, diplôme ES	Diploma federale, diploma SSS

Note 1: Flow charts

Flow charts of the school system are available in four languages, English,[222] German,[223] French[224] and Italian.[225] Many of the terms used above can be found there.

Note 2: Use of terminology

Various other terms are used around the country to describe the different stages of school in the local languages. Please see the cantonal tables in chapter 27 for more details. When talking generally about types of school in English, I have tried to use the official terms recommended by the EDK and OPET as much as possible. An exception is when referring to upper-secondary school qualifications. The EDK and OPET refer to the Gymnasial, Vocational, and Specialised Maturity as types of *Baccalaureate* and use the term *baccalaureate schools* to describe gymnasium. Locally, school authorities, teachers and parents may not be familiar with these official terms. They are more likely to borrow a term from the local language when speaking English, or else use a word in English that is close to it.

As my aim is to help incoming parents communicate effectively with the local school, I looked for a pragmatic compromise across the cantonal and linguistic divide. I chose the terms closest to those used most often in German, French and Italian. I use the word *gymnasium* in English as the term that is used most often by local teachers and parents in German (*Gymnasium*) and is closest to the French *gymnase*. I use the term *Maturity* in English as the word closest to *Maturität* or *Matura* (D), *maturité* (F) or *maturità* (I). I write the name of the type of Maturity in capitals to remind readers that I am referring to an official qualification, rather than how mature their children are. I add the official term, *Baccalaureate*, in brackets.

It is, however, helpful to know the terms recommended in English by the EDK and OPET as they are on their official national websites and are well-understood by educationalists internationally. They are worth using when applying to a university abroad or for a job abroad (possibly in addition to naming the qualifications in the school language). If admissions officers or recruiters refer to an official Swiss web site to check someone's qualifications, they will find further information about them there.

Appendix 3 Useful school terms in Swiss German

Parents trying to translate letters written in High German by their child's teacher may not understand words like *Znüni* and *Finkli*. They will be even more perplexed to discover these words are not even in their German dictionary. They are dialect words that are commonly used by German-speaking Swiss when speaking High German. The informal list below is based on important words suggested to me by foreign parents around the country via the Yahoo Swiss Schooling group. It is by no means comprehensive, and the terms may be different in your canton. You will probably find that you start using these words too when you speak English.

Swiss German	English
Bäbiecke	dolls corner
Baschtle	handicrafts, making things
Etui	pencil case
Finkli	slippers for classroom (usually with a heel)
Ganztägige	day trip (requires a picnic)
Heftli	notebook
Huusi, Ufzgi	homework
Kindsgi, Kindi	kindergarten
Kindsgibändl, Bändeli, Drüeck, Lüüchtsgi, Streifeli	luminous safety band worn by child when walking to kindergarten
Mäppli	folder, file
Posttäschli	bag to carry notes from teacher
Schläppli, Täppeli	elasticated slippers for physical education class
Thek or Schulthek	school bag
Znüni	morning snack
Znüni-box	snack box
Znünitäschli	bag to carry snack

Table 26   School terms in Swiss German

Appendix 4 Acronyms used in this book

Table 27

Acronym	Stands for
ACT	American College Test
AFC	Attestato federale di capacità
AI	Canton of Appenzell-Innerrhoden
AI	Assurance-invalidité
AO	Canton of Appenzell-Ausserrhoden
AG	Canton of Aargau
ASEP	Association Suisse pour les Enfants Précoces
ASP	Alta scuola pedagogica
BAEP	Bureau d'accueil pour l'école primaire
BE	Canton of Bern
BL	Canton of Basel-Landschaft
BS	Canton of Basel-Stadt
DELF	Diplôme d'Etudes en Langue Française
CAS	Certificate of Advanced Studies
CAS	Creativity, Action, Service
CDIP	Conférence suisse des directeurs cantonaux de l'instruction publique
CDPE	Conferenza svizzera dei direttori cantonali della pubblica educazione
CFC	Certificat fédéral de capacité
CIIS	Convention intercantonale relative aux institutions sociales
CPNV	Centre professionelle du Nord vaudois
CRUS	Rectors' Conference of the Swiss Universities

D	German
DAS	Diploma of Advanced Studies
DaZ	Deutsch als Zweitsprache
ECG	Ecole de culture générale
EDK	Schweizerische Konferenz der kantonalen Erziehungsdirektoren
EDK	Conference of Cantonal Ministers of Education
EFZ	Eidgenössisches Fähigkeitszeugnis
EPFL	Ecole Polytechnique Fédérale de Lausanne
ES	Ecole supérieure
ETHZ	Eidgenössische Technische Hochschule Zürich
F	French
FfF	Förderung für Fremdsprachige
FH	Fachhochschule
FMS	Fachmittelschule
FR	Canton of Fribourg
GE	Canton of Geneva
GL	Canton of Glarus
GM	Gymnasium am Münsterplatz
GR	Canton of Graubünden (or Grisons)
H	HarmoS
HEP	Haute école pédagogique
HES	Haute école spécialisée
I	Italian
IB	International Baccalaureate
IBO	International Baccalaureate Organisation

INSOS	Soziale Institutionen für Menschen mit Behinderung Schweiz
ISCED	International Standard Classification of Education
ISF	Integrative Schooling
IQ	Intelligence Quotient
IV	Invalidenversicherung
IVSE	Interkantonale Vereinbarung für soziale Einrichtungen
JU	Canton of Jura
KiTs	Bilingual private school in St Gallen
KJPD	Department of Child and Adolescent Psychiatry
LAVI Centre	Loi fédérale sur l'Aide aux Victimes d'Infractions
LU	Canton of Lucerne
MAS	Master of Advanced Studies
MBA	Master of Business Administration
NE	Canton of Neuchâtel
NW	Canton of Nidwalden
OB	Canton of Obwalden
OFFT	Office fédéral de la formation professionnelle et de la technologie
OPET	Federal Office for Professional Education and Technology
OS	Orientierungsschule
OW	Canton of Obwalden
PES	Procédure d'évaluation standardisée
PET	Professional Education and Training
PhD	Doctor of Philosophy
SAT	Scholastic Aptitude Test
SAV	Standardisiertes Abklärungsverfahren

SER	State Secretariat for Education and Research
SG	Canton of St Gallen
SH	Canton of Schaffhausen
SMS	Scuola media specializzata
SO	Canton of Solothurn
SRK	Swiss Red Cross
SSS	Scuola specializzata superiore
SUPSI	Scuola universitaria professionale della Svizzera italiana
SZ	Canton of Schwyz
TG	Canton of Thurgau
TI	Canton of Ticino
TOK	Theory of knowledge
UASA	University of Applied Sciences and Arts
UFFT	Ufficio federale della formazione professionale e della tecnologia
UR	Canton of Uri
ÜK	Übergangsklasse
VD	Canton of Vaud
VET	Vocational Education and Training
VS	Canton of Valais
WBS	Weiterbildungsschule
WMS	Wirtschaftsmittelschule
ZG	Canton of Zug
ZH	Canton of Zurich

Endnotes

1. 'Public' is used here in the sense of being offered free of charge to the general public. In other countries, this might be called a 'state school'. There is no national Ministry of Education in Switzerland and schools are either municipal or cantonal.

2. www.bfs.admin.ch or Google 'map, gallery, Switzerland, languages'.

3. Throughout the book I provide terminology in the local languages, first in German, then French, then Italian.

4. In lists I refer to the names of cantons by the official abbreviations used for them. Please see Appendix 1 for a full list of the abbreviations and the cantons to which they refer.

5. EDK Cantonal school structures and cantonal offer. http://www.edk.ch/dyn/11550.php

6. "Heile, heile Segen, morgen gibt's Regen, übermorgen Schnee, und jetzt tut's nie mehr Weh." Translation: "Heal, heal, blessing, tomorrow it will rain, the next day it will snow, and now it doesn't hurt any more."

7. Margaret Oertig. (2011). *Beyond chocolate – understanding Swiss culture*. Basel: Bergli Books. www.bergli.ch.

8. '6+ ist noch nicht gut genug'. Alexandra Muz. *Das Magazin*, no 42, 2011.

9. www.readysteadyrelocate.com

10. http://swissfamilytaylor.blogspot.com/

11. See note 7.

12. www.englishforum.ch

13. http://groups.yahoo.com/group/Expat-Moms-In-Switzerland/join

14. http://groups.yahoo.com/group/Swiss-Schooling/

15. http://www.elternlobby.ch/deutsch/initiative/

16. http://www.psi.org.uk/publications/archivepdfs/Recent/CENLOC4.pdf

17. 'Eltern können Schule als Kunden mitgestalten'. Esther Ugolini. *Basler Zeitung*, 25 April 2008.
18. http://www.bista.zh.ch/ms/MSQuote_Map.aspx, http://www.bista.zh.ch/ms/Uebertritte.aspx
19. Mind Matters coaching (telephone and face-to-face). val. alexander2@googlemail.com.
20. www.alivetochange.com
21. This observation was made by an American manager in a company course I gave.
22. www.learnfrenchathome.com
23. Estimates provided by The Association of Language Testers of Europe, www.alte.org
24. Council of Europe, Common European Framework of reference for languages: Learning, teaching, assessment.
25. Katz, L.G. (2011). 'Current perspectives on the early childhood curriculum'. In Richard House (Ed.). *Too much too soon? Early learning and the erosion of childhood*. Hawthorn Press.
26. www.plandetudes.ch
27. www.lehrplan.ch
28. 'Lehrplan Kindergarten für den Deutschsprachigen Teil des Kantons Bern'. Erziehungsdirektion des Kantons Bern.
29. Stufenlehrplan Kindergarten Kanton Basel-Landschaft.
30. See Wikipedia on Waldorf education.
31. 'Childhood being eroded by modern life, experts warn'. Education news. *Daily Telegraph*, 24 September 2011.
32. Krenz, A. (2003). *Elementarpädagogik aktuell: Die Entwicklung des Kindes professionell begleiten*. Gabel Verlag.
33. Remo H. Largo. (2000). *Kinderjahre*. Piper Verlag.
34. Interview with Muriel Djéribi Valentin about Françoise Dolto: 'Quand l'enfant est un sujet à part entière'.
35. See note 33.
36. Remo H. Lago & Martin Beglinger. (2010). *Schülerjahre*. Piper Verlag.
37. http://www.hlgr.ch/docs/Largo_Individ_Fideris.pdf http://www.lch.ch/dms-static/1645ded6-275c-4b9d-8065-be9815843eae/1_Folien_Largo.pdf
38. 'EDK-OST 4 bis 8. Schlussbericht 2010'. www.schulverlag.ch
39. www.plandetudes.ch
40. Introductory pages to the school record book (i).

Enseignement primaire, Direction générale, Service de la scolarité. Geneva.

41. Google 'EDK, Nationale Bildungsziele' (D), or 'CDIP, Objectifs nationaux de formation' (F) or 'CDPE, Obiettivi formativi nazionali' (I).

42. In German: 'Grundkompetenzen für die Schulsprache. Nationale Bildungsstandards'. EDK, 2011. In French: 'Compétences fondamentales pour la langue de scolarisation. Standards nationaux de formation'. CDIP, 2011.

43. In German: 'Grundkompetenzen für die Naturwissenschaften'. Nationale Bildungsstandards. EDK, 2011. In French: 'Compétences fondamentales pour les sciences naturelles. Standards nationaux de formation'. CDIP, 2011.

44. German version: 'Grundkompetenzen für die Mathematik. Nationale Bildungsstandards'. EDK, 2011. French version: 'Compétences fondamentales pour les mathématiques. Standards nationaux de formation'. CDIP, 2011.

45. See www.ilz.ch ->"Lehrmittelübersicht" for an overview of which German-speaking cantons use which books for reading, maths, the school language and the first foreign language.

46. www.schulschrift.ch

47. 'Wenn Mama Ufzgi macht'. Andrea Fischer Schulthess. *Migros Magazin* 15, 11 April 2011.

48. 'Frust mit dem Wochenplan'. Veronika Bonilla Gunzeler. 2011. www.wireltern.ch

49. See note 33.

50. Carl Honoré (2008). *Under pressure. Rescuing our children from the culture of hyper-parenting*. Orion Books. www.carlhonore.com.

51. Allan Güggenbühl. (2002). *Die PISA-Falle*. Herder.

52. Amy Chua. (2011). *Battle Hymn of the Tiger Mother*. Penguin Press.

53. 'Kind und Velo, aber sicher'. Stadtpolizei Zürich. http://www.velofahrkurs.ch/assets/files/Broschueren/Kind_und_Velo.pdf

54. See note 7.

55. Clotaire Rapaille. (2006). *The Culture Code*. Broadway Books.

56. See note 36.

57. http://www.edudoc.ch/static/web/bildungssystem/grafik_bildung_e.pdf

58. http://www.edudoc.ch/static/web/bildungssystem/grafik_bildung_d.pdf
59. http://www.edudoc.ch/static/web/bildungssystem/grafik_bildung_f.pdf
60. http://www.edudoc.ch/static/web/bildungssystem/grafik_bildung_i.pdf
61. EDK Cantonal school structures and cantonal offer. http://www.edk.ch/dyn/11550.php
62. www.plandetudes.ch
63. www.lehrplan.ch
64. 'Swiss Education Report, 2010'. SKBP-CSRE. www.skbf-csre.ch
65. See note 41.
66. 'OECD (2010), PISA 2009 Results: What students know and can do – student performance in reading, mathematics and science (Volume I)'. www.oecd.org/edu/pisa/2009
67. 'PISA 2009. Leseförderung bleibt ein Thema'. Education ch, No 1, March 2011. www.edk.ch -> Dokumentation ->Newsletter.
68. Moser, U., Buff, A., Angelone, D. & Hollenweger, J. (2011). 'Nach sechs Jahren Primarschule. Deutsch, Mathematik und motivational-emotionales Befinden am Ende der 6. Klasse'. Zürich: Bildungsdirektion Kanton Zürich.
69. I use 'six-year gymnasium' as a generic term for all 11 cantons, as the names vary from one canton to another.
70. See note 64.
71. See note 64.
72. 'EDK. Übertritt aus der obligatorischen Schule in Gymnasiale Maturitätsschulen'. Informationszentrum IDES, January 2009.
73. From 2014, gymnasium will last six years in the old system which is being phased out.
74. Pallas, A. M. (2003). 'Educational transitions, trajectories, and pathways'. In J. T. Mortimer & M. J. Shanahan (Eds.), *Handbook of the Life Course* (pp. 165-184). New York: Kluwer Academic/Plenum Publishers.
75. With the exception of Basel-Stadt in the old system.
76. 'Parents, it's time to let go'. Barbara Kantrowitz. p 4-7. *Newsweek. Finding the right college for you.* Spring 2011.
77. Neuenschwander, M.P. & Garrett, J. L. (2008). 'Causes and consequences of unexpected educational transitions in Switzerland'. *Journal of Social Issues*, 64, 1, 41-57.

78. See note 51.
79. www.zeller-beratungen.ch
80. www.lerntherapie.ch
81. Article 5 of Neue Maturitätsanerkennungsreglement of 15 February 1995, revised 27 June 2007.
82. Franz Eberle und Mitarbeitende (2008). 'EVAMAR II Evaluation der Maturitätsreform 1995 (EVAMAR) Phase II'. Universität Zürich, Institut für Gymnasial- und Berufspädagogik.
83. http://www.bfs.admin.ch/bfs/portal/de/index/themen/15/06/dos/blank/05/01.html or google 'Gymnasiale Maturitätsquote' (D) 'taux de maturités gymnasiales'(F).
84. See note 82.
85. See note 64.
86. 'Wenn Wissenschaft begeistert'. *Roche Nachrichten*, Ausgabe 3/2011. Page 11.
87. Elmiger, D. (2008). 'Die zweisprachige Maturität in der Schweiz'. SBF.
88. www.ibo.org
89. www.nagc.org
90. www.gmbasel.ch
91. See note 24.
92. See note 82.
93. See note 50.
94. 'Use of an aptitude test in university entrance: a validity study'. Kirkup, C., Wheater, R., Morrison, J. and Durbin, B. (2010) Slough: NFER.
95. www.jugendarbeitslosigkeit.ch Change settings for French.
96. http://epp.eurostat.ec.europa.eu/statistics_explained/index.php/Unemployment_statistics#Youth_unemployment_trends
97. http://bls.gov/news.release/youth.nr0.htm
98. http://www.weforum.org/issues/global-competitiveness
99. Symonds, W.C., Schwartz, R.B., Ferguson, R. (2011). 'Pathways to Prosperity: Meeting the challenge of preparing young Americans for the 21st century'. Harvard Graduate School of Education.
100. 'Die Lehrlingslücke', *NZZ am Sonntag*, 26 June, 2011. Page 23.

101. www.worldskills.org
102. 'Swiss skills win medals galore in London'. Andrew Littlejohn. 10 October 2011. www.swissinfo.ch
103. www.apprenticeships.org.uk
104. 'Bildungsabschlüsse 2010. Sekundarstufe II und Tertiärstufe'. Bundesamt für Statistik (D). 'Examens finals en 2010. Degré secondaire II et degré tertiare'. Office fédérale de la statistique (F). www.bfs.admin.ch
105. Stamm, M. (2007). *Kluge Köpfe, goldene Hände*. Rüegger Verlag.
106. For a detailed overview in English, see 'Vocational Education and Training in Switzerland'. 2011. Facts and Figures. FDEA, OPET.
107. www.berufsberatung.ch (D); www.orientation.ch (F); www.orientamento.ch (I).
108. Either google 'Berufsberatung, information in foreign languages' or go to http://www.berufsberatung.ch/dyn/bin/8188-9345-1-englisch_schule_beruf_2011_04_15.pdf
109. Two examples in German: (1) Erwin Egloff and Daniel Jungo. (2009). *Berufswahltagebuch*. Schulverlag plus AG. (2) Rainer Schmid and Claire Barmettler. 2009. *Wegweiser zur Berufswahl*. S & B Verlag.
110. See www.adressen.sdbb.ch (D), www.adresses.csfo.ch (F), www.indirizzi.csfo.ch (F)
111. See note 79.
112. www.multicheck.ch (google 'Multicheck, Junior')
113. www.lex.dbk.ch (D, F, I). See also www.berufsbildung.ch (D), www.formationprof.ch (F), www.formazioneprof.ch (I) for more facts, figures and documentation about the VET system.
114. www.ichmachwas.sdbb.ch
115. For a full list of jobs, see the document: 'Kein EFZ- und trotzdem eine Berufsprüfung machen'. 04.05.2011, Schweizerisches Dienstleistungszentrum Berufsbildung / Berufs-, Studien- und Laufbahnberatung. www.swissdoc.sdbb.ch
116. See note 64.
117. http://www.edudoc.ch/static/web/arbeiten/diplanerk/liste_akabschlfms_df.pdf
118. See note 107
119. http://www.edudoc.ch/static/web/arbeiten/fktbl_fms_d.

pdf (German); http://www.edudoc.ch/static/web/arbeiten/fktbl_fms_f.pdf (French)

120. www.ict-berufsbildung.ch (D and F).

121. 'UNESCO Global Education Digest, 2011. Comparing Education Statistics Across the World'. UNESCO Institute for Statistics.

122. International Standard Classification of Education.

123. See note 122.

124. http://www.crus.ch/information-programme/study-in-switzerland/page.html?L=2

125. Please see www.crus.ch for further information on general admission requirements for students from abroad.

126. http://www.arwu.org

127. http://www.topuniversities.com/university-rankings

128. http://www.timeshighereducation.co.uk/world-university-rankings/

129. See note 64.

130. www.kfh.ch

131. See the website of each UASA for specific information on its fees structure.

132. 'Studying in Switzerland. Universities. 2011'. Edited by Rectors' Conference of the Swiss Universities (CRUS), Bern.

133. See note 106.

134. See www.bbt.admin.ch or google 'Professional Education and Training' (PET).

135. For a full list, see http://www.bbt.admin.ch/bvz/hbb/index.html?lang=de. Changes settings to French or Italian.

136. 'Machen Titel Leute?' Bildungsmarkt Schweiz. Claude Meier. *Organisator*, 8 April 2011.

137. Based on information found in www.berufsberatung.ch, www.orientation.ch, www.orientamento.ch.

138. For a list of schools across the country, google 'Passarellen Schulen' (D) or 'Ecoles passerelle' (F).

139. For further information, google 'Passarellen' (D) or 'passarelles' (F) in the national jobs and careers advice website: www.berufsberatung.ch (D); www.orientation.ch (F); www.orientamento.ch (I).

140. ETH (Zurich) and EPFL (Lausanne) are federal universities.

141. http://www.sbf.admin.ch/htm/themen/bildung/matur/ ch-matur_de.html (D), Change settings to French or Italian.
142. See note 107.
143. There are of course exceptions, such as medicine and law.
144. www.globaluniversitychoices.com
145. 'Maturanoten und Studienerfolg. Eine Analyse des Zusammenhangs zwischen Maturanoten und der Basisprüfungs der ETH Zürich'. Data evaluated by B. Spicher. University of Freiburg 2008.
146. CRUS Recommendations for the Assessment of Foreign Upper-Secondary School-Leaving Certificates. 7 September 2007. www.crus.ch
147. 'Wenn Eltern Schule machen'. Speech by Isabelle Chassot at the delegates' meeting of Schule und Elternhaus Schweiz, 2 April 2011. www.schule-elternhaus.ch
148. 'Elternarbeit für die Schule'. Peter Bächle. Forum, Basler Zeitung, Friday 2 May 2008, page 24.
149. www.alivetochange.com
150. See note 80.
151. 'Die Probleme müssen auf den Tisch'. Birthe Homann & Daniel Benz. Beobachter, 11, 2011.
152. 'Wenn Venus auf Mars trifft'. Daniel Benz. Beobachter, 11, 2011.
153. See note 152.
154. Nägeli, Ch. & Alsaker, F.D. (2005). 'Beschimpft, geplagt und ausgelacht – Mobbing Im Kindergarten'. Institut für Psychologie, Abteilung Entwicklungspsychologie, Universität Bern. www.praevention-alsaker.unibe.ch.
155. http://www.praevention-alsaker.unibe.ch.
156. Google 'Be Prox' for International studies in English.
157. www.oslihowil.ch ->Wir über uns -> Prävention-> Gewaltprävention.
158. www.chili-srk.ch (change language settings to French or Italian as required).
159. Ask at your school or google 'Schulpsychologischer Dienst' (D), 'Psychologie scolaire' (F), and the name of your canton to find the telephone number.
160. Google 'Opferberatung' (D) or 'Centre LAVI' (F) or 'UIR' (I) and the name of your canton.

161. www.schulsozialarbeit.ch (German and English).
162. 'Schulsozialarbeit. Wir sind nicht dazu da, jedes Problemchen wegzuwischen'. Diana Frei. *Surprise* No. 259, 2011.
163. Behindertengleichstellungsgesetz, or BehiG in German, Loi sur l'égalité pour les handicapés, or LHand in French, Leggi sui disabili or LDis in Italian. http://www.admin.ch/ch/d/sr/151_3/index.html.
164. 'Interkantonale Vereinbarung über die Zusammenarbeit im Bereich der Sonderpädagogik', 25 Oktober 2007. http://edudoc.ch/record/87689/files/Sonderpaed_d.pdf.
165. Standardisiertes Abklärungsverfahren, or SAV in German and Procédure d'évaluation standardisée or PES in French. www.szh.ch/sav-pes.
166. www.sodk.ch/it/la-cdos/ivse.html Change language settings as required.
167. Sonderpädagogisches Konzept für die Kantone Basel-Landschaft und Basel-Stadt, 2010.
168. Liesen, C. (2011). 'Making schools responsible for students with special needs: Swiss country report'. Interkantonale Hochschule für Heilpädagogik, Zürich. http://www.hfh.ch/projekte_detail-n70-r79-i1880-sD.html
169. www.insos.ch. Google 'INSOS' and 'praktische Ausbildung' (D) or 'formation pratique' (F).
170. Google 'KJPD' and 'Autismus'. The KJPD diagnoses children from the whole of Switzerland, but there is a long waiting list.
171. Adapted from table: 'Integration als Kontinuum – eine Herausforderung für die Statistik'. Bericht der Arbeitsgruppe Statistik der Sonderpädagogik. SZH, 2011.
172. 'Und welche Macke hast du?' Tanja Polli. *Wir Eltern*. 6/2011
173. See note 172.
174. See note 172.
175. www.furerkarrer.ch/cms/en/ (website in English)
176. See note 159.
177. 'Früher, schneller, schlauer'. Caren Battaglia. *Wir Eltern*. 2011. www.wireltern.ch
178. Benjemia, C. 'Intellectually gifted children'. ASEP 2010. www.asep-suisse.org. Click on 'publications'.

179. Brunner, E., Gyseler, D. and Lienhard, P. (2005) *Hochbegabung (k)ein Problem*. Zug: Klett und Balmer Verlag.
180. Joëlle Huser (2011). *Lichtblick für helle Köpfe*. Lehrmittelverlag Zürich.
181. http://www.lehrmittelverlag-zuerich.ch/Portals/1/ Documents/shop/downloads/Lichtblick_English.pdf
182. See note 178.
183. See note 179.
184. 'More Parents 'Redshirting' Kindergartners'. Stephanie Pappas. *Live Science*. 5 September 2010.
185. www.talenta.ch
186. www.kits-dayschool.ch
187. www.asep-suisse.org Mesures prises par l'école, par Anonyme. 26 November 2008.
188. www.swissolympic.ch Schulangebote für Sporttalente (D), Programmes scolaires adaptés aux talents sportifs (F).
189. For the names of the school authorities in each canton, google 'EDK Schulaufsichtsbehörden' (D), 'CDIP Autorité chargée du contrôle de l'enseignement'(F). http://www.edudoc.ch/ static/strukturdaten/pdf_rohdaten/105.pdf
190. Walter Noser. (2011). *Hilfe im Schulalltag*. Beobachter Buch-Verlag.
191. www.beobachter.ch Another publishing house with a similar offer is Saldo Verlag, www.saldo.ch
192. www.anwaltskanzlei-imthurn.ch
193. If you wish to add to any of the information here for the next printing of the book, please write to margaret.oertig@bluewin.ch.
194. A list of the abbreviations and full names of cantons can be found in Appendix 1.
195. Please see Chapter 28 for further information on cantons undergoing a change of structure.
196. a.c. = attendance compulsory; o.c. = offer compulsory.
197. Note: The 8th transition year (H8) is held in the lower secondary school building. Pupils still experience it as "moving up" to lower-secondary school.
198. The exception is Leimental, where primary school lasts for 5 years only. This will change in 2015.
199. It may also be possible to send younger children to kindergarten. They may start in August or February.

200. This is for reference only as there is no official starting date.

201. 'EDK. Übertritt Primarstufe-Sekundarstufe I'. Informationszentrum IDES, Dezember 2009. http://edudoc.ch/record/35910/files/Prim_sek1.pdf. (Document written in German and French).'CIIP. Structures de l'enseignement Suisse romande et Tessin. Année scolaire, 2011-2012'. http://www.irdp.ch/documentation/dossiers_comparatifs/structures/2011_2012/structuresdocumentcomplet1112.pdf

202. 'Sekundarstufe' is an official term that tends to be used if there is a range of school types with different names.

203. See note 197.

204. Each canton has a legal basis for selection (Rechtliche Grundlage, base juridique) and the document should be available on the canton's website. See also note 201.

205. Please see chapter 14 for a discussion on what the teacher's judgment can include.

206. Canton-wide comparisons of performance (e.g. tests) are well-established in French-speaking Switzerland and are on the increase everywhere. Test subjects tend to be the school language and maths, followed by the second language taught at school. These subjects are therefore gaining importance for the selection process.

207. In some cantons, if parents do not agree with the school's decision, the pupil may take an external entrance exam to settle the matter.

208. Where cantonal law states that the teacher's judgment or recommendation is the official entrance criterion, class work and/or marks normally play an informal role in the decision. I therefore include them in this table in brackets where they are not explicitly stated as one of the criteria in the canton's law.

209. In the German-speaking part only.

210. http://www.avs.bl.ch

211. http://www.ed.bs.ch (> Aktuell > Das Schulsystem in Basel-Stadt).

212. Gymnasium lasts 3.5 years in the old system. This will be changed to 4 years from 2014.

213. See note 72.

214.   See note 207.
215.   See note 208.
216.   See note 210
217.   See note 211.
218.   Google: 'Basel-Stadt bisheriges Schulsystem' to see a diagram of the old system and 'Basel-Stadt neues Schulsystem' to see a diagram of the new system.
219.   Gymnasium will last one year longer from 2014.
220.   To be confirmed by the canton. See note 211.
221.   To be confirmed by the canton. See note 211.
222.   See note 57.
223.   See note 58.
224.   See note 59.
225.   See note 60.

List of Tables

		Topic	Page
Table	1	Hours required to learn a language	61
Table	2	Primary school subjects in canton Geneva	83
Figure	3	Numbers wall	88
Table	4	Specialised Maturity (or Baccalaureate) focus and future prospects	165
Table	5	Swiss universities in the top 200 in the world rankings of 2011-2012	171
Table	6	Qualifications required for universities and UASA	176-177
Table	7	Integration as a continuum	213
Table	8	Legal terms in French and German	235
Table	9	Kindergarten and primary school by canton	240-241
Table	10	Date school year begins by canton	242
Table	11	Minimum age to start kindergarten in a particular year by canton	243
Table	12	Minimum age to start school in a particular year by canton	244
Table	13	Cantons changing the minimum age to start kindergarten	245
Table	14	Cantons changing the minimum age to start school	245

Index

Acknowledgements

Prior to writing this book, I spoke to many people over a period of several years about issues related to Swiss schooling. I would like to thank them all – my family, friends, neighbours, clients, colleagues and students – for helping me to clarify and think through the most important issues. I am grateful to my husband Hans for encouraging me as I initiated and carried out this project. I also appreciated the perspectives of my daughters. Sarah helped bring me back to a whole system perspective when I got too caught up in details. Fiona provided me with an insider perspective of a range of values and attitudes of Swiss young people in the school context.

I was greatly encouraged at the outset by ETAS, the English Teachers Association of Switzerland, who allowed me to contact its 400 Swiss and international members across the country. Many of them provided rich insights as both observers and participants in educational processes. Many thanks to Ann Humphry-Baker and Stephen Lander for facilitating this. I also interviewed and corresponded with many members of the Yahoo Swiss Schooling group and Expat-Moms-In-Switzerland and would like to thank Carmen Crenshaw, the moderator of both. These conversations with people from all over the world helped me expand the topic range to address the concerns of incomers from a wide range of backgrounds.

All in all, I conducted over 120 conversations with parents. I would like to thank them all. I also appreciated hearing about the experiences of many young people, and passing on their advice. The perspectives of dedicated teachers on the front line were invaluable too. I am indebted to all these 'co-producers of knowledge' (who are too numerous to name here) for their openness and generosity in sharing their stories, insights and wisdom.

As well as the contributions of parents, pupils and teachers, I obtained extensive information from the websites of Swiss departments of education at municipal, cantonal and national levels. If information is power, then the Swiss approach of making so much information freely available really empowers the people, provided they can speak the local language. Professionals and experts from fields such as education administration and management, law and coaching provided additional information and suggestions that I could not have obtained from websites. Their names appear throughout the book.

I would like to thank the following people for reading and commenting on parts or all of my manuscript: Rudolf A, Kirstin Barton, Rachel Benzies, Rainer Buechele, Christian Liesen, Natalie M, Lukas Moesle, Kate Taylor and Dagmar Voith. Mark Hanks and Loretta Koch merit special thanks for proof-reading the whole book.

Lastly, my gratitude goes to the team at Bergli Books. My publisher, Dianne Dicks, worked on this book with her usual professionalism, combining exactness and flexibility. Monica Vischer was both humorous and encouraging, and Heidi Scherz did an excellent job, finding ways to handle the intricacies of the layout of text, boxes, tables and endnotes. I would also like to thank Marc Locatelli for so carefully considering the themes of the book and for his humour and attention to detail in designing the cover and illustrations.

My daughter's teacher taught her the 80/20 rule. It can be more efficient to do a job only 80% perfectly, as it could take just as long to achieve the last 20% as it took to achieve the first 80%. Although there is a disclaimer in this book, saying that we assume no responsibility for errors or omissions, I have done my best to check that everything is correct as we go to press. It was my aim to get the facts around 95% correct. If I have managed to achieve this I will be more than satisfied. If I have not, and there is a significant error somewhere, or something important has changed, do write to me at margaret.oertig@bluewin.ch and let me know.

Margaret Oertig
Basel, May 2012

About the author

Margaret Oertig, M.A, M.Ed, originates from Scotland and lives with her Swiss husband near Basel. She has lived and worked in Switzerland since 1987. Her two daughters, who are now adults, went through the Swiss school system. Margaret has worked for many years delivering intercultural training programmes to international companies. Since 2002, she has worked for the Fachhochschule Nordwestschweiz (UASA), lecturing, writing and working on projects related to intercultural collaboration.

About Bergli Books

Bergli Books publishes books in English that focus on living in Switzerland and on intercultural matters:

Beyond Chocolate – understanding Swiss culture by Margaret Oertig-Davidson, enables you to immerse yourself in the cultural attitudes of Switzerland's fascinating, multifaceted society and understand your Swiss neighbours, friends and international business colleagues. ISBN 978-3-905252-21-7.

Schokolade ist nicht alles – Ein Leitfaden zur Schweizer Kultur von Margaret Oertig-Davidson ist die deutsche Ausgabe von *Beyond Chocolate*. ISBN 978-3-905252-10-1.

Ticking Along Too – stories about Switzerland, edited by Dianne Dicks, is filled with entertaining and informative personal experiences of living with the Swiss written by authors of nine nationalities and various professions. ISBN 978-3-9520002-1-2.

Ticking Along Free, edited by Dianne Dicks, with more stories about living with the Swiss from residents who enjoy figuring out how Swiss German or the laundry room key work. Also includes stories from Swiss writers: Franz Hohler, Hugo Loetscher, minu, Gisela Widmer and others. ISBN 978-3-905252-02-6

Cupid's Wild Arrows – intercultural romance and its consequences, edited by Dianne Dicks, contains personal experiences of 55 authors living with two worlds in one partnership. ISBN 978-3-9520002-2-9.

A Taste of Switzerland, by Sue Style, with over 50 recipes showing the richness of this country's diverse gastronomic cultures. This award-winning international food writer takes you to dairies, vineyards, butchers and bakers as well as to some of the great restaurants and hotels. ISBN 978-3-9520002-7-4.

Cheese – slices of Swiss culture by Sue Style. Meet the country's prize-winning and most talented artisan cheese makers and discover fine cheeses, cheese recipes, and cheese trails. ISBN 978-3-905252-20-0.

Swiss Cookies – biscuits for Christmas and all year round, by Andrew Rushton and Katalin Fekete. Discover the delicious secrets of the most famous and traditional Swiss cookies and baked goods. ISBN 978-3-905252-17-0.

Inside Outlandish, by Susan Tuttle, illustrated by ANNA, a collection of 25 essays that take you to the heart of feeling at home in new places as a mother, friend and member of a new community. ISBN 978-3-9520002-8-1.

*Lifting the Mask – your guide to Basel Fasnacht by Peter Habicht, illustrations by Fredy Prack. Whether you are a first-time visitor or a life-long enthusiast, here's all you need to know (and more) about Basel's famous carnival. English edition: ISBN 978-3-905252-04-0.

*Pfyffe ruesse schränze – eine Einführung in die Basler Fasnacht von Peter Habicht mit Illustrationen von Fredy Prack. Ob erstmaliger Besucher oder begeisterter Stammgast, hier finden Sie alles, was Sie über die Basler Fasnacht wissen müssen. ISBN 978-3-905252-09-5.

*At Home – a selection of stories by Franz Hohler, one of Switzerland's most popular and respected writers. His endearing tales delight readers of all ages. Enjoy story-telling at its best – with wit, compassion and integrity. ISBN 978-3-905252-18-7.

*Swiss Me by Roger Bonner, illustrations by Edi Barth. Ever tried socializing at the bottle bank? Or finding the Röstigraben? Want to improve your Swiss German in 30 minutes? Ever run into Mr. Tell looking for his son? Need to check if you are becoming too Swiss? These playful stories will give new perspectives and pleasures to your life with the Swiss. ISBN 978-3-905252-11-8.

Hoi – your Swiss German survival guide by Sergio J. Lievano and Nicole Egger. With this survival guide and its over 200 cartoons and illustrations, it is downright fun for speakers of English to learn all about Swiss German as it is spoken in the region of Zurich. ISBN 978-3-905252-13-2.

Hoi Zäme – Schweizerdeutsch leicht gemacht by Sergio J. Lievano and Nicole Egger, for German speakers: ISBN 978-3-905252-22-4.

Hoi! Et après... – manuel de survie en suisse allemand by Sergio J. Lievano and Nicole Egger, for French speakers who would like to enjoy communicating in Swiss German. ISBN 978-3-905252-16-3.

Sali zämme – your Baseldütsch survival guide by Sergio J. Lievano and Nicole Egger, for English speakers wanting to get to grips with day-to-day communication in the Swiss German dialect spoken in Basel. ISBN 978-3-905252-26-2.

Ticking Along with Swiss Kids by Dianne Dicks and Katalin Fekete. Children from ages 6 to 12 can learn all they need to enjoy making friends and feeling at home in Switzerland. ISBN 978-3-905252-15-6.

Swiss History in a Nutshell by Grégoire Nappey, cartoons by Mix & Remix, showing the key historical events that have created Switzerland as it is today. ISBN 978-3-905252-19-4.

Swissellany – facts and figures about Switzerland by Diccon Bewes, illustrations by Mischa Kammermann. Fact-lovers will enjoy this treasure-trove of serious and not-so-serious facts and figures about Switzerland. This collection of lists will amuse and enlighten you with interesting facts you never dreamed you'd enjoy knowing. ISBN 978-3-905252-24-8.

*Also available as an Ebook.
www.bergli.ch

Dear Reader,

Your opinion can help us. We would like to know what you think of *Going Local – your guide to Swiss schooling*.

Where did you learn about this book?

Had you heard about Bergli Books before reading this book?

What did you enjoy about this book?

Any criticism?

Any corrections?

Check this book's listing on **www.bergli.ch** to see about any updated information about *Going Local*.

Would you like to receive more information about the books we publish and distribute? If so, please give us your name and address and we'll send you a catalogue.

Name:
Address:
City
Country

Cut out page, fold here, staple and mail to:

Bergli Books
P.O. Box
CH-4001 Basel
Switzerland